Beginnings

BEGINNINGS

EARLY AMERICAN JUDAICA

ABRAHAM J. KARP

Philadelphia   5736/1975
The Jewish Publication Society of America

Designed by Adrianne Onderdonk Dudden

For Deborah

Contents

Foreword

In this Bicentennial year, when all Americans are stimulated to reflect on the origins of the Republic, it is only fitting that American Jews, too, share in the general festivities. For Jews, moreover, there is a special resonance to the occasion. A people that has known persecution so long and so intimately has particular reason to commemorate the birth of a nation that was the first to extend to Jews full religious, political, and cultural freedom, as well as to reexamine the early history of the American Jewish community.

The booklets that form this Bicentennial collection are thus offered in a spirit of celebration and reflection. They afford tangible evidence of a creative, though numerically small, Jewish presence in colonial and post-Revolutionary society. To be sure, from the total perspective of Jewish history these ten publications would hardly loom as monuments. They are products of a young and obscure community on the fringes of a Jewish world still centered in Europe and the East. Within the evolution of the American Jewish community, however, each pamphlet represents a milestone of achievement and a significant augury for the future.

These publications, we trust, will yield many pleasures. At the most immediate level there is the satisfaction of holding history in one's hands, so to speak, of perusing documents that are faithful reproductions of their often rare originals. Their contents will enrich the reader with vivid insights into personality and historical detail. But above all there is the joy of recognition, of seeing our contemporary selves reflected in the past, of discovering that the archetypal American Jewish experience—fidelity to Jewish tradition joined to an almost intuitive embracing of the American ethos—is already manifest in the thought and conduct of forebears of two centuries ago.

We have called this collection of early American Judaica "Beginnings." Each item marks a pioneering effort of one kind or another—the first Jewish liturgy and the first Jewish sermon printed in the New World, a paradigm of future charity appeals, the debut of American Jewish journalism, a precedent-setting protest meeting of international Jewish concern, a prophetic Zionist manifesto. Together they evoke the problems, preoccupations, and triumphs of an emerging American Jewish society.

When the pioneer prayer book—the first publication in the present series—made its appearance in 1761, American Jewry numbered about one thousand persons. The American Jew viewing the facsimile of this prayer book today is a member of a community of almost six millions, the largest Jewry in the history of the Diaspora. In the intervening centuries much has changed, of course; but there is also evident a constancy of purpose and concern, even of expression. The American Jew of 1761 and his counterpart in 1975 would somehow recognize one another. We offer this collection of early American Judaica as our contribution to the American Bicentennial observance, in the hope that its varied contents will serve once more to inspire and instruct.

We extend our thanks to the American Jewish Historical Society for its aid in the preparation of this project, particularly to Dr. Nathan M. Kaganoff, the Society's Librarian-Editor, and to Prof. Abraham J. Karp, who, in the following pages, provides a detailed description of each of the ten facsimiles.

The Jewish Publication Society of America
Tishri 5736 / September 1975

I

Pioneer Prayer Book

One of the earliest references to a Jewish presence in what later became the United States is contained in a letter, dated March 18, 1655, from Dominie Johannes Megapolensis, a *predikant* of the Dutch Reformed Church of New Amsterdam, to his superiors, the classis of Amsterdam. Among other matters of interest he noted:

> Last summer some Jews came here from Holland, in order to trade. Afterwards some Jews, poor and healthy, also came here. . . . Now again in the Spring some have come from Holland, and report that a great many of that lot would yet follow and then build here their synagogue.

More Jews did indeed follow, though not in the numbers anticipated by the dominie, and in due course—in 1730, three-quarters of a century later and after New Amsterdam had become New York—Congregation Shearith Israel of New York built its first synagogue, on Mill Street. A generation later Shearith Israel's sister congregation in Newport,

Rhode Island, erected its handsome synagogue building, now a national shrine. By the end of the colonial period, there were congregations as well in Savannah, Charleston, and Philadelphia. All followed the Sephardic rite, despite the fact that by the beginning of the eighteenth century Ashkenazim began to outnumber Sephardim. Thus, a draft of a constitution for Philadelphia's Congregation Mikveh Israel was composed in Yiddish, but the synagogue ritual and liturgy accorded with the Sephardic practice. The later-arriving German Jews (Ashkenazim) accepted the Spanish-Portuguese (Sephardic) rite rather than advancing their own partly because it was already established in the congregation, but mainly because it seemed to them so much an *American* mode.

The general social climate of colonial America, it must be remarked, was notably sympathetic to the fostering of Jewish religious development. Several of the colonies had been founded by religious groups, some for religious purposes. In all the colonies, religious forms were adhered to and religion was esteemed. It is not surprising, therefore, that in early America the synagogue came to occupy a more central position in Jewish communal life than it did in Europe. For the Jews of eighteenth-century colonial America, the congregation was the locus of all Jewish affiliation and activity: religious, cultural, social, and philanthropic. It solemnized marriages, educated the young, consecrated burial grounds, and dispensed charity for needs at home and abroad.

Although there was considerable social integration in the various frontier communities and intermarriage was not uncommon, most Jews married within the fold. Religious laxity was vigorously fought. Violators of the Sabbath and the dietary laws were held to account. For most early American Jews the need for community was stronger than the lure of religious deviation. The synagogue, as the preeminent Jewish institution, was able to maintain discipline within the community through denial of the basic religious rites—circumcision, marriage, burial. As Jacob R. Marcus, the foremost historian of colonial Jewry, has summed up:

> The Jews [of colonial America] were loyal to their faith; they were determined to survive as an integral part of the world Jewish fellowship. The community organization which they improvised with their synagogue as the hub and the Sephardic prayer service as the new American rite gave them group cohesion.

In the mid-eighteenth century there lived in New York a Jew who must have felt that a prayer book translated into English and printed in America would serve to weld the small community even closer together. His effort—the first of these Bicentennial offerings—appeared in 1761 under the title *Evening Service of Roshashanah, and Kippur; or The Beginning of the Year, and the Day of Atonement.* The name of the printer is given as W. Weyman, of Broad Street, New York. The name of the translator is nowhere to be found, nor is there any note of introduction or explanation, as might be expected in a publication of this order. Who was the anonymous translator and why the omission of his name?

But before we hazard an opinion, there is an antecedent question to be asked: why did the first published translation of any part of the Jewish liturgy into English for synagogue use—for such indeed is the distinction of this little volume —make its appearance in colonial New York, with its meager community of a few hundred Jews, rather than in metropolitan London, which boasted a flourishing community of some ten thousand?

The answer is really quite simple. London Jewry at this time had no pressing need for an English translation of the Hebrew prayer book and therefore none was forthcoming.

Because of its size the London community was able to support schools whose function it was to prepare the young for worship in Hebrew. As for those Jews who required translations, there were the Spanish and Judeo-German (Yiddish) versions for the edification, respectively, of Sephardic and Ashkenazic Jews, among whom the use of these languages was still widespread. However, in the colonies a different situation prevailed. There the Jewish community, as we have seen, consisted of an Ashkenazic majority and a Sephardic minority. Neither of these groups was absolutely proficient in Hebrew, and for neither were the existing Spanish and Yiddish translations of any practical use. Even if they were fluent in Yiddish, the Ashkenazim, preponderantly members of the older Sephardic congregations, could not take advantage of the Judeo-German translations, which only accommodated the Ashkenazic rite. Many of the Sephardim, by now second- and third-generation American Jews, no longer understood Spanish. Moreover, owing to the small numbers of the New York Jewish community, linguistic acculturation proceeded at a far more rapid pace than in the mother country. Clearly, here was another instance of necessity dictating innovative procedure.

As Isaac Pinto—of whom we shall soon have more to say —put it in the introduction to his (credited) translation of *Prayers for Shabbath, Rosh-Hashanah, and Kippur* (published in New York in 1766, also preceding a British translation):

> [Hebrew] being imperfectly understood by many, by some not at all; it has been necessary to translate our Prayers, in the Language of the Country wherein it hath pleased the divine Providence to appoint our Lot. In Europe, the Spanish and Portuguese Jews have a Translation in Spanish, which as they generally understand, may be sufficient, but that not being the Case in the British Dominions in America, has induced me to Attempt a Translation in English.

This statement is explicit enough and would seem also to account for the appearance of the 1761 volume. But the question of the translator's identity remains to be answered. Who *was* the pioneer translator of *Evening Service of Roshashanah, and Kippur*—and why, unlike the proclaimed translator of *Prayers for Shabbath, Rosh-Hashanah, and Kippur*, did he choose to remain anonymous?

Here we can only presume, although there is a near consensus among scholars that the mysterious translator in all likelihood was the aforementioned Isaac Pinto. Israel Abrahams *(By-paths in Hebraic Bookland)* refers to "Isaac Pinto's translations of the Hebrew prayerbook (1761 and 1766)," and Hyman B. Grinstein *(The Rise of the Jewish Community of New York)* notes "the printing of Isaac Pinto's English translation of the prayerbook in New York in 1761 and 1766." Jacob R. Marcus *(The Colonial American Jew)* is more cautious: "It [the 1761 translation] has been ascribed to Isaac Pinto, but there is no proof that the work was prepared by him."

Proof there is none, and indeed a textual comparison of the two works reveals many variations in translations of identical Hebrew passages. Here are some examples:

Passage	*1761 prayer book*	*1766 prayer book*
Ps. 92:1	Praises	Psalms
Ps. 92:2	Benevolence	Benignity
Ps. 92:3	Upon the Harp with a solemn sound	Upon the Harp with Meditation
the *Sh'mah*	Hear, O Israel, the Lord, our God, is one Lord	Hear O Israel the Lord, Our God, the Lord, *is* One
Eloheno she-ba-shamayim	Our God who art in Heaven, suffer us not to perish through the Length of our Captivity.	Our God who art in Heaven, waste us not through the length of our Captivity.

Passage	1761 prayer book	1766 prayer book
the *Amidah*	The Great GOD, Powerful and Tremendous: the Most High GOD! Bountifully dispensing Benefits; the Creator and Possessor of the Universe.	the great God, powerful and tremendous, the *most* high God! Bountifully dispensing Benefits; the Creator of all Things.

Nevertheless, a case can be made for Isaac Pinto as the putative translator of the 1761 volume. First, the 1761 prayer book and the 1766 one complement each other in content. Since they appeared in the same small community only five years apart, it is reasonable to assume that they are both parts of one translation by a single translator. Further, it is a matter of no small astonishment that the mid-eighteenth-century Jewish community of New York should have counted among its tiny numbers a man of such scholarship and enterprise as to be able to fashion a liturgical translation and to undertake its publication. That there might have been two such individuals is difficult to imagine.

The question persists: if both volumes did indeed issue from the same hand, how can we account for the variations of language? Here some more textual analysis would seem to be in order. When we compare the translations of identical Hebrew passages *within the same volume,* we find that the translator in both cases, 1761 and 1766, has permitted himself a certain latitude, varying the language from one place to another. Consider, for example, the following translations of identical passages occurring in the *Amidah* prayer for both the Rosh Hashanah and Yom Kippur services:

The 1761 prayer book

Roshashanah, p. 11	*Kippur, p. 24*
Thou, O Lord, art for ever Powerful. Thou restorest the Dead to life; and art Mighty to save; causing the dew to descend . . . animatest the Dead.	Thou O Lord art forever Powerful, restoring the Dead to Life; Thou art Mighty to save; caused the Dew to descend . . . animating the Dead.
Or who may be compared with Thee, O King, the Lord of Death and Resurrection; causing also salvation to flourish.	Or who may be compared with Thee, O King, who killest and again restorest unto Life, and causest salvation to flourish.

The 1766 (Pinto) prayer book

Rosh-Hashanah, p. 65	*Kippur, p. 100*
. . . setting at liberty those that are in Bonds; . . . unto those that sleep in the Dust.	. . . setting the Prisoners at Liberty . . . unto them that sleep in the Dust.
who is like unto thee, O Lord most mighty, or who may be compared with thee.	who is like unto thee, the Lord of Mighty Acts, or who may be compared with thee.

The translator of the 1761 prayer book and Isaac Pinto, it would seem, share the same peculiarity of style: a proclivity for variation—one time rendering the Hebrew *mehaye metim* as "Thou restorest the Dead to life," another, "restoring the Dead to Life"; in one case translating *matir asurim* as "setting at liberty those that are in Bonds," in another, "setting the Prisoners at liberty." It is a consistency of inconsistency, so to speak, and it strongly suggests a unity of authorship. If there can be variant versions of identical passages within the same volume, then why not variation from volume to volume, particularly in translations made five years apart?

Why did Isaac Pinto, assuming him to be the translator

of both prayer books, hide behind anonymity in the first instance and declare himself in the second? We venture a conjecture. In 1761 the small Jewish community of New York had not yet entirely shaken off its feelings of colonial inferiority. Congregation Shearith Israel, a tiny outpost of Jewish life on the fringes of the civilized world, looked to London, and particularly to the formidable Bevis Marks Congregation, for direction. The translator of *Prayers for Shabbath, Rosh-Hashanah, and Kippur* may have felt that he would be thought a usurper, preempting the prerogative of scholars more expert than he and more qualified to carry out the task at hand. Might he not have been inhibited from divulging his identity both by provincial diffidence and by concern over incurring the possible displeasure of the London authorities?

However, between 1761 and 1766 something occurred that might have led Isaac Pinto to throw off the cloak of anonymity. These years saw a mounting tension between the colonies and the mother country. The various British repressive measures—the Proclamation Act of 1763, the Sugar Act of 1764, the Stamp Act of 1765, the Mutiny Act —were answered by a growing resentment of overseas domination and an increasing expression of nondependence. Isaac Pinto, a signatory to resolutions favoring the Nonimportation Agreement, may have placed his name boldly on the 1766 volume as an expression of the same spirit: a declaration to the elders in London that their brethren in the "British Dominions in America," though small in number, were independent in will, that they were developing their own religious requirements and possessed the means to satisfy them.

Isaac Pinto, whether or not he was the translator of both the 1761 and 1766 prayer books, was certainly an adornment of the eighteenth-century American Jewish community. Ezra Stiles, president of Yale College, described him as "a learned Jew at New York," and indeed he was. In 1773

PRAYERS

FOR

SHABBATH, ROSH-HASHANAH, AND KIPPUR;

OR

The SABBATH, the BEGINNING of the YEAR,

AND

The DAY of ATONEMENTS;

WITH

The AMIDAH and MUSAPH of the MOADIM,

OR

SOLEMN SEASONS.

According to the Order of the Spanish and Portuguese Jews.

TRANSLATED BY *ISAAC PINTO*.

And for him printed by JOHN HOLT, in New-York.
A. M. 5526.

Title page of the Pinto prayer book (1766)

Pinto corresponded with Rabbi Haim Isaac Carigal of Hebron, then visiting Newport, Rhode Island (see page 11), on the meaning of Arabic words in Abraham Ibn Ezra's commentary on the Bible. Pinto's proficiency in languages is attested to by his advertisement in the *Journal and Patriotic Register* of New York: "The Spanish language taught by Isaac Pinto, No. 14 Duke Street."

That he was esteemed in the New York community is indicated by his epitaph and obituary notice. The Hebrew inscription on his tombstone reads: "Tombstone of the great man of his generation / the venerable and honored Isaac Pinto / who went to his eternal home 13 Shebat 5551 [January 17, 1791] / the years of his life were seventy years and seven months."

A contemporary New York newspaper extolled his life and memory:

> Mr. Pinto was truly a moral and social friend. His conversation was instructive, and his knowledge of mankind was general. Though of the Hebrew nation, his liberality was not circumscribed by the limits of that church. He was well versed in several of the foreign languages. He was a staunch friend of the liberty of his country. His intimates in his death have lost an instructive and entertaining companion; his relations, a firm friend; and the literary world, an historian and philosopher.

Isaac Pinto, staunch friend of liberty, instructive and entertaining companion, historian and philosopher—and, we may safely assume, first translator of a Hebrew prayer book into English.

2
Emissary from Hebron

On March 8, 1773, the Reverend Ezra Stiles, then minister
of the Second Congregational Church of Newport, Rhode
Island, attended a Purim service in the local synagogue. He
recorded the occasion in his diary:

> There I saw Rabbi [Haim Isaac] Carigal I judge aet.
> 45. lately from the city of Hebron, the Cave of the
> Macpelah in the Holy Land. He was one of the two
> persons that stood by the Chusan at the Taubauh or
> Reading Desk while the Book of Esther was read. He
> was dressed in a red garment with the usual Phylacter-
> ies and habiliments, the white silk Surplice; he wore a
> high brown furr Cap, had a long Beard. He has the
> appearance of an ingenious & sensible Man.

The visitor from the Holy Land so colorfully described
by Stiles was no stranger to the New World. A native of
Hebron—he was born in 1733 and ordained as a rabbi
twenty years later—Carigal had traveled widely in the Near
East and Europe and in the Americas, acting on occasion
as an itinerant rabbinic functionary. He had spent two years

in Curaçao and then returned to Hebron in 1764. In 1768 he again took off on his travels. For two and a half years he served as a teacher in London and then spent a year in Jamaica. In the summer of 1772 he made his way to Philadelphia. After tarrying there a month and five and a half months in New York, he arrived in Newport on March 3, 1773, in time to celebrate the Purim holiday and to make the acquaintance of Ezra Stiles.

Stiles had a vast curiosity about all manner of things and an inordinate interest in Jews and Judaism. Fortunately for the student of history he kept voluminous diaries, which have survived as a unique repository of eighteenth-century information, including much Jewish information. Thus we learn from him that no less than six foreign rabbis visited Newport between 1759 and 1775. Stiles sought them all out and made suitable entries in his diaries.

Of the six, Carigal impressed him the most. The two divines spent much time together and over the months conversed on a variety of topics:

[March] 30. This afternoon the Rabbi came to visit me in Company with Mr. Lopez. . . . We conversed largely on the Gemara, the 2 Talmuds (of which he preferred the Babylonish) the Changes of the Hebrew Language in different Ages &c. &c. . . . He . . . shewed me a passage in the *Zohar* which he said predicted that the *Russians should conquer the Turks.* . . . We talked upon the differences of the Dialects of the Chaldees, Syriac, and rabbinical Hebrew, on the Targum &c.

[June] 14. In the Forenoon I went to visit the Rabbi— discoursed on Ventriloquism & the Witch of Endor and the Reality of bringing up Samuel. He had not heard of Ventriloquism before and still doubted it.

[July] 15. Spent the afternoon with the Rabbi, partly at the Redwood Library and partly at my house. I asked him whether the Rabbins of this Age thought themselves to have any particular Reason for expecting the Messiah immediately? He said not; but he thought it was high Time for him to come.

Carigal supplied Stiles with information about Jews in other lands, especially the Holy Land, noting that there were about one thousand families of Jews and twelve synagogues "in all Judea or Holy Land A. D. 1773." Stiles also learned from him that there were three rabbis "settled in America, one in Jamaica, one in Surinam and one in Curaçao," but "none on the Continent of North America." Carigal himself planned to settle ultimately in Antigua.

Ezra Stiles continued his visits to the Newport synagogue, particularly on festival days. Passover (April 8, 1773) found him once more attending the services, where again he encountered Rabbi Carigal, this time even more elegantly attired:

> The Rabbi's dress or Apparel: Common English Shoes, black leather, Silver Buckles, White Stockings. His general Habit was Turkish. *A green silk Vest . . .* reaching down more than half way the Legs. . . . A Girdle or Sash of different Colors red and green girt the Vest around his Body. . . . When he came into the Synagogue he put over all, the usual *Alb* or white *Surplice,* which was like that of other Jews, except that its Edge was striped with *Blue Straiks,* and had *more Fringe.* He had a white cravat around his neck. . . . On his Head a high fur (Sable) Cap, exactly like a Womans Muff, and about 9 or 10 Inches high, the Aperture atop was closed with green cloth.

On May 28, the festival of Shavuot, Stiles also was in the synagogue, and this time he had the pleasure of hearing a sermon preached by Carigal in "Spanish"—although it may very well have been Ladino—which lasted for forty-seven minutes. Though few present were able to understand any part of the lengthy discourse, whose theme was "the salvation of Israel," the occasion was an auspicious one for the twenty-five families who formed the Jewish community of Newport. Dignitaries from the general community had been invited—Stiles noted Governor Wantan, Judge Oliver, and Judge Auchmuty—and all listened respectfully to the exotically garbed preacher speaking in a strange yet impressive tongue. "There was a Dignity and Authority about him, mixt with modesty," observed Stiles. It must have been an exhilarating experience for the small group of Jewish immigrant merchants, raising them, in the eyes of their fellow citizens of Newport, to the status of scions of an ancient and noble tradition.

It was certainly a moment that demanded preservation for posterity. Abraham Lopez, a native of Portugal and a former Marrano who had entered the Covenant of Abraham six years earlier, was entrusted with the task of translating the sermon into English. It was published later that year—the first Jewish sermon in America, insofar as we know, to be accorded the honor.

Rabbi Carigal shows himself to be a skillful preacher who must have held his auditors enthralled, not only because of his colorful costume but also (at least to those who understood him) by dint of his homiletic art. Like all good preachers, he seeks to engage the attention of his listeners by entering into their familiar world: in this case, the pursuit of a livelihood—a universal preoccupation, but one of special concern, no doubt, to the Newport congregants. All creation and the Creator Himself, Carigal begins simply, labor to provide sustenance—bread. From this homely starting point he launches into the elaboration of his theme. Quoting Scripture and the Sages, bread becomes "the holy law, which subsists man in this world and in the world to come." Reminding his listeners of the occasion for the sermon, the Festival of the Giving of the Law, he pleads for "the study of the law." He upholds traditional interpretation against "some authors, touched with a vehement desire to finding out new methods of commentary upon the

Portrait of Haim Isaac Carigal, made for Yale College

sacred Scriptures." In a burst of passion he reminds the assemblage that the classic enemies of the Jewish people all went down in defeat. (What the distinguished non-Jews in the audience made of this bit of intelligence, we do not know.) Finally, the sermon builds to a climax with an expression of faith in the Restoration and an ethical exhortation. In the fashion of the time, it concludes with a prayer.

The sermon was published after Carigal left Newport, contrary to his wishes. Stiles, ever the faithful diarist, reports:

> The Rabbi told me that he had nothing written when he preached at the Synagogue—but that he had *sealed* it first in his head and so delivered it—that he was able to recollect it and to gratify the Jews here he should write it in Spanish, and they would translate it into English, and then he would give me a copy. But he would not consent that it should be printed.

Fortunately, the Jews of Newport paid no heed to his instructions.

Carigal died four years later in Barbados. The affection which Stiles bore for him survived parting and death. When the Newport clergyman was called to become the fifth president of Yale College, he suggested to Aaron Lopez, the leader of the Newport Jewish community, that a portrait of Carigal be "deposited in the Library of the College." Lopez was pleased that the likeness of the rabbi would be preserved "in so distinguished a seminary," and in due time a portrait painted by Samuel King was hung in the Yale library (where, regrettably, it is no longer on view). It is a compelling representation. Arrayed in all his splendor, displaying an air of "Dignity and Authority," and looking very much as he must have appeared that morning of May 28, 1773, Rabbi Haim Isaac Carigal, emissary from the holy city of Hebron to the Jews of the New World, continues to command our attention.

Interior of the Newport synagogue

3
Patriot Preacher

The Revolutionary War ended, independence achieved, a government established, the new American nation turned to the mother country with an affection born of remorse. The elected leaders of the Republic looked to England for friendship and turned against America's former ally, France, which in the wake of the successful American struggle had mounted its own revolution. As the eighteenth century was drawing to an end, the United States was divided between Federalists and Republicans, between those who favored traditional stability, as represented by England, and those hailing revolutionary change, as fostered by France. International sympathies were cloaks for domestic commitments. It was the first testing of the meaning and promise of America, whether the nation would be fired by the vision of the Declaration of Independence or ruled by the compromise of the Constitution.

The publication of the XYZ correspondence, which disclosed a demand by French political leaders for a bribe, turned anti-French sentiment into a passion and laid the ground for the Alien and Sedition Acts. Suspicion, sup-

pression, bitterness, and recrimination poisoned the at-
mosphere.

On March 23, 1798, President John Adams designated
May 9 as a day of fasting, prayer, and national "humiliation." The citizens were enjoined to repair to their houses
of worship. The Jews of New York gathered in their synagogue on Mill Street, recited appropriate psalms, and attended to a discourse delivered by their minister, the Reverend Gershom Mendes Seixas.

Unlike the great majority of his non-Jewish colleagues
who also spoke from the pulpit that day, Seixas did not
attack the French. To be sure, he affirmed that "we are
threatened with all the horrors of war by a great, a con-
quering nation," but, he reminded the congregation, only
"a few years past" the same nation "was looked upon to
have been highly instrumental in procuring liberty and independence to the United States of America, when we
were oppressed by the ravages and devastations of an en-
raged enemy, who sought to deprive us of our invaluable
rights and privileges." Seixas did not mention either
France or England by name, but the reference was clear
to all.

Nor did he consider foreign threats to be the only perils
that confronted the new nation. Equally dangerous, and to
his mind more distressing, were internal division and en-
mity. In the manner of a preacher, citing precedent and
verse, he pleaded for "friendly disposition toward each
other." Noting the diversity of the American populace
("collected from different countries, each bringing with
him the prejudices of the government he was brought up
in"), he averred that such a society, more than others, must
adhere to "the grand principles of benevolence towards all
our fellow creatures."

The sermon, as was customary for the period, is a ram-
bling affair, touching upon many themes, from the pious to
the apocalyptic. Striking a note that was to be echoed again

and again by future spokesmen for American Jewry, Seixas pays tribute to the special blessing of America for Jews:

> It hath pleased God to establish us in this country where we possess every advantage that other citizens of these states enjoy, and which is as much as could in reason expect in this captivity, for which let us humbly return thanks for his manifold mercies, and sincerely pray for a continuance of his divine protection.

In the wars that plague the nations, and the depravity that corrupts the individual, Seixas perceives the "pangs of the Messiah" and declares that "we must necessarily be led to believe that the glorious period of redemption is near at hand, and that our God will make manifest his intentions of again collecting the scattered remnants of Israel, and establishing them according to his divine promise."

But above all there is Seixas the revolutionary patriot, who cannot forget who was friend and who foe in the War of Independence. A man of democratic tendencies, he is loath to attack the Jacobin sentiments and is aware of the danger of the suppression of liberal expression in the new and developing nation.

The discourse, as we read on the title page, was "Printed by William A. Davis & Co. for Naphtali Judah, Bookseller and Stationer. No. 47 Water street."(A printer's error gives the date of publication as 1797; the correct date, of course, is 1798.) At the time Davis was the publisher of *The Time Piece,* a triweekly Republican newspaper. Naphtali Judah was a leader of Congregation Shearith Israel, a member of the anti-Federalist Democratic Society and the Society of Tammany.

The introductory statement by "The Editor" that "the solicitation of several of the Author's friends . . . has induced him to have it [the discourse] printed" seems more than the customary formula. Among the friends soliciting

Medal bearing likeness of Gershom Mendes Seixas,
struck by Columbia College
American Jewish Historical Society

publication of what must have been considered a pro-Republican sermon were no doubt Naphtali Judah and certainly Solomon Simpson, who served as parnass of Shearith Israel in 1773, 1776, and in the postwar years of 1787, 1790, and 1791. At the time of the publication of the discourse, Simpson was president of the Democratic Society, which he had helped found in 1794.

Gershom Mendes Seixas was the first native-born Jewish clergyman to serve an American congregation. He was both a product of the American milieu and a participant in the young nation's developing society and culture. Born in New York on January 15, 1746, he was educated in the synagogue school of Shearith Israel. Following his bar mitzvah he went out to learn a trade, but at the age of twenty-two he was engaged as hazzan by Shearith Israel. In the course of time he came to be called "the reverend" and "minister" and, on occasion, "rabbi." Together with members of his congregation, he left New York when it was occupied by the British during the War of Independence, and served Congregation Mikveh Israel in Philadelphia. When peace was established he returned to his New York congregation, which he served with faithfulness and increasing distinction until his death in July 1816.

In 1784 Seixas became a regent of Columbia College, serving in this capacity until 1815. In grateful tribute, the college struck a medal bearing his likeness, with the legend "Gershom M. Seixas Congregationis Hebraeae Sacerdos Novi Eboraci" (Priest of the Hebrew Congregation of New York).

As his name indicates, Gershom Mendes Seixas was a member of a noted Sephardic family, but his mother's family were all Ashkenazim. And although he served a congregation that followed the Spanish-Portuguese rite (albeit largely Ashkenazic in membership), as his letters disclose he was far more fluent in Yiddish than in the Iberian tongues. Seixas was thus not only a Jew integrated into the general culture and society, but a representative as well of an early amalgam of the discrete national backgrounds that fused to form the American Jew.

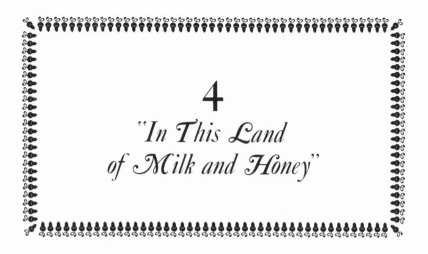

4

"In This Land of Milk and Honey"

The oration ended with a prayer:

> And now, oh, thou God of Israel! thou High and
> Mighty Father of Mankind! from whom emanates all
> that can be perceived of Mercy and Goodness, permit
> one of thy servants, in humble supplication, to address
> thy throne. . . . O! Omnipotent God . . . collect to-
> gether thy long scattered people of Israel, and let their
> gathering place be in this land of milk and honey.

The occasion for this flight of eloquence was the fifth anniversary of the founding of the Hebrew Orphan Society,
established in Charleston, South Carolina, on July 15,
1801. The impassioned orator of the day (October 15,
1806) was the gifted Myer Moses, then twenty-seven years
old.

The stated purpose of the Hebrew Orphan Society, as
laid down in its charter was

> relieving widows, educating, clothing and maintaining
> orphans and children of indigent parents; making it a

particular care to inculcate strict principles of piety, morality and industry; and designing at the same time to cultivate any indication of genius they may evince for any of the arts and sciences, that they may thereby become qualified for the enjoyment of those blessings and advantages to which they are entitled—kind Heaven having cast their lot in the United States of America where freedom and equal rights, religious, civil and political, are liberally extended to them, in common with every other class of citizens.

At the time of the founding of the Hebrew Orphan Society, Charleston was the largest Jewish community in the United States, and remained so for the next two decades. The chief seaport and commercial capital of the South, the city was enjoying a postwar prosperity, and its Jewish citizens joined in the general well-being, becoming increasingly integrated into the social and cultural fabric of the community. As Philip Cohen, a "respectable merchant," wrote in 1811:

> The Jews of Charleston enjoy equal literary advantages with other members of the community. . . . The dress and habits . . . do not distinguish them from other citizens. . . . They have built an elegant synagogue. . . . They also have societies for the relief of strangers, for attending the sick, and for administering the rites of humanity, and burial to the dying and dead. The most modern institution is a society for the relief of orphans. The capital is already considerable and it is yearly increasing [quoted in *History of the Jews,* by Hannah Adams, Boston, 1812].

The Charleston congregation, Beth Elohim, was organized in 1749, although Jews had lived in the city since 1695. In 1784 the Hebrew Benevolent Society was founded, but was not incorporated until 1830. "An Act to Incorporate the *Abi Yetomim Ubne Ebyonim,* or Society for the Relief of Orphans and Children of Indigent Parents" was passed by the General Assembly of South Carolina on

December 18, 1802, making the Hebrew Orphan Society (as the institution came to be known), in the words of Jacob R. Marcus, "the oldest *incorporated* Jewish charitable organization in continuous existence in the United States." It seems only fitting therefore that the Myer Moses oration should, among other things, represent the earliest known published appeal for charitable funds on behalf of an American Jewish institution.

Myer Moses was born in Charleston on February 12, 1779, the son of a merchant and revolutionary patriot who bore the same name. In time he carved out a distinguished career in commerce and public service, a testament both to his considerable talents and to the opportunities available to Jews in American society. He was a member of the South Carolina legislature (1810), commissioner of free schools (1811), commissioner of public schools (1823), active member of the South Carolina Society for Promotion of Domestic Arts and Manufactures, director of the Planters and Mechanics Bank, and major in the South Carolina volunteers. He married Esther Phillips, daughter of Jonas Phillips of Philadelphia, and thus became a brother-in-law of the New York publisher Naphtali Phillips and an uncle of Mordecai Manuel Noah (see below, page 59).

In about 1825 Myer Moses moved to New York, where his family connections as well as his reputation gave him immediate entry into the city's political life. His writings include *Remarks on the Supplementary Vendue Act of 1815, Addressed to the Legislature of South Carolina* (Charleston, 1822); the *Full Annals of the Revolution in France* (New York, 1830), to which was appended *Full Account of the Celebration of Said Revolution in the City of New-York*, and *Oration Delivered at Tammany Hall, on May 12, 1831*.

The oration before the Hebrew Orphan Society reveals a young man who is already a most accomplished speaker, skilled in all the arts of rhetoric and able to evoke sentiments of strong patriotism mingled with Jewish concern:

> No country can boast more of an adoption of virtuous principles, than can this blessed land, in which it has pleased the Almighty to place us in, and, in fact, many concomitant causes render it just why it should be so.
> The mild and liberal constitution of our country knows no distinction of its citizens. . . . They all partake alike of the blessings it imparts: it holds up a free toleration in religious pursuits and licences a general exercise of rational liberty, free from the control of a polluted and mercenary police. . . . The distinctions of rank and nobility, known in other countries, are abolished, and we hail each other by no other appellation than that of fellow citizen. . . . To us, my brethren, should particularly belong a sacred love to this our country; for, when we look back to the oppressed days of our forefathers, we cannot but feel a self importance arising from our happy lot, and duly appreciate the source from whence it came.

Master of a style whose force can still be felt across the centuries, Myer Moses, like all gifted, self-confident, serious speakers, is not afraid to pull out the emotional stops:

> Can the eye witness, or the heart beat stronger with pity, than in beholding a helpless child, forlorn and deserted, wandering from door to door, and craving a morsel to ease the pinching call of hunger. . . . Its tender frame exposed at one season to the bleaking cold, at another to the parching heat. . . . For its covering it has the starry element; for its pillow the cold earth. . . . It knows no tender mother's embrace; it wants a father's anxious solicitude. . . . This helpless innocent, fatherless and motherless, stands as a lonely bush, placed obscurely in the midst of a great forest: thousands will daily pass it; nay, even crush its rise, when it would only need some kind solace, some little care to make it flourish, perhaps, a lofty tree.

FULL ANNALS

OF THE

REVOLUTION IN FRANCE,

1830.

TO WHICH IS ADDED,

A FULL ACCOUNT

OF THE

CELEBRATION OF SAID REVOLUTION

IN THE

CITY OF NEW-YORK,

ON THE 25TH NOVEMBER, 1830:

BEING THE FORTY-SEVENTH ANNIVERSARY OF AN EVENT THAT RESTORED
OUR CITIZENS TO THEIR HOMES, AND TO THE ENJOYMENT
OF THEIR RIGHTS AND LIBERTIES.

—◆—

BY MYER MOSES.

===

NEW-YORK:

PRINTED BY J. & J. HARPER, 82 CLIFF-STREET.

SOLD BY COLLINS AND HANNAY, COLLINS AND CO., G. AND C. AND H. CARVILL, O. A.
ROORBACH, WHITE, GALLAHER, AND WHITE, A. T. GOODRICH, W. B. GILLEY, E.
BLISS, C. S. FRANCIS, G. C. MORGAN, M. BANCROFT, W. BURGESS, N. B. HOLMES,
M'ELRATH AND BANGS, E. B. CLAYTON, J. E. BETTS, AND J. T. K. PORTER;—ALBANY,
STEELE AND LITTLE AND CUMMINGS.

1830.

Title page of a pamphlet by Myer Moses

However, his greatest effects are reserved for his unblushing love of America:

> I am so proud of being a sojourner in this promised land, that, had I to subsist on the spontaneous production of the earth, and each day to search a running stream to quench my thirst at, I should prefer it to all the luxuries and superfluities of the most brilliant court which ill fated Europe can boast of.

Giving full rein to his impulse, he rises to a crescendo:

> May we not fondly cherish the pleasing hope, that, from among the Hebrew Society, there may spring a WASHINGTON for the field; a JEFFERSON for the cabinet, and a PREBLE for the navy? . . . Nay, may we not indulge this hope, and let our imagination carry us still further, in pronouncing that the ABI YETOMIM may, one day, pluck from its promising stock a branch suitable for either of those dignified stations.

(The hope was indeed granted. A well-founded tradition has it that a student at the school of the Hebrew Orphan Society was Judah P. Benjamin, a son of "indigent parents," who rose to serve in the cabinet of the Confederate States as attorney general, secretary of war, and from 1862 to 1865, secretary of state.)

Myer Moses is listed as a "Vice-President of the Institution." His duties with the Hebrew Orphan Society apparently included what was to become the prime communal activity of American Jewry, namely, engaging in acts of charitable benevolence, or what later generations were to call fund raising. All the more surprising, then, that the various histories of the Jews in the South scarcely mention his Jewish leadership activities. Indeed, *Oration Delivered before the Hebrew Orphan Society* seems to have eluded the attention of the standard bibliographies in the field. It is therefore good to be able to restore Myer Moses to his rightful place in American Jewish history, as an early exemplar of the American Jewish fund-raising tradition, and to give long-denied credit for participation in Jewish affairs to one who heretofore had been noted only for his involvement in the civic and political life of Charleston and New York.

5

The "Jew Bill"

In 1776, the year the Declaration of Independence proclaimed that "all men are created equal," the state of Maryland adopted a constitution. Its preamble, known as the Declaration of Rights, stated (section 33): "It is the duty of every man to worship God is such manner as he thinks most acceptable to Him: all persons professing the Christian religion are equally entitled to protection in their religious liberty." Article 35 of this declaration, which took a rather restricted view of religious liberty, provided that "no other test or qualification ought to be required on admission to any office of trust or profit than such oath of support and fidelity to the State . . . and a declaration of belief in the Christian religion."

In 1797, following the establishment of the new nation, the adoption of the federal Constitution, and the enactment of the Bill of Rights, "Solomon Etting and others" petitioned the Maryland Assembly: "A sect of people called Jews . . . are deprived of invaluable rights of citizenship and praying to be placed on the same footing as other good citizens." The petition was termed "reasonable," but was not acted upon, a fate also suffered by subsequent submissions. In 1804 the struggle was suspended, not to be pressed again for fourteen years.

In 1818 a champion arose in the person of Thomas Kennedy, who asked the legislature, of which he was a member, to appoint a committee "to consider the justice and expediency of placing the Jewish inhabitants on equal footing with the Christians." An eight-year struggle ensued in the legislature, in the press, and at the polls. Kennedy was joined by Ebenezer S. Thomas, Judge Henry Brackenridge, and Colonel William G. D. Worthington. The Jewish community of Baltimore, now grown to some 150 persons, were led in the endeavor by Solomon Etting and Jacob Cohen, prominent members of the leading families.

A vote in 1819 defeated what was now called the "Jew Bill" 50–24, the Republicans voting in favor, the Federalists against. Four years later a broader bill was again defeated, and Kennedy lost at the polls in 1823. Elected a year later, he continued to press his campaign. Finally in 1825 an enfranchising bill was passed and confirmed the following year. It provided

> that every citizen of this state professing the Jewish Religion . . . appointed to any office of public trust . . . shall . . . make and subscribe a declaration of his belief in a future state of rewards and punishments, in the stead of the declaration now required.

The spoken and printed words had played their part in the achievement of the victory. There had been newspaper editorials supporting the Jew Bill and numerous orations, many of which were rushed into print. Of the latter, none was more effective than Colonel Worthington's *Speech on the Maryland Test Act 1824.*

William Worthington, described on the title page of his speech as a "member of the General Assembly of Maryland, from the City of Baltimore," held a variety of positions in government service. His titles of "colonel" and "governor" were honorific. He was obviously acquainted with many Jews, and it seems most likely that Solomon Etting provided him not only with information about the Jewish situation in Maryland but also with the motivation for support of the bill.

Worthington's argument to include the Jews in Maryland's bounty was based on legal, historical, and practical considerations. Religious restriction, he contends, "is against the genius and character of the government of our State and Union, and the age in which we live." When the Maryland constitution was framed, the country was still under the sway of "monarchical . . . prejudice, and narrow-mindedness." The War of Independence liberated the spirit of man, and in its wake came the Constitution of the United States, which is more expressive than the Maryland document of true democratic sentiments. No such restrictions would be imposed today, he argues, so why persist in retaining them?

A pamphlet opposing the Jew Bill, bearing the signature "Orthodox," had been placed on the desk of every Maryland legislator. Worthington attacks the document on factual grounds and then proceeds to the heart of his argument, which is "practical" in nature. The well-being of a growing and an expanding community, he posits, is based on its ability to attract capital and men of enterprise who know how to use it for economic good. The anti-Jewish restrictions would not only discourage the immigration of "moral, enterprising, and affluent citizens," but might also drive those already in residence to "some other state, where they enjoy equal rights and favor"—why, even Rothschild himself, "with his immense wealth . . . driven to seek an asylum in this western hemisphere . . . would turn in loathing from you to live in some *Free State.*"

Worthington cites the letters of mutual respect between

Portrait of Solomon Etting (1764–1847), by John Wesley Davis

George Washington and the Jews of his day. He invokes the political philosophy of Fox and Pitt and appeals for justice. He reminds his auditors of the separation of church and state and avers that the issue is larger than the Jew Bill, as indeed it was. However, the most forceful plea remains that of self-interest. Again he stresses that unless the Jews are made welcome in Maryland, other states will stand to benefit from their wealth and enterprise.

Truth to tell, the appeal to justice by Kennedy and the skillful legal argument by Brackenridge were more lofty and idealistic, but Worthington's emphasis on the "practical" was more persuasive and carried the day.

To aid the reader in a better understanding of Colonel Worthington's *Speech on the Maryland Test Act,* some brief notes are included:

Page 13 (line 6): The "person . . . , some year or so past, elected in the North Carolina legislature"—"a Jew"—was Jacob Henry. This happened in 1809. A challenge had been raised to his election, and Henry defended his rights in a speech that has become somewhat of a classic ("Conduct alone is the subject of human laws . . . man ought to suffer civil disqualifications for what he does and not for what he thinks"). Jacob Henry was finally allowed to take his seat, by an act exempting legislative office from restrictions in the state constitution, which were not removed until 1868.

Page 17 (line 19): Solomon Etting (1764–1847) was born in York, Pennsylvania, and bears the distinction of having been the first native-born *shohet* (ritual slaughterer). He subsequently moved to Baltimore, organized the Baltimore East India Company, and served as a director of the first American railroad company, the Baltimore and Ohio. He was also active in the civic life of the city and led the struggle for the Jew Bill.

Page 18 (line 16): For "John Burk" read "Solomon Bush." (This erratum, as the reader can see, has been corrected in the margin in script.) Born in Philadelphia in 1753, Bush was appointed deputy adjutant general for the state militia of Pennsylvania in 1777. He fought in the Revolution, and when wounded was retired with the rank of lieutenant colonel. A fervent patriot and abolitionist, he was unsuccessful in his quest for public office.

Page 18 (line 24): Reuben Etting (1726–1848) was the elder brother of Solomon. In 1801 he was appointed by President Jefferson as marshal of Maryland. As a Jew, he could not hold any state office.

Page 20 (line 9): Uriah P. Levy (1792–1862), of Philadelphia and New York, served in the navy in a variety of posts. Court-martialed six times and twice dismissed, he attributed his troubles to anti-Semitism and jealousy. Reinstated, he retired with the title of commodore, the navy's highest rank at the time. He led the battle for the abolition of flogging in the navy.

Page 33 (line 22): The "youth" referred to here is Elijah Etting, son of Reuben, who went on to become district attorney of Cecil County in Maryland.

Page 34 (line 16): Another erratum, also corrected by hand. For "Juda Probah" read "Judah Touro" (here spelled "Torah"). Touro was a leading philanthropist, whose last will and testament reads, in effect, like a directory of all the Jewish institutions in the United States in 1855. His beneficence enabled Sir Moses Montefiore to build the first Jewish housing in Jerusalem outside the walls of the Old City.

In his personal copy of the speech, Colonel Worthington wrote in his own hand:

This speech was highly spoken of by Jared Sparks, Esq., Editor of the North American Review. As I was told by a Rabbi it was translated into Hebrew. The facts stated in it and its profuse circulation throughout the state, it was said, mainly aided in repealing that part of the Constitution of Maryland in a year or two afterward.

The Jews always treat me with great politeness and friendly attention, which I attribute to this speech.

W. G. D. W.

If a Hebrew translation was indeed made, it has not yet been found.

6

The Haggadah— "First American Edition"

The Passover Haggadah has been reprinted more often and in more places than any other Jewish classic. One of these places, of course, is the United States, where over the years there have been countless editions in a vast variety of forms. But whether it be a lavish oversize volume with original illustrations or a more modest booklet issued by some organization or institution, all of these "American" Haggadahs must trace their origin to a small 86-page publication (included among the present offerings), printed in New York in 1837—the "First American Edition," as it proclaims itself, of a *Service for the Two First Nights of the Passover, in Hebrew and English.*

This is not say that prior to 1837 American Jews were bereft of this essential Jewish text. There were many European editions of the Haggadah available to the early Jewish community in America, including editions with accompanying English, Spanish, or Yiddish translations (if the Hebrew alone proved insufficient). Indeed, the translation carried in the 1837 publication—"by the late David Levi of London"—had long been available to American Jews in its

various British editions. Be that as it may, for some reason
the printer, Solomon Henry Jackson, decided that the time
was ripe to bring out an American edition. The event may
very well mark yet another instance of American Jews de-
claring their cultural independence from the mother country (albeit with a translation done by an English Jew!).

Jackson, had he wanted to, could have prepared his own
translation. In 1826 he had printed a prayer book that bore

Hebrew and English title pages of the Jackson prayer book

THE FORM

OF

DAILY PRAYERS,

ACCORDING TO THE CUSTOM

OF THE

SPANISH AND PORTUGUESE JEWS.

AS READ IN THEIR SYNAGOGUES, AND USED IN THEIR FAMILIES

Translated into English from the Hebrew, by
SOLOMON HENRY JACKSON.
The Hebrew Text carefully Revised and Corrected by
E. S. LAZARUS.

FIRST EDITION.

NEW-YORK:
PRINTED BY S. H. JACKSON, AT THE HEBREW AND ENGLISH PRINTING
OFFICE, 23 MERCER-STREET.
A. M. 5586.

סדר התפלות

כמנהג ק"ק ספרדים יזי"א

מתוקן בסדר נאה ויפה והוגה בעיין וברקדוק והשגחה פרטית כאשר
עיני הקורא התחזינה מישרים
ע"י המדקדק התוארני
כהרר אליעזר ב"י מוהרר שמואל

להדים מכשול ולסקל המסילה ולהסיר כל טעות ושגיאה למען חתיה תפלותנו קרובה לכל
בשפה ברורה ותהי לרצון לפני מלך שומע עתירה ואז נזכה לקולות לציין ברנה
יכוני עולם וכשנים קדמניית נעברהו ביראה

נו-יארק

רפס על ידי הצעיר שי:מה בן כה"ר צבי הדוש ז"ל מלונדן

פ:ה

ואת דכאי רוח יושיע

לפ"ק

the ascription: "Translated into English from the Hebrew, by Solomon Henry Jackson," and an English rendering of the Haggadah was certainly within his capacity. Apparently the Levi translation of the Haggadah was held in such esteem that Jackson, surveying the market, thought it wisest to take advantage of its fame and acceptance. Indeed, the Levi translation was so widely used that it ultimately became the standard translation in later American editions of the Haggadah, often without credit to the translator.

The story of Solomon Henry Jackson is interesting in itself and instructive about early Jewish life in America. A native of England, Jackson came to these shores about 1787. His later activities indicate that he arrived with a good background in Jewish and secular studies. He settled in Pike County, Pennsylvania, where he married the daughter of a Presbyterian minister, who bore him five children. After some twenty years of marriage Jackson was widowed, and he moved to New York. Apparently he was smitten with remorse for his marital lapse, for not only did he raise his children as Jews, but he devoted his life to the defense of Judaism against Christianity and service to the Jewish community. In the years 1823–25 he edited an antimissionary monthly, *The Jew; Being a Defence of Judaism Against All Adversaries, and Particularly Against the Insidious Attacks of Israel's Advocate.* "Not to defend our character as a people," he declared, "would be a dereliction of duty."

Jackson was the first Jewish printer in New York, doing work in both English and Hebrew. As mentioned above, he published his own translation of the Hebrew prayer book, *The Form of Daily Prayers, According to the Custom of the Spanish and Portuguese Jews.* He was active in a number of congregations in New York and in the Hevrat Hinnukh Ne'arim, a society for the promotion of Jewish education. In 1837 he led a movement to settle Jews on the land. After his death in 1847 his son carried on his printing trade.

David Levi (1742–1801), the translator of the "First American Edition" of the Haggadah, was a native of London. He was intended for the rabbinate, but circumstances forced him to work as a hatter. Nevertheless, he managed to pursue a busy career as a scholar, translator, and polemicist. He translated the Pentateuch into English, as well as the Sephardic and Ashkenazic prayer books. He published a Hebrew grammar and dictionary, *Rites and Ceremonies of the Jews,* and in print defended the Jewish religion against an attack by Joseph Priestley and the Bible against the onslaught of Thomas Paine.

Thus it was that an impoverished London hatter and the repentant son-in-law of an American Presbyterian minister begot, so to speak, the first Haggadah published in the United States.

By way of postscript: In 1850 there appeared a second edition of this Haggadah, published by Jackson's son. Altogether there have been over 210 separate editions of the Haggadah published in the United States up to 1960 (according to Abraham Yaari, *Bibliography of the Passover Haggadah*). These include curiosities, departures from the traditional text, parodies, and, of course, edition after edition of the familiar traditional version.

7
"Meeting of the Israelites Resident at Philadelphia"

The event was deemed of such interest that the *Pennsylvania Inquirer and Daily Courier* gave it six columns of space in the issue of August 31, 1840, fully two-thirds of the news page. Under the headline, PERSECUTION OF THE JEWS/THE MEETING IN PHILADELPHIA, readers could find "the official account of the recent meeting in this city, in relation to the persecuted Jews of Damascus." ("We have printed a few extra copies," a note stated, "for the accommodation of such of our citizens as desire to forward copies to friends at a distance.")

The meeting had taken place on August 27 of that year. Eight days before, a similar meeting had been called in New York. A day following the Philadelphia gathering there was a general meeting of citizens of Charleston, South Carolina, followed the next evening by a meeting of the city's Jewish community. Meetings were also held in Richmond, Savannah, and Cincinnati.

The outrage that had called forth this unprecedented outpouring of protest and petition was the so-called Damascus affair, a mid-nineteenth-century recrudescence of the medieval blood-libel accusation. Following the disappearance of a Catholic priest on February 5, 1840, the Jewish community of Damascus was accused of his murder, "in order to take his Blood, it being ordered by their religion to make use of Christian Blood in their unleavened Bread at Easter" (in the language of a contemporary account). Scores of Jews were thrown into prison and tortured until they confessed to the false accusation. Throughout the city Jews hid in terror. ("The inquisition against the Jews . . . continues with much vigour and no jew can show his face out in the streets," the same account reported.)

The unfortunate Jews of Damascus had been caught in the vise of an international conflict, victims of a power struggle between the viceroy of Egypt and the Turkish sultan. The viceroy, sponsored by France, had seized Syria from the sultan, who was backed by a coalition of powers headed by Britain. The French consul in Damascus actively promoted the accusation with the support of his government, which sought to exploit the incident for its own imperial design.

In Great Britain there was a huge public outcry against the events, for humanitarian as well as political reasons. The world press seized on the affair, and the world Jewish community was caught up in a sense of common destiny, determined to act in defense of their hapless Damascus brethren. British Jewry, taking their cue from the general response, assumed the lead. Backed by the Jewish Board of Deputies, Sir Moses Montefiore undertook negotiations with the Foreign Office to intervene. Accompanied by Adolphe Crémieux, representing French Jewry, Sir Moses set out for Egypt on July 21 to plead the cause of the accused Jews of Damascus. The mission, happily, was a success.

News of the outrage apparently was slow in reaching the Jews in America. The New York meeting, for instance, took place almost two months after a meeting in London called by Jewish Board of Deputies. Once aroused, however, American Jewry moved with dispatch and boldness. Meeting followed meeting, and strong representations were made to the State Department and to President Van Buren, who was petitioned by the Jews of New York to "use every possible effort to induce the Pasha of Egypt to manifest more liberal treatment towards his Jewish subjects."

The Damascus meetings were notable as expressions of shared international Jewish concern. They were also significant as indications of the growing American Jewish self-confidence, as evidenced by the willingness to petition the government to take action, as a matter of duty and right, on behalf of a Jewish interest. Finally, the meetings marked a growing sense of American Jewish unity ("the unanimous opinion of the Israelites throughout the Union," as the Richmond meeting put it).

All these sentiments find expression in the pamphlet offering, *Persecution of the Jews in the East,* which contains the full proceedings of the Philadelphia meeting, held, as noted, on August 27, 1840, at Mikveh Israel Synagogue. The contents are identical to those found in the aforementioned newspaper account, except for some additional correspondence (pages 26–29), including a copy of a letter sent by Secretary of State John Forsyth to the U. S. consul at Alexandria:

In common with all the civilized nations, the people of the United States have learned with horror the atrocious crimes imputed to the Jews of Damascus, and the cruelties of which they have been victims. The President fully participates in the public feeling. . . . He is . . . anxious that the active sympathy and generous interposition of the Government of the United States should not be withheld from so benevolent an object, and he has accordingly directed me to instruct you to employ, should the occasion arise, all those good offices and efforts which are compatible with discretion and your official character, to the end that justice and humanity may be extended to those persecuted people, whose cry of distress has reached our shores.

The gathering at Mikveh Israel was described as a "very numerous and respectable meeting of the Israelites resident at Philadelphia." It was indeed that. The participants, presiding officers and speakers as well as the audience, represented the widest community spectrum.

Hyman Gratz, who called the meeting to order, was born in Philadelphia in 1776. He made his fortune in the insurance industry and became one of the leading Philadelphia citizens of the day. He was very active in all manner of civic and Jewish affairs, with a particular attachment to Mikveh Israel Synagogue. His largesse helped to establish the Gratz College for Jewish studies.

Abraham Hart, who opened the meeting, was only thirty years old at the time, but he was already a prominent figure in the community. Hart became one of the most successful and highly esteemed book publishers in the United States and was, as described in *The History of the Jews of Philadelphia* (Edwin Wolf 2nd and Maxwell Whiteman), "without question the leading Jewish layman of Philadelphia" of his day. He was active in the affairs of Mikveh Israel Synagogue and served as one of its presidents.

The major address was delivered by the Reverend Isaac Leeser, the spiritual leader of Mikveh Israel and a prominent figure in the cultural and religious life of nineteenth-century American Jewry (we shall have more to say of him later). His remarks, as was to be expected, were notably appropriate to the occasion:

> We, the inhabitants of a land where a benevolent Providence causes to prevail an equality of rights and an entire freedom in religious pursuits, have met for the purpose of publicly expressing our sympathy for those

Hyman Gratz (1776–1857)

of our brothers who, living where the "bond of slavery twineth," have lately been subjected to persecutions at which the blood runs cold, and this for the sake of false accusations brought against them, not as men, but as members of the Jewish community. . . . As citizens, we belong to the country we live in; but as believers in one God, as the faithful adorers of the Creator, as the inheritors of the law, the Jews of England, and Russia, and Sweden, are no aliens among us, and we hail the Israelites as a brother, no matter if his home be the torrid zone, or where the poles circle the earth with the impenetrable fetters of icy coldness. We have therefore met for the purpose of expressing our abhorrence of the calumny cast on our religion in another part of the world, and to offer our aid, in conjunction with our brothers in other towns both of this country and elsewhere, to those who have been subjected to such unmerited barbarities.

Thus it was that a tragic event in a distant part of the world evoked dormant feelings of kinship among American Jews and brought them to the realization that American Jewry, dispersed as it was throughout a broad land and grouped into disparate congregations, nevertheless formed one community of concern.

Isaac Leeser seized the opportunity and in 1841 attempted to organize a Union of American Israelites, for the purpose of bringing some semblance of unity into American Jewish religious life. A circular signed by representatives of "the Sephardim, . . . the Ashkenazim and [members] of the Polish synagogues" was circulated among several communities, urging the convening of a planning conference, but the scheme came to naught. As Leeser later wrote, "the conference did not meet; no rabbinical authority was instituted, and the incipient division and party strife were permitted to take what shape they pleased." Leeser blamed the failure on the opposition of the leaders of Congregation Shearith Israel of New York, who feared that the proposed Union would be dominated by the numerically superior German Jews. Nevertheless, the unity initiated by the response to the Damascus affair persisted. In agreement and dissent, in concerted action or intramural strife, after 1840 American Jewry knew itself to be *one* community.

8

A Journal for American Jewry

The appearance in April 1843 of a new monthly journal, *The Occident and American Jewish Advocate*—devoted to the "spread of whatever can advance the cause of [the Jewish] religion, and of promoting the true interest of that people which has made this religion its profession"—can be said to mark the real beginning of Jewish journalism in America. To be sure, Solomon Henry Jackson's periodical, *The Jew,* had appeared for two years two decades earlier, but its efforts were directed exclusively to antimissionary polemics. *The Occident,* on the other hand, from its very inception reflected the totality of Jewish concern. In this it was very much the creature of its editor, the tireless Isaac Leeser, minister of Congregation Mikveh Israel in Philadelphia, whose own broad Jewish interests and activities the journal expressed.

The first issue, volume I, number 1—herewith presented —can very well serve as a prototype for the many that followed (*The Occident* appeared regularly for twenty-six years). It contains a sermon ("On Miracles," one of Leeser's own preachments); translated excerpts from a French work, *Les Matinées du Samedi* (Saturday Mornings), "a book

of moral and religious education for the use of young Israelites"; news items ("chiefly from the latest European papers"); articles touching on Jewish life in the United States;
a juvenile department; and assorted notices. Three items
are of more than passing interest.

In the first ("On the Establishment of a Jewish Colony in
the United States"), Julius Stern, a Philadelphia Jew given
to synagogue reform and publisher of a short-lived Ger-
man-language newspaper, *Israelit,* proposes a kind of pre-
Zionist scheme for Jewish autonomy in the United States—
the establishment, with a view to its becoming a state, of a
"colony in one of the western territories" where immigrant
Jews might devote themselves to "the pursuits of agricul-
ture and the breeding of cattle, which occupations are the
best props of every state." Relieved of economic worry and
in a position to shape their own society, they would then be
free to practice their "holy religion"—"for never will [the
religion] be able to appear in all its dignity, glory and
greatness, so long as our people live dispersed among the
followers of other creeds." Editor Leeser, introducing this
utopian proposal, takes occasion to voice his disagreement
and to express his own view regarding the direction of the
American Jewish society:

> Independently of the consideration . . . that it is not
> very likely that a sufficient number of Jews would settle
> in any one district to entitle them to compose a sepa-
> rate commonwealth; we ought not to desire it if we
> could succeed. All we need is that we form communi-
> ties, not states, where we could act in harmony for a
> general good; for the rest the equitable laws of the
> United States and the freedom of opinion, equality,
> and protection guaranteed by the Constitution must
> satisfy us whilst we are scattered in small numbers all
> over the world.

The second item is a report on the "fifth anniversary
examination" of the Sunday-School of Religious Instruc-

tion of Israelites of Philadelphia, a pioneering educational institution of 140 young students, drawn from all three of the city's congregations. Following a description of the preliminary exercises (the reading of a portion of the thirty-sixth chapter of Ezekiel, delivery of the annual report, and so on), there is an account of the examination of the young scholars:

> We are sure that we do not exaggerate in saying that seldom did scholars, many of them scarcely five years old, answer more promptly and understandingly the questions which were propounded to them. . . . Several of the scholars next gave recitations of pieces committed to memory, which were received with marked approbation by the audience; especially the performances of two little boys, one about six and the other five years old, the first of whom recited a piece of poetry, describing the finding of Moses on the banks of the Nile, the latter the hundred and fifteenth psalm. One young lady, also a scholar, afforded a good deal of pleasure by the recitation of a poem in reference to the parting of Rebecca with Jacob.

In the course of this engaging report, we also find a hard nugget of historical fact: "The whole population of the Jews in Philadelphia is scarcely more than fifteen hundred."

The third item deals with "The American Society for Meliorating the Condition of the Jews, and Its Organ, The Jewish Chronicle." This was the same missionary group that had prompted the appearance of the aforementioned periodical, The Jew, and indeed missionary activities were a source of recurring aggrievance to American Jews of the time. This was not Leeser's first confrontation with missionaries (or his last, for that matter). Earlier, on January 31, 1836, he had written a letter, published in the United States Gazette, in which he reported an incident of a missionary agent's handing out tracts to the worshipers of Mikveh Israel as they left the synagogue following Sabbath services. He warned the offenders that

Isaac Leeser (1806–68)

another visit from your agent, or one distributing con-
troversial tracts, emanating from you or any body, may
be received rather unkindly; and much as we depre-
cate any violence or disturbance, we cannot answer for
the forbearance of the zealous ones amongst us, who
might perhaps be induced in their honest indignation,
to eject an impertinent meddler, mildly if they can,
forcibly if they must.

Born in Germany in 1806, Isaac Leeser was brought to
America in 1824 by an uncle living in Richmond. There he
helped the Reverend Isaac B. Seixas in the religious school,
and together with him first advocated the founding of a
Sunday school. He came to the attention of the larger Jewish community in the United States through his masterful
defense of Judaism, published in a Richmond newspaper.
This in turn led to his appointment, in 1829, as hazzan of
Mikveh Israel Synagogue in Philadelphia. A year later he
published his first volume, *Instruction in Mosaic Religion.*
This was followed, in 1833, by *The Jews and Mosaic Law.* His
prodigious literary output also included a translation of the
Sephardic prayer book (in six volumes), an English translation of the entire Bible (the first by a Jew), as well as numerous textbooks, catechisms, volumes of sermons, addresses,
and assorted other translations.

Equally important were his pioneering efforts to organize the American Jewish community and its institutions. As
early as 1841, as we have noted, he began to address public
pleas toward this end and to issue proposals for a united
American Jewish community. His persistent advocacy resulted in the formation, in 1859, of the Board of Delegates
of American Israelites, the first representative body of
American Jewry. In addition to being the first to propose
a Sunday school, he was also the first to suggest that "it
would be best to establish elementary schools in every district." He helped found the Hebrew Education Society and
also Maimonides College, the first Jewish theological seminary in the United States.

Isaac Leeser's fruitful life came to a close on a Sabbath morning, February 1, 1868. In fulfillment of a promise, his friend and disciple Mayer Sulzberger continued to edit *The Occident* for another year. In the valedictory statement that concluded the publication of this pioneer effort of American Jewish journalism, Sulzberger noted: "Periodical literature is not our great want; for the number of ably-edited Jewish papers, already proportionately greater than any other denomination, is continually increasing by fresh accessions." For this happy situation, as for so many other cultural and communal amenities, American Jewry had Isaac Leeser to thank.

9

For "the Rising Generation of Israel"

A graceful little work, *The Teachers' and Parents' Assistant,* contains "Thirteen Lessons Conveying to the Uninformed Minds the First Ideas of God and His Attributes." As the pseudonymous author notes, the effort was intended "expressly for the benefit of the rising generation of Israel, by assisting mothers and teachers in the duty of imparting to their minds the first ideas of the Deity." Isaac Leeser, in his introduction, describes it: "This small guide . . . is the very thing needed to make the parent or teacher think, and gives to the intelligent child the means of gradually entering the task of developing his own ideas, and to print the important truth of religion indelibly on his soul."

In content the work is similar to other popular catechisms of the period, but there the resemblance stops. These lessons are distinguished not only by their greater charm, but also by their attractive directness and pedagogic validity. One does not find here the standard questions and answers meant to be learned by rote. Indeed, the author warns: "The design in arrangement, &c. will be entirely defeated if the book be put into the hands of children, either to commit any portion of it to memory, or even to be read aloud to a teacher." Rather, the purpose was to establish a creative partnership, a Socratic situation whereby instructor and student, working together, arrived at the desired understanding.

The instruction proceeds in such a way as to make basic theological concepts—*creatio ex nihilo,* for example—comprehensible to the young scholar. There is none of the talking down, coyness, or evasion that are to be found in so many other texts of this sort. The level is simple, to be sure, but the approach is always honest and clear. A brief sample:

> There is a word which means to make something where before there was nothing. No child and no man can think how great He is.
> This word is "to create." Now tell me the meaning of "to create."
> *After the child has answered as well as he can, let the teacher say:*
> It means, to make something, where before there was nothing. God *created* all His works, because *He* made them at first out of nothing. What is God called because He made all things out of nothing?
> *Let the child think for a moment, and then let the teacher answer for him:*
> He is called the Creator.
> Now tell me the meaning of Creator.
> *After the child has given such a definition as he is capable of, let the teacher say:*
> Creator means one who has made something where before there was nothing. Who is the only Being who can make something out of nothing?
> *The child will readily answer,*
> God.
> God then, you see, is the Creator.

The material is a sheer delight to read, and many a teacher or parent must have felt tempted to ignore the author's instructions and place the booklet in the child's hands. The author, however, is strict in insisting that the teacher hew to her method:

> The instruction . . . is intended to be conveyed *orally,* as if proceeding immediately from the mind of the teacher; and the author flatters herself that she has so arranged it as to enable the most unpractised teacher, with the aid of a little preparation and an occasional

Building of the Hebrew Sunday-School Society

reference to the book, during the lesson, to accomplish this. Some experience in the interesting task of conveying knowledge to uninformed minds has convinced her that the grand secret of instruction is, not to think for the child, but to make him think for himself; not so much to impart ready-formed ideas, as to enable the child to awaken those that lie dormant in his own mind.

Proper educational advice, and quite modern-sounding, too.

Who was the author of *The Teachers' and Parents' Assistant*, who signed herself only "An American Jewess"? It is generally accepted that the credit belongs to Rebecca Gratz, a member of Philadelphia's most distinguished Jewish family and founder and superintendent of the Hebrew Sunday-School Society in that city. There is reason, however, to reject Miss Gratz's authorship.

Henry S. Morais, who had a firsthand knowledge of the history of Philadelphia Jewry, does not attribute any publications to Miss Gratz, either in *Eminent Israelites of the Nineteenth Century* (1880) or in *The Jews of Philadelphia* (1895). In the earlier volume he writes: "Miss Gratz, in the pursuit of her educational designs, induced the writing and compilation of text-books for instruction in the Jewish faith." There is no evidence that she ever advanced from inducing writing in others to writing herself.

Further, in his notice about *The Teachers' and Parents' Assistant*, in *The Occident* (June 1845), Isaac Leeser wrote: "We hope that our friend ["An American Jewess"] will meet with a very favorable reception, and that her merits may speedily and properly be appreciated by all our readers." Miss Gratz at that time was already in her sixty-fourth year and her merits had long been properly esteemed. It is hardly conceivable that Leeser, if indeed he was referring to Miss Gratz, would couch the matter in quite such terms.

His attitude toward the formidable Miss Gratz, his honored patron, was always one of reverential deference, as we know from other sources.

Finally, a study of the files of *The Occident* reveals that "An American Jewess" was a regular contributor to the journal. There is an essay under that pseudonym in the issue of January 1845, another in the issue of January 1846, still another in the issue of December 1846. No one has ever suggested that these efforts issued from Rebecca Gratz— who did, however, once sign herself "A Daughter of Israel," in a letter to *The Occident* advocating the establishment of a Jewish Foster Home (cited in *The Jews of Philadelphia*).

It would, of course, be most fitting if we could acknowledge Rebecca Gratz—a gracious lady and a pioneer in Jewish religious education—as the pseudonymous author of *The Teachers' and Parents' Assistant*. Nevertheless, the evidence points otherwise and there is nothing to indicate that "A Daughter of Israel" and "An American Jewess" were one and the same. Still, whoever the latter author may be, we pay tribute to both women, for their abundant qualities of heart and mind and devotion to their community.

IO
From Ararat to Zion

On Friday evening, April 17, 1818, Mordecai Manuel Noah, editor of the *National Advocate* and former United States consul to Tunisia, delivered the principal address at the consecration of Congregation Shearith Israel's new synagogue in New York. He touched on a variety of pertinent topics, but his most impassioned remarks were reserved for a theme to which he was to return often, a theme that became his obsession: "the restoration of the Jewish nation to their ancient rights and dominion."

"There are upward of seven millions of Jews . . . throughout the world," he declared, "possessing more wealth, activity, influence, and talents, than any body of people on earth"—and never were the prospects for the Jewish return to Zion "more brilliant than they are at present." Speaking almost eighty years before Theodor Herzl raised the Zionist banner, Noah held forth an equally stirring vision:

[Jews] will march in triumphant numbers, and possess themselves once more of Syria [as the region was then generally called], and take their rank among the governments of the earth. This is not fancy. I have been too much among them in Europe and Africa—I am too well acquainted with their views and sentiments in Asia, to doubt their intentions. They hold the purse-strings, and can wield the sword; they can bring 100,-000 men into the field.

Alas, "fancy" it was, as Noah soon realized. However, an alternate notion occurred to him: a Jewish commonwealth in America, an interim "city of refuge" that would serve the purpose of Jewish polity pending the restoration in Zion. Accordingly, in 1820 he petitioned the state of New York to sell him Grand Island in the Niagara River, near Buffalo, where he proposed to establish such a settlement, to be called, fittingly, Ararat. A committee of the state legislature reported favorably on his request, but no bill was passed. The following year he proposed a Jewish settlement in Newport, Rhode Island, but this never went beyond the suggestion stage.

Noah turned again to Grand Island. He was able to persuade a friend to purchase a section, and the date of dedication was announced for September 25, 1825. Noah concocted a ceremony worthy of the occasion. Cannon boomed, and military and Masonic formations led government officials and representatives of various organizations and institutions in a grand march to a local church, where the dedication was to take place. (There were not enough boats to convey this large assemblage to Grand Island.) Presiding over this splendor, garbed in crimson judicial robes trimmed with ermine, was Mordecai Manuel Noah, "Citizen of the United States of America, late Consul of the said States for the City and Kingdom of Tunis, High Sheriff of New York, Counsellor at Law, and by the grace of God Governor and Judge of Israel," as he described himself. The band blared out the grand march from *Judas Maccabeus*, the organ pealed a *jubilate*, a biblical lesson was read by the minister, psalms were recited, and the new "Judge of Israel" delivered his *Proclamation to the Jews.* It urged the immigration of the Jewish youth of the world to the commonwealth of Ararat, declared that polygamy was abolished and that prayer "shall be forever in the Hebrew language," and levied a poll tax of three shekels or one Spanish dollar

> upon each Jew throughout the world, for the purpose of defraying the various expenses of re-organizing the government, of aiding emigrants in the purchase of agricultural implements, providing for their immediate wants and comforts, and assisting their families in making their first settlements . . . in the furtherance of the laudable objects connected with the restoration of the people and the glory of the Jewish nation.

Noah was a dramatist as well as a practicing politician, and Ararat reflected both of his aspects. Ararat, unlikely as the scheme may appear today, seemed to make good, even practical, sense at the time. These were years of upheaval in Europe following the Napoleonic defeat, and the Jews, as usual, were among the chief sufferers. Their resettlement in a "city of refuge," handily located at the western terminal of the newly opened Erie Canal, was something deserving of serious consideration. The rest, however—the robes, the rhetoric, and all the other trappings—was pure theater. It was all most typical of Mordecai Manuel Noah— creative artist and man of action, a mixture of the practical and the imaginative, not unlike Theodor Herzl, who was also a playwright, one might observe.

Born in Philadelphia in 1785, to a father who was an immigrant from Germany and to a mother descended from one of the early Sephardic American families, Noah was raised by his maternal grandfather, Jonas Phillips. His early years were spent in Philadelphia, Charleston, and finally New York. From 1813 to 1815 he served as consul to Tunis, and on his return he became editor of the *National Advocate,* owned by his uncle, Naphtali Phillips, a leader of Tammany. Noah himself became something of a political force in New York, and served as sheriff, surveyor of the port, and associate judge of the Court of Sessions. In all, he cut an important figure in the civic and cultural life of New York.

His Jewish commitments were equally intense. A leading member of Shearith Israel, he was also a founder of New York's first Ashkenazic congregation, B'nai Jeshurun. He wrote widely on Jewish subjects in the general press and in Jewish periodicals, and was active in many Jewish charitable and civic enterprises. However, as noted, his abiding interest was the reconstitution of Jewish statehood. Ararat, envisioned as a way station on the road to a restored Zion, did not progress much beyond the dedication ceremonies and the proclamation. But the dream remained, and Noah held fast to his Zionist vision.

In 1837 he published a *Discourse on the Evidences of the American Indians Being the Descendants of the Ten Lost Tribes of Israel,* which contains a passage that is a remarkable prefigurement of the Herzlian program:

> The Jewish people must now do something for themselves; they must move onward to the accomplishment of that great event, long promised, long expected. . . . Syria will revert to the Jewish nation by *purchase.* . . . Under the co-operation and protection of England and France, this re-occupation of Syria . . . is at once reasonable and practicable. . . . A just and liberal government . . . [will] be a bulwark to the interests of England and France.

Seven years later the return to Zion became the subject of a talk twice delivered at the Tabernacle in New York, on October 28 and December 2, 1844. This lecture—our final

Mordecai Manuel Noah (1785–1851)

Bicentennial presentation—was published the following year as *Discourse on the Restoration of the Jews.* It is Noah's consummate Zionist statement.

"I confidently believe in the restoration of the Jews," he writes in the preface ". . . and believing that political events are daily assuming a shape which may finally lead to that great advent, I consider it a duty to call upon the free people of this country to aid us in any efforts which, in our present position, it may be prudent to adopt."

The discourse was addressed to professing Christians, and Noah, marshaling biblical quotations and other telling evidence, seeks to demonstrate to his audience why it is in the Christian interest to "facilitate the return of the Jews to Jerusalem, and the organization of a powerful government in Judea," which would "lead to that millennium which we all look for, all hope for, all pray for." But over and above that, he stresses the special affinity between America and the Jewish national aspirations. This remarkable kinship of feeling and understanding, which has proven so durable over the years, was given early and moving expression by Noah. It is worth quoting in some detail:

> Where, I ask, can we commence this great work of regeneration with a better prospect of success than in a free country and a liberal government? Where can we plead the cause of independence for the children of Israel with greater confidence than in the cradle of liberty? Where ask for toleration and kindness for the seed of Abraham, if we find it not among the descendants of the Pilgrims? Here we can unfurl the standard, and seventeen millions of people will say, "God is with you; we are with you: in his name, and in the name of civil and religious liberty, go forth and repossess the land of your fathers. We have advocated the independence of the South American republics, we have given a home to our red brethren beyond the Mississippi, we have combated for the independence of Greece, we have restored the African to his native land. If these

nations were entitled to our sympathies, how much more powerful and irrepressible are the claims of that beloved people, before whom the Almighty walked like a cloud by day and a pillar of fire by night; who spoke to them words of comfort and salvation, of promise, of hope, of consolation, and protection; who swore they should be *his* people, and he would be *their* God; who, for their special protection and final restoration, dispersed them among the nations, without confounding them with any!"

Elsewhere in the *Discourse on the Restoration of the Jews*—echoing the statement in *Sayings of the Fathers,* "It is not thy duty to complete the work, but neither art thou free to desist from it"—Noah observes: "We in this generation may be impelled to commence the good work, which succeeding generations will accomplish."

This seems altogether a fitting quotation with which to conclude these series of remarks about the early writings of the American Jewish community. Suffice it to say that if the "succeeding generations" have any accomplishments to their credit, then that is due in no small measure to the good works of their precursors—Isaac Pinto, Gershom Mendes Seixas, Isaac Leeser, Mordecai Manuel Noah, and all the rest. It is to their instructive texts that we now turn.

A Selected Bibliography

Abrahams, Israel. *By-paths in Hebraic Bookland*. Philadelphia, 1920.

Adams, Hannah. *History of the Jews*. 2 vols. Boston, 1812.

Blau, Joseph L., and Baron, Salo W. *The Jews of the United States, 1790–1840, A Documentary History*. 3 vols. New York, 1963.

Elzas, Barnett A. *Jews of South Carolina*. Philadelphia, 1905.

Fein, Isaac M. *The Making of an American Jewish Community: The History of Baltimore Jewry from 1773–1920*. Philadelphia, 1971.

Goldberg, Isaac, *Major Noah*. Philadelphia, 1937.

Grinstein, Hyman B. *The Rise of the Jewish Community of New York*. Philadelphia, 1945.

Gutstein, Morris A. *The Story of the Jews of Newport, 1658–1908*. New York, 1936.

Karp, Abraham J., ed. *The Jewish Experience in America*. 5 vols. New York, 1969.

Learsi, Rufus (Isaac Goldberg). *The Jews in America*. New York, 1972.

Leeser, Isaac. "The Jews in the United States." In *An Original History of the Religious Denominations . . . in the United*

States, edited by I. Daniel Rupp. Philadelphia, 1844.

Morais, Henry S. *Eminent Israelites of the Nineteenth Century.* Philadelphia, 1880.

————. *The Jews of Philadelphia.* Philadelphia, 1895.

Marcus, Jacob R. *American Jewry, Documents, Eighteenth Century.* Cincinnati, 1959.

————. *The Colonial American Jew.* 3 vols. Detroit, 1970.

————. *Early American Jewry.* 2 vols. Philadelphia, 1951–53.

————. *The Handsome Young Priest in the Black Gown: The Personal World of Gershom Seixas.* Cincinnati, 1970.

————. *Jewish Americana.* Cincinnati, 1954.

Phillipson, David, ed. *The Letters of Rebecca Gratz.* Philadelphia, 1929.

Pool, David de Sola, and Pool, Tamar de Sola. *An Old Faith in the New World.* New York, 1955.

Pool, David de Sola. *Portraits Etched in Stone.* New York, 1952.

Reznikoff, Charles, and Engelman, Uriah Z. *The Jews of Charleston.* Philadelphia, 1950.

Rosenbach, A. S. W. *An American Jewish Bibliography.* New York, 1926.

Rosenbloom, Joseph R. *A Biographical Dictionary of Early American Jews: Colonial Times through 1800.* Lexington, Ky., 1960.

Schappes, Morris U. *A Documentary History of the Jews in the United States.* New York, 1950.

Stern, Malcolm. *Americans of Jewish Descent: A Compendium of Genealogy.* Cincinnati, 1960.

Tobias, Thomas J. *The Hebrew Orphan Society of Charleston, S.C.* Charleston, 1957.

Whiteman, Maxwell. "Isaac Leeser and the Jews of Philadelphia." *American Jewish Historical Quarterly* 48 (1959).

Wolf, Edwin, 2nd, and Whiteman, Maxwell. *The History of the Jews of Philadelphia: From Colonial Times to the Age of Jackson.* Philadelphia, 1957, 1975.

ABRAHAM J. KARP is professor of history and religious studies at the University of Rochester. He is a corresponding
member of the Institute of Contemporary Jewry of the Hebrew University, and has served as president of the American Jewish Historical Society (1972–75).

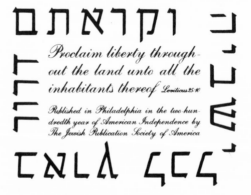

וקראתם

דרור

בארץ לכל יושביה

Proclaim liberty through-
out the land unto all the
inhabitants thereof *Leviticus 25:10*

Published in Philadelphia in the two-hun-
dredth year of American Independence by
The Jewish Publication Society of America

Praise for
Mom Brain

"Dr. Dobrow DiMarco is the wise, funny, relatable, and brutally honest girl-friend that every new mom needs—and she's also a seasoned psychologist who shows how tested clinical techniques can be used to address the worries, fears, frustrations, and feelings of loneliness that inevitably attend motherhood. *Mom Brain* is an outstanding contribution and a gift to new moms everywhere."

—Lisa Damour, PhD, *author of* Untangled
and Under Pressure

"I can't wait to recommend *Mom Brain* to my friends—both moms-to-be and those who have been around the block a time or two! This book has helped me define and prioritize what is important to me, and look at my relationships through a different lens. Most important, I no longer feel like I'm letting my baby and others down when I stand up for myself and my needs. I rarely reread books, but this one is different. I look forward to using it as a resource as both my son and I grow."

—*Blair B., Raleigh, North Carolina*

"This is a terrific book that all mothers should read. With a healthy dose of humor, Dr. Dobrow Dimarco shows you that it is normal to sometimes feel anxious and depressed about parenting—but that there are tools available to help. I'm a mother *and* a psychologist, and I still learned some new strategies for managing my own 'mom brain' by reading this book!"

—*Shireen L. Rizvi, PhD, ABPP, Graduate School
of Applied and Professional Psychology,
Rutgers, The State University of New Jersey*

"Dr. Dobrow DiMarco gets me—and that's not easy! Finally, someone has written about 'mom brain' with both impressive knowledge and self-deprecating compassion, acknowledging the complexity while simultaneously keeping things simple. As both a clinical psychologist and a mother of young kids, I have only two things to say to Dr. Dobrow DiMarco: Bravo, and thank you."

—*Rebecca Schrag Hershberg, PhD,
author of* The Tantrum Survival Guide

MOM BRAIN

Mom Brain

Proven Strategies to Fight the Anxiety,
Guilt, and Overwhelming Emotions
of Motherhood—and Relax into Your New Self

Ilyse Dobrow DiMarco, PhD

THE GUILFORD PRESS
New York   London

To my boys—Chris, Matty, and Sam

Copyright © 2021 The Guilford Press
A Division of Guilford Publications, Inc.
370 Seventh Avenue, Suite 1200, New York, NY 10001
www.guilford.com

The information in this volume is not intended as a substitute for consultation with healthcare professionals. Each individual's health concerns should be evaluated by a qualified professional.

Printed in the United States of America

Last digit is print number: 9   8   7   6   5   4   3   2   1

Library of Congress Cataloging-in-Publication Data

Names: DiMarco, Ilyse Dobrow, author.
Title: Mom brain : proven strategies to fight the anxiety, guilt, and
    overwhelming emotions of motherhood—and relax into your new self /
    Ilyse Dobrow DiMarco, PhD.
Description: New York : The Guilford Press, [2021] | Includes
    bibliographical references and index.
Identifiers: LCCN 2020058587 | ISBN 9781462543212 (hardcover ; alk.
    paper) | ISBN 9781462540266 (paperback ; alk. paper)
Subjects: LCSH: Motherhood—Psychological aspects. | Mother and child. |
    Mothers—Psychology.
Classification: LCC HQ759 .D547 2020 | DDC 306.874/3—dc23
LC record available at *https://lccn.loc.gov/2020058587*

Contents

Author's Note

All illustrations in this book are composites or have been disguised to protect the privacy of the individuals described.

I use feminine pronouns when referring to individual moms to promote ease of reading as our language continues to evolve and not out of disrespect toward readers who identify with other personal pronouns. I sincerely hope that all will feel included.

Acknowledgments

My mother, Diane Stein Dobrow, taught me everything I know about being a loving mom (and a loving human). She, along with my father, Harvey, brother, Larry, and sister, Julie (herself an outstanding mother), raised me in a home filled with love, warmth, and laughter, and they continue to provide me with unconditional love and encouragement.

Thank you to three other important mothers in my life—my grandmothers, Eleanor "Grandma Teeth" Dobrow and Eleanor "Grandma Hearts" Stein (who would have bragged so much about this book!), and my mother-in-law, Rita DiMarco. These amazing women have had a significant impact on my life and parenting.

I was fortunate to marry into a terrific family—thank you to the DiMarcos, and especially to Rob DiMarco, who provided considerable help and encouragement.

Many people helped me on my path to writing this book. Terry Wilson shared his passion for cognitive-behavioral therapy and remains my mentor to this day. Saul Austerlitz read my early work and advised me about book writing. Valerie Dobrow walked me through the publishing process. My wonderful extended family (the Dobrow, Stein, Narcisi, and Rosenberg crews) have always been my cheerleaders. Thanks to my super-supportive friends, especially Krupa Desai, Amanda Kerins, Abby Pressel, and Becky Silber (who came up with the title!). Friends who shared their expertise included Sherrie Delinsky, Deborah Glasofer, Shelby Harris, Samantha Lutz, and Allison Topilow. Tom Johnson took the wonderful author photo. With her characteristic warmth and humor, Rebecca Schrag Hershberg imparted everything she knew about writing a book and introduced me to my editors at The Guilford Press, Kitty Moore and Christine Benton.

And speaking of Kitty and Chris: They guided me through every step of this process, providing spot-on advice, insightful feedback, and unwavering encouragement, all with kindness and good humor. All writers should be lucky enough to work with editors like them. Thank you also to Lucy Baker, Guilford's publicist, who, in addition to publicizing the book, read the whole manuscript in its early stages and provided extremely helpful feedback.

I am also so grateful to the many mom patients I've worked with over the years, who shared their most private experiences and trusted me to help them navigate the often choppy waters of early motherhood.

A big thank-you to my children, Matty and Sam—you won't find two more hilarious, loving, and joyful boys. And finally, to Chris DiMarco, without whom this book, and everything else significant I've ever done in my life, would not have happened. There are truly no words to express my admiration, gratitude, and love.

Introduction

A scene from my life, 9 years ago: My newborn son Matty is nursing for an hour, and I don't know how to get him to stop. I am poring over three different nursing books (yes, I can read books while I nurse; I can also drink coffee and watch reality TV on my phone), looking for advice about how to deal with Matty. But I also need advice about how to deal with myself. I've been crying for an hour and am so stressed I can't eat. Where's the book to help me with that?

This scene replayed itself, in a variety of different forms (me crying because I couldn't get Matty to nap, me crying because Matty threw a Lego piece at another kid, me crying because I'd inadvertently given Matty scrambled eggs with an ant fried into them), many times during Matty's early years. It always went the same way: I'd become overwhelmed by yet another parenting challenge and start frantically searching books and the Internet for answers (picture me googling "What happens when babies eat ants?"). While I was focused entirely on Matty's needs, I never stopped to consider my own.

Of course, my own needs were considerable, as are the needs of all new mothers. Becoming a mother causes a seismic shift in your priorities, identity, and relationships. You're tasked with keeping a little person alive and figuring out all of the things you need to do to make this happen. Because you've never parented before, you truly don't know what you're doing and constantly question whether you're getting anything right. Your former identities—as a professional, say, or a sports enthusiast or music lover—are abruptly swallowed up by your maternal identity. Your perception of the world and its dangers shifts dramatically because you suddenly have a little person to protect. Your responses to social media posts are now filtered through your mom lens, as you're evaluating how other moms' lives appear to compare with yours. Your relationships with partners, extended family members, and friends are put to the test, forced to accommodate the new little person who is now at the center of everything.

And, thanks to our highly judgmental culture, all of these dramatic changes occur against a backdrop of relentless mom-shaming. Mothers are evaluated for practically everything: for being too attached to their children, or not attached enough; for working too hard, or not working enough; for helicoptering or free-range parenting or God knows what else. So at the same time as you're trying to figure out what you're doing as a mom, and mourning the loss of the person you once were and the relationships you once had, you're contending with criticism and opinions from multiple sources—social media, other moms, and even close family members and friends. Everyone seems to care so much about what you're doing to help your kid and so little about what you're doing to help yourself.

So it's no wonder that as a new mom I felt totally overwhelmed. My mom brain was consumed, at times, with anxiety, guilt, self-criticism, loneliness, shame, and self-judgment, as well as indescribable love, joy, and gratitude.

It was in this state that I returned to work after my first maternity leave. As a clinical psychologist based in the suburbs of New York City, I started seeing a lot of women like me: moms with young kids who were experiencing drastic changes and wildly swinging emotions. Most had minimal support and few coping skills.

I hadn't been trained to work with moms specifically, but I did have a long history of treating anxiety and stress, as I was an expert in cognitive-behavioral therapy (CBT) for anxiety. The results of countless research studies, as well as my own clinical experience, indicated that CBT and related evidence-based strategies worked extremely well in the treatment of anxiety, mood issues, perfectionism, and other emotion regulation difficulties. Why not, I figured, adapt these strategies for new moms, who, by virtue of all the stressors I mentioned above, struggle with all of the issues that CBT was designed to treat? I realized that CBT skills could greatly help moms manage the tidal waves of thoughts and feelings moving through their mom brains every minute of every day.

Let me take a moment to tell you what CBT is. CBT is a short-term, action-focused form of psychotherapy comprised of specific techniques that have been supported by research findings. The aim of CBT work is to improve your functioning by making changes in the way you think about a situation, the way you behave, and the way you interpret and respond to your emotions. CBT skills are often used in tandem with skills from two other evidence-based treatments, dialectical behavior therapy (DBT) and acceptance and commitment therapy (ACT). Like CBT, DBT and ACT offer specific coping strategies, with an emphasis on emotion regulation, mindfulness work, and values-based action.

It turned out that CBT strategies, and related tools from DBT and ACT, were a perfect match for me and other overwhelmed new moms, for a number of reasons:

1. **They are easy to learn.** Moms can learn CBT, DBT, and ACT skills quickly and easily, without having to spend years in therapy talking about their mothers. Plus these tools are clear and straightforward, so that even the most exhausted, brain-fried moms can learn them.

2. **They are easy to use.** Once moms understand CBT/DBT/ACT skills, they can use them immediately, in the moment, whenever they need them. For example, a mom who reads a friend's highly curated Instagram post about her 4-year-old tennis pro daughter can immediately engage in cognitive and mindfulness strategies to help her manage her comparison making and resulting anxiety.

3. **They are enduring.** Moms can continue to use CBT/DBT/ACT tools as their children age. Matty is now 9, and my younger son, Sam, is now 6, and I still use my skills on a daily basis to manage my own feelings of overwhelm. Just yesterday I forced myself to take a mindful "adult time-out" when my sons came to blows over which Harry Potter spell would be most useful in real life. (For the record, I'm partial to Accio. What mom wouldn't covet the power to summon anything she needed at a moment's notice? Can you imagine how many hours you'd save if you didn't have to continually look for stuff your kids misplaced?)

Once I recognized how well CBT was working for me and for the moms in my practice, I decided to make it my mission to help make CBT available and accessible to as many moms as possible. I started writing short pieces for popular parenting websites but quickly realized that I had a lot more to say; CBT, after all, offered strategies for managing a wide range of maternal issues. I decided to present all of these strategies in one comprehensive book. *Mom Brain* is the result.

Mom Brain is written for mothers of young children (ages birth to 5) who are contending with the unique challenges of new motherhood (which is to say, *all* mothers of young children!). I chose the title *Mom Brain* to reflect the profound cognitive and emotional changes that occur when you have a child and the many aspects of your life (identity, relationships, work life, self-care) that are strongly impacted by these changes. As we'll discuss in Chapter 1, mom brain is about a whole lot more than just forgetting where you left your phone.

Mom Brain focuses on moms themselves and *not* on kids or parenting, offering concrete coping strategies for a wide range of maternal stressors. Throughout the book, I share many of my own personal stories, as well as stories inspired by the patients with whom I work (for confidentiality purposes, I do not share any personal information that would identify them).

Mom Brain is organized so that foundational issues are discussed first, followed by deeper dives into a number of common maternal stressors. Chapter 1 discusses the many aspects of mom brain and provides a more detailed introduction to CBT, DBT, and ACT. Chapter 2 delves into the complicated emotional lives of new mothers. Chapter 3 explores maternal identity issues, including work identity, and details how values work can help moms come to terms with their new identities. Chapters 4 and 5 present strategies for coping effectively with anxiety. Chapter 6 focuses on maternal self-care. Chapters 7 and 8 tackle social media comparison making and perfectionism. Chapters 9–11 are all about managing relationships post-kids. And Chapter 12 delves into vacations, holidays, and special events.

A note about how to use this book: You can certainly plan to read it from cover to cover (and frankly, if you can find the time to do this, I salute you!). As an alternative, consider reading Chapters 1–3, which describe core concepts that will inform your thinking about your new life as a mom. Once you've done this, you can pick and choose which of the other chapters you most want to focus on, based on the particular challenges you're experiencing at a given moment.

Mom Brain is composed of easily digestible sections, so even if you only have 10 minutes to read, you'll be able to pick up at least one or two solid coping skills. And *Mom Brain* is one of those books that you can revisit throughout your little one's early years when the need arises, without having to start from the beginning each time.

Each chapter contains a variety of coping strategies. It's important to remember that not every coping strategy we discuss will be helpful for you. This is because every mom is unique, and every kid is unique, and no two households are the same. You'll find that certain strategies will work better in certain situations (and with certain individuals) than others. As you read, take note of the strategies that you think will be helpful for you, try them out, and determine whether and how they work best for you. CBT is experimental by design—it assumes that you'll explore a variety of different coping skills until you home in on the tools that are most effective for you. Once you've got those tools, they'll be with you for life.

As I noted earlier, this book is for moms contending with the everyday stressors and anxieties of new motherhood. It is not designed to treat more significant mood or anxiety issues and is not a substitute for psychotherapy. In Chapters 1 and 5, I discuss when you should consider seeking further help from a licensed mental health practitioner. In the Resources at the back of the book, I include a list of sources to help you connect with a helpful professional.

If my years treating mothers and being a mother myself have taught me anything, it's that mom brain is a permanent condition—once you have kids on the brain, you always have kids on the brain (according to my 76-year-old mother, this remains true even after your kids are grown). My hope is that I can teach you some tools that will help you embrace all of the changes—both positive and negative—that come with mom brain.

So put aside all those books about how to best take care of your kid and devote some time to learning how you can best take care of yourself. I promise you'll be a better mother for it.

"What's Happened to My Head?"

"Mom Brain" and How CBT Can Help

What do you think about when you hear the term "mom brain"?

If you're like most of the moms I see in my practice (and the ones I know in my personal life), you probably subscribe to the pop culture notion of mom brain, which suggests that new moms are prone to memory lapses, concentration difficulties, and general mental cloudiness. No doubt you've seen those #mombrain memes, featuring a confused, disoriented mom with two different shoes on and a breast pump hanging from one of her nipples. The implication is that our brains don't work as well once small children (and the sleep deprivation that comes with them) enter the picture.

There's no question that all of us moms experience periods of mental cloudiness and forgetfulness (I can cite here my chronic inability to remember to send Matty to baseball practice with his baseball glove). But contrary to popular belief, there is no compelling evidence that mothers suffer from significant declines in brain functioning when they have kids. According to the emerging research on the topic, a mother's brain adapts so that she becomes acutely attentive to her baby's needs, thereby ensuring that the baby becomes a top mental priority. Basically, babies take up a lot of brain space, crowding out some of the other people and tasks demanding our attention. Which is why we might be a little forgetful or have some difficulty focusing on non-kid-related things.

The research findings are completely consistent with my own experience as a parent. When I had Matty, he instantly became my top mental priority (and remains so to this day—along with his little brother, of course). No longer were the decisions I made solely about me. Now, and forevermore, my kids were always going to be a consideration.

What does this look like, practically speaking? To illustrate, let me provide a window into my current mom brain. Below you'll see two graphics illustrating the contents of my brain in the year before I became a parent, and today.

Before having Matty, I probably had a chic haircut, a recently expanded wardrobe, and a Caribbean vacation looming on the horizon. Currently I have an unruly tangle of split-ended hair, bras that date back to the first Obama administration, and a season pass for Legoland.

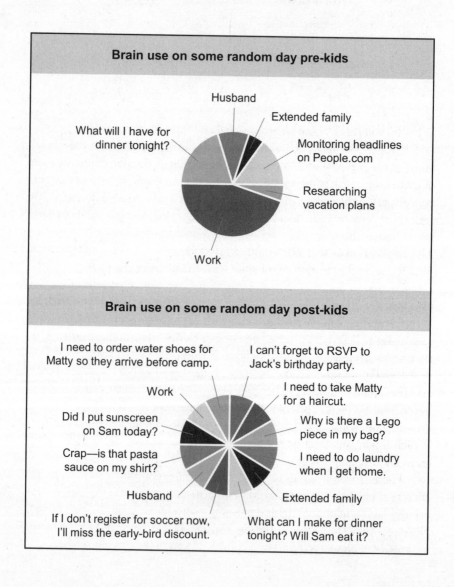

Brain use on some random day pre-kids

Husband

Extended family

What will I have for dinner tonight?

Monitoring headlines on People.com

Researching vacation plans

Work

Brain use on some random day post-kids

I need to order water shoes for Matty so they arrive before camp.

I can't forget to RSVP to Jack's birthday party.

Work

I need to take Matty for a haircut.

Did I put sunscreen on Sam today?

Why is there a Lego piece in my bag?

Crap—is that pasta sauce on my shirt?

I need to do laundry when I get home.

Husband

Extended family

If I don't register for soccer now, I'll miss the early-bird discount.

What can I make for dinner tonight? Will Sam eat it?

Clearly, mental prioritization is a big part of mom brain—you've got lots to think about and an ever-expanding to-do list. But it certainly isn't the only part. In recent years, mental health professionals, researchers, and curious journalist moms alike have been trying to expand our definition of mom brain, acknowledging that mom brain is about a whole lot more than just occasional memory lapses and shifts in mental priorities (for some interesting writing on this topic, see the Resources).

Mom Brain and Your Emotions

Mom brains are constantly awash in a sea of mixed emotions. We vacillate between heart-stopping love, gut-wrenching anxiety, soul-crushing boredom, and mind-blowing anger (sometimes, all over the course of one tuck-in). As we'll discuss in Chapter 2, this emotional roller coaster is powered by a number of different things: physiological changes, our sudden exposure to completely new and unfamiliar environments, our failure to meet the unrealistic expectations we set for ourselves, and our tendency toward negative self-judgment. Anxiety is a particularly pernicious maternal emotion. When we become moms, we suddenly find ourselves responsible for the life of another human being (an anxiety-provoking prospect if I've ever heard one). Our anxiety is often fueled by social media, which subjects us to relentless comparison making and mom-shaming.

Even those of us who specialize in treating anxiety aren't immune to this. Before I had kids, I prided myself on being one of those people who could easily dismiss alarmist posts and stories that came across my social media feeds. But during those long nights of scrolling through social media while nursing Matty, I found myself getting sucked in by every alarmist post I read. Whatever the crisis du jour, I immediately assumed Matty was at risk. Had I drunk too much caffeine in my early days of nursing? Had Matty spent too much time mouthing a toy made of non-BPA-free plastic? What if I got cancer like my Facebook friend's friend and died and left Matty motherless? Every threat that came across my feed felt so much more terrifying and possible now that I had a little baby in my care.

Mom Brain and Your Identity

After you become a mother, your sense of who you are profoundly changes. Take Jenn, for example. Pre-kids, Jenn defined herself primarily by her work, and always approached her job with single-minded focus. She pitied those parents who had to decline work opportunities and rush out of meetings early because of kid-related responsibilities and vowed that when she had kids she would never let them get in the way of her career. Cut to Jenn at 5 months postpartum, calling in to a work meeting (late) while walking up and down the streets of her neighborhood with her stroller-bound son, who was sick and would sleep only when in motion. Strolling past her house for the 12th time, she wondered, "How on earth did I get here?"

Motherhood profoundly affects work life, of course, with moms having to figure out whether and how work will fit into their lives as parents. New moms also lose touch with aspects of themselves that they no longer have the time or energy to explore. Former social butterflies, movie buffs, gourmet chefs, and travel junkies often find themselves reduced to one role: mom.

Mom Brain and Your Relationships

Another central aspect of mom brain concerns the profound relationship changes that new moms often experience. Maria, for example, struggled with the significant resentment she felt toward her husband. Historically, she and her husband had always managed to achieve an equal division of labor at home. But when their daughter was born, her husband, intimidated by this new little person in his life, let Maria take the lead on most tasks relating to their daughter. By the time their daughter was a year old, Maria found herself doing virtually all of the child care. While Maria was extremely angry about this, she felt powerless to fix it. Her husband truly did not know how to perform many child care tasks, because he didn't have any experience with them. And Maria did not have the time or energy to teach him. She felt stuck in a relationship dynamic that was not working for her (or for her husband).

Like Maria, many moms have difficulty relating to their partners and struggle to communicate and problem-solve effectively. Extended family relationships may suffer as well, as grandparents/uncles/aunts/etc. may turn out to be more overinvolved or underinvolved than anticipated. Friendships, too, often change, as moms don't have the time and energy they once did to devote to friends and might want different things from their friendships now that they have children.

Mom Brain: The Bottom Line

So this is where we find ourselves when we become mothers: responsible for the life of a helpless child, overwhelmed with complex emotions, juggling 800 competing priorities, and experiencing dynamic changes in our relationships with others and our sense of who we are as people. Our mom brains are undergoing profound changes and working overtime to adapt to our dramatically altered circumstances.

So how do we adapt effectively? Often, our go-to coping strategies cease to be effective or even feasible after kids come into the picture. Take the popular "sleep in and binge-watch *Friends*" strategy—it's simply not an option for, say, a stay-at-home mom with an infant and toddler in her charge.

New brains require new coping strategies. Fortunately, cognitive-behavioral therapy (CBT) and related evidence-based treatments offer a wide variety of tools ideally suited to helping new moms navigate the myriad and dramatic changes of motherhood.

CBT for Moms

As I mentioned in the Introduction, CBT is a form of therapy that has been shown in countless research studies to be effective for managing anxiety, mood, and emotion regulation difficulties, among many other issues. CBT involves making changes in the way you think about a situation, the way you behave, and the way you interpret and respond to your emotions.

Here are some important features of CBT:

1. It is **present-moment focused.** If you come to my office for a session, I won't have you lie down on a couch and talk about your childhood. Instead, I'll have you sit upright (unless you really want to lie down—I do have a couch) and tell me what your **current** difficulties are. CBT is less concerned with past problems and more concerned with helping you manage your problems in the here and now. This is not to say that we CBT therapists don't talk about childhood; and in fact, new moms often find it helpful to discuss how they were raised and how their parents coped with the many challenges of parenting. But generally speaking, we talk about present-moment issues (such as how to avoid murdering that mom who won't stop asking you to volunteer for the nursery school spirit committee).

2. It is **goal directed.** Related to the here-and-now nature of CBT is its mission to target well-defined problems that can be approached in a clear, focused manner. In this book, I'll encourage you to spend time identifying the problems you're experiencing and setting specific goals for tackling those problems.

3. It is **strategy based.** CBT is comprised of a collection of strategies that are effective for managing different types of difficulties. My goal is to present these strategies in an accessible manner, so that they are easy for you to learn. Unlike other self-help books, this one is light on clinical jargon and heavy on *Real Housewives* references.

4. It requires **practice.** Once you read about CBT strategies, the next step is to try them out at home, in real time, so you can figure out which ones work best for you, and in which circumstances. The more you practice using new strategies, the better you'll become at using them. The nice thing about the CBT tools I'll be sharing is that they are user-friendly, so even the most overscheduled mom can incorporate them into her daily routine.

Strategies in CBT tend to fall into one of two categories: cognitive and behavioral.

Cognitive Strategies: Rethinking Your Thoughts

Cognitive strategies help you explore the ways you think and challenge any problematic patterns that might be maintaining your difficulties. Certain types of thinking patterns are very common among new moms (always thinking of things in terms of what you "should" be doing, for example, or assuming that small incidents will have catastrophic outcomes). Moms can benefit greatly from using cognitive skills to change these patterns.

Take Yael, for example. Yael forgot about the highly anticipated "pajama day" at her son's day care. When Mason walked into school and saw his buddies decked out in their nighttime finest, he began sobbing uncontrollably and continued to do so as Yael slowly eased her way out of his classroom. She presented this to me as evidence that she was clearly the "world's worst mom." Obviously, there was something off in Yael's thinking about this: in focusing on the pajamas incident, she was considering only one piece of data (a thinking pattern we call "overgeneralizing"—more on that in Chapter 4) to arrive at her assessment of herself as a mother. Cognitive work with Yael involved encouraging her to consider the many other pieces of evidence that suggested she was a terrific mother—her ability to make Mason laugh, for example—and use this evidence to make a more realistic assessment of her maternal success.

Evidence is a key term in cognitive therapy: at the core of cognitive work is trying to determine whether there is enough evidence to support a negative thought that you might be having. My mom patients and I work as scientists, trying to amass facts to either support or refute negative thoughts. There are lots of different effective methods for amassing these facts, which I'll be sharing throughout the book.

Behavioral Strategies:
Changing How You Act to Change Your Mood

Not surprisingly, the goal of behavioral strategies is behavior change. It is often the case that changes in thoughts and emotions *result from* changes in behavior, as opposed to *lead to* changes in behavior. The phrase "fake it till you make it" (or what we like to call "acting as if" in CBT) is a great illustration of this concept. If you initially act as if you know what you're doing, you'll eventually gain experience and as a result confidence that you actually know what you're doing.

Behavioral tasks in CBT can be something as simple as setting an alarm to remind you to engage in daily self-care or something as complicated as limiting the time you spend looking at your baby's video monitor at night (trust me, that one is *a lot* more involved than it sounds).

Recently many of my patients have worked to develop a behavior change plan around phone/social media usage. So many moms cannot resist the pull of the phone but recognize that constant use is impairing their ability to focus on their parenting (and work, and conversations, and so on and so on . . .). I often create "phone plans" with these moms, in which we lay out when and how often they will check their phones each day. I tell moms that I'm essentially preparing them for when their children are teenagers and they'll have to impose such a schedule on their kids. (More on this in Chapter 7.)

The behavioral strategies we'll discuss in *Mom Brain* will mostly fall into one of two categories. The first, exemplified by the "phone plan" story, is scheduling/prioritizing. Because our mom brains are so overtaxed, we can no longer rely on our brains to remember everything we need to do. We also have to come to terms with the fact that we will never be able to complete all of the items on our to-do list and have to figure out a way to rank these items in order of importance. This is why I still don't have a new hair dryer, even though for the past 6 weeks mine has been purring like a 40-year-old pickup truck and smells like something is burning. In the book we'll talk about how to use strategies like creating daily schedules, setting alarms, and strategically prioritizing our daily tasks.

The second type of behavioral strategy we'll discuss in the book is exposure. You may have heard of exposure therapy for things like phobias, where someone with, say, a fear of spiders faces her fear by spending a bunch of time with spiders. But exposure therapy is much more than reaching into a tank full of insects. Typically, whenever we are fearful of anything (be it spiders, germs, or the judgment of others), we try to avoid what we're fearful of. But oftentimes avoidance can be extremely problematic.

Consider Logan, who sometimes avoided driving her son around in her car. Logan had never been a confident driver, and after having her son she began to fear that she would get into a car accident with him in the back seat. As a result, Logan often turned down invitations for playdates that required driving, even though these events provided opportunities for some much-needed adult interaction. In her exposure work, Logan tasked herself with saying "yes" to all playdate invites, despite her fear of accidents, and challenged herself to drive progressively longer distances. With time, she realized that she could manage her anxiety and successfully drive wherever she needed to.

The goal of exposure for moms like Logan is to face what you are fearful of. Exposure practice can occur in person, when you practice your fears in "real life," as Logan did, and/or in your imagination, when you imagine yourself facing your fears. Sometimes it can even help to expose yourself to bodily sensations (like dizziness, shortness of breath, or sweating) that might be causing or maintaining your anxiety. We'll talk about exposure throughout the book, and I'll describe how you can tailor an exposure plan to help manage any anxiety that might be consuming your mom brain.

DBT, ACT, and Mindfulness: Accepting Negative Emotions to Manage Them Effectively

Along with CBT, we'll be discussing mindfulness and a number of other strategies from dialectical behavior therapy (DBT) and acceptance and commitment therapy (ACT). Like CBT, these are research-supported, skill-based, goal-directed treatments that are extremely effective.

Mindfulness: Focusing on the Present, without Judgment

You've no doubt heard about mindfulness, a practice that can help people manage anxiety, depression, and stress, among other things. Being mindful simply means being fully focused on the present moment, without judging the moment or trying to change it. According to that definition, lots of things qualify as mindfulness activities, such as concentrating on your breathing, paying attention to (but not judging) the thoughts or feelings that move through your mind, and listening for sounds during a mindful nature walk.

I use mindfulness all the time to cope with mom-related (and also non-mom-related) stress. Yesterday, for example, I was trying to watch a *Parks and Recreation* rerun (my go-to brain clearer) when I noticed that I wasn't paying any attention to the episode. Instead, I was thinking about how I needed to set a calendar reminder to take clipboards home from work so I could use them at my son's back-to-school night. I realized that *Parks and Rec* wasn't helping me quiet the noise in my head, so I turned it off, went into my living room, closed my eyes, and just mindfully listened to the tick-tock of our grandfather clock for a few minutes. It helped me focus my attention and clear my mind enough so that when I returned to the TV, I was able to actually appreciate what I was watching.

I think moms are the perfect candidates for mindfulness work. We always have a million things in our heads at once, we're often distracted by social media and/or screaming children, and we rarely give ourselves the opportunity to take "mental time-outs" during our day. Life with kids can be so chaotic, and having a method for quickly decompressing, refreshing, and refocusing in the middle of a busy day is extremely valuable.

Also, as we'll discuss in detail in Chapter 2, moms experience complex and at times seemingly contradictory emotions. There are a number of mindfulness activities that encourage you to take a nonjudgmental stance toward your feelings and thoughts, to simply notice them and allow yourself to have them without judging yourself. This is tremendously helpful for moms. Moms need to be able to show themselves compassion and accept all of their emotions as valid, even the not-so-pleasant ones.

DBT: Learning Skills for Navigating Strong Emotions and Interpersonal Relationships

Pioneered by psychologist Dr. Marsha Linehan, DBT was originally developed to help individuals with borderline personality disorder and suicidality.

It has since been adapted as a treatment for a host of other issues, and DBT-skill-based treatment has been shown to lead to improvements in emotion regulation in adults with depression and anxiety. A major tenet of DBT is that one must aim for both acceptance and change; that is, accept one's problems as they are in the moment, while at the same time work to make changes. DBT treatment teaches skills addressing four target areas: mindfulness, emotion regulation, distress tolerance, and interpersonal effectiveness.

I recently used DBT skills to help Sarah manage her stress about an upcoming family visit. Sarah was dreading her parents' imminent weeklong stay at her house, as her parents had historically "taken over" her home when they visited; they flouted her rules, oversugared her kids, and generally left a path of destruction in their wake. I taught Sarah how to communicate "house rules" to her parents using the DBT interpersonal effectiveness skill of DEAR MAN (much more on DEAR MAN in Chapters 9, 10, and 11). We then role-played the discussion she would have with her parents in advance of their visit.

ACT: Committing to Taking Actions Consistent with Your Values

Created by psychologist Dr. Steven Hayes, ACT stresses two major goals: acceptance of thoughts, feelings, and circumstances; and commitment to behavior change. Regarding the former, in ACT, as in DBT, individuals are taught to mindfully accept their thoughts, emotions, and circumstances just as they are, without judgment. ACT also stresses the need to distance oneself from one's thoughts and emotions, rather than assuming that these thoughts and emotions represent the objective truth. Regarding the "commitment" piece of ACT, individuals are asked to articulate their values and then commit to taking action consistent with these values. As in CBT, behavior change is an important component of ACT work. Research has shown ACT to be an efficacious treatment for anxiety and depression, among other issues.

I used ACT strategies with LaTonya, who valued being athletic and fit but stopped exercising entirely once she had her son. We discussed how important her value of athleticism was to her and considered all of the barriers keeping her from honoring this value. We then made a behavioral plan to which LaTonya could commit: she would join a local softball league and arrange kid coverage with her partner and mother-in-law. In Chapter 3, and throughout the book, we'll spend a significant amount of time talking about your values and what you can do to continue to honor them.

Coping with Mom Brain: Use What Works

In *Mom Brain*, you'll learn strategies from CBT, ACT, and DBT. There are some who argue that these are completely separate treatments whose strategies should not be combined, as they have different aims (e.g., CBT tells you to refute your thoughts; ACT tells you to distance yourself from them). Personally, I've always gone with the "use what works" approach, and I think all three treatments have wonderful strategies that can be extremely useful for moms.

In my experience, some of these techniques work better than others in certain situations and/or with certain people. As you read the book, you will find that particular strategies really speak to you—perhaps they are a good match for the difficulties you're having, or you can see how you can easily incorporate them into your daily routine. I'd recommend you try out those strategies first and practice them as much as possible. Include those that work well for you in your mom brain "tool kit." If you find that the strategies you expected to work are not as helpful as you had hoped, try out some others. By the time you're finished with this book, you'll have a host of tools at your disposal for managing all kinds of mom-brain-related stress.

How Do You Know If You Need More Help?

Hopefully by now you've gotten the message that mom brain, with all of its attendant emotional upheavals and relationship changes, is a condition that affects all new moms. However, some new moms find it particularly difficult to navigate the challenges of motherhood and struggle to function on a day-to-day basis as a result. These moms might meet criteria for a perinatal mood or anxiety disorder (PMAD). PMAD is a relatively new term, encompassing both postpartum depression and postpartum anxiety disorders (such as postpartum obsessive–compulsive disorder and postpartum posttraumatic stress disorder).

While people commonly talk about PMADs developing during the early days of motherhood, you may experience significant mood and anxiety symptoms throughout the course of your children's lives. Further, in addition to anxiety and depression there are many negative emotions that can become disabling, including anger, guilt, irritability, and resentment. You may also find that you're struggling with *emotion regulation*—that is, that you are unable to successfully manage and respond to your emotions.

It can be difficult to tell the difference between the "normal" negative feelings that come with new motherhood and symptoms that require more serious intervention. It's not typically the case that moms either have these bad feelings or don't. Most of us have these feelings, to varying degrees of frequency and intensity. You should consider seeking mental health treatment if you experience persistent anxiety, panic, depression, sadness, anger, irritability, or any other negative emotions that interfere with your ability to:

- Parent effectively
- Take care of yourself effectively (shower, brush teeth, spend some time each day outside the house)
- Sleep (either sleeping too much or too little, beyond the typical sleep issues that are expected in new mothers)
- Eat
- Perform relatively minor daily tasks
- Work

Other important indicators that you should seek mental health treatment include:

- Thinking about hurting yourself or your child
- Feeling like you are constantly reexperiencing a traumatic birth experience, pregnancy loss, or any other past traumatic event
- Frequent crying
- Feeling hopeless or worthless
- Experiencing persistent scary thoughts, including thoughts of your baby being harmed or you harming your baby
- Worrying that you're "losing your mind" or "going crazy"
- Feeling like you have not been able to bond with your child and/or that you are not fit to be a mother

The term "mental health treatment" is deliberately broad, encompassing both therapy and medication management (seeing a psychiatrist who prescribes psychiatric medications). Depending on your individual situation, therapy or medication (or a combination of both) might be right for you.

A caveat here: I know that all new mothers often struggle with daily self-care stuff like sleeping, eating, and showering. We expect moms to experience these difficulties. What you (and your loved ones) need to determine is whether you are struggling to the point where you cannot function and perform day-to-day tasks. If so, it's critical that you seek outside help.

If you are in pain, please know that you are not alone and that great treatment is available. See the Resources section of the book for more information about seeking help. Also, see Chapter 5 for a more in-depth discussion of maternal anxiety.

2

"What's Happened to My Heart?"

Understanding the Emotional
Roller-Coaster Ride of Motherhood

As a mom-to-be, I felt ready to withstand the emotional ups and downs that come with new motherhood. I was a psychologist, after all, and had a sister who'd already been through it twice. If anyone was emotionally equipped to handle a new baby, I was.

Unfortunately, I quickly learned that years of psychology training and vicarious mothering were no match for a real-deal baby. Sure, I experienced many of the "classic" emotions of motherhood that I had come to expect—the complete joy, the bone-crushing fatigue, the feelings of inadequacy. But I had no idea how intense and complex my emotional experiences would be.

Let me describe a few such experiences for you. For example, the **"5 P.M. predinner low point"**: I'm covered in poop/spit-up/vomit (or all three); I am hungry, but not for any food in my fridge; I am desperate for my husband to get home from work to relieve me but also kind of hoping he never comes home because then I can binge-watch several episodes of *Friday Night Lights* while the baby sleeps; and I am about to go insane from the baby's constant wailing, courtesy of a phenomenon called "The Witching Hour," which apparently happens to all babies around dinnertime.

Or how about the **"Sunday-morning grocery store run"**? I'm thrilled to be out but also despairing at what being "out" now means for me; I'm racing through the aisles to make it back home to nurse my kid, feeling like an escaped convict with the police on my trail; I feel hopeless, and desperate, like I will never be able to live my life on my own terms again; and yet I already miss my kid and can't wait to get him back in my arms.

And then there's the **"Trip to the moms' play group"**: I'm thrilled that I actually showered and did my hair, but feel so exhausted by this process that as soon as I get to the play group, I want to go home and go to sleep; I watch the projectile boogers from another kid's nose fall on my son's hand, which my son swiftly puts in his mouth, prompting me to panic about my son getting sick; I see some kid doing what appears to be Shakespeare recitations and I start to fret that maybe my kid is behind developmentally, and should I be putting him in one of those hard-core academic preparedness programs? Also while this is happening I am trying to make small talk with another mom who I am 100% sure I will never see again.

All of us, parents and nonparents alike, experience countless emotions every day, both negative and positive. But new motherhood is one of those times in our lives when our emotions go into overdrive, when biological and life changes converge in an epic way, leaving us completely and helplessly awash in feelings. If human emotional experiences are like roller-coaster rides, motherhood is a trip on one of those coasters where the ride starts off with a 450-foot drop and loops you around and around until you end up throwing up on your shoes (or, if you're me, passing out—a very public embarrassment that marked my final trip to Six Flags Great Adventure).

A critical task for all of us moms is to learn to understand and accept all of our emotions, the good, the bad, and the ugly. Because, as we'll discuss throughout this chapter (and throughout the book), once you strap into the insane emotional roller-coaster ride of parenthood, you never get off. Sure, your emotional experiences change as your kids age—the anxiety about whether you are inadvertently harming your infant, for example, might slowly morph into anxiety about whether or not your school-age kid is being harmed by a bully—but your emotions remain intense and complicated.

Like me, so many new moms are initially surprised by their strong and varied emotional experiences, which feel so different from the types of experiences they've had before. My initial reaction, and that of many of my patients, was to judge myself for being "emotional" and figure out how to control my feelings. But I quickly learned that I had to accept these up-and-down emotions as a hallmark feature of mom brain. Only by accepting these feelings would I be able to figure out how to cope with them effectively.

In this chapter, we'll discuss where all of these mom brain emotions come from and highlight some initial steps you can take to respond to them. We'll end with a special section on coping with negative emotions about your kids.

What Muddies the Emotional Picture for Moms?

Do you remember what it felt like after you first moved out of your child-hood home and started living on your own? I vividly recall the beginning of my freshman year of college, when I struggled to adapt to a new environ-ment and routine. I had to figure out how to feed myself (which explained my all-cereal diet), how to get where I needed to go, and who to turn to when I needed emotional support. I felt completely lost and unmoored.

I'd argue that new motherhood is like those first few weeks of living independently (or like any other major life shift, such as a big move or new job), except that while you're trying to figure out how to adjust to your new routine and take care of yourself you're also trying to figure out how to take care of a tiny little person. New motherhood is disorienting in a way few other life experiences are.

The story of Sherrie's first trip out with her new baby perfectly illus-trates the emotional disorientation of new motherhood. She decided to go to Target (naturally), to buy a bunch of baby supplies and return some baby gifts. When she arrived, she spent 10 minutes in the parking lot getting her baby into the stroller and shoving all of the baby gifts into the way-too-small stroller basket. By the time she made it into the store, she was already sweat-ing and frustrated. While she was waiting on line to make her returns, her daughter started to wail, so she picked her up in one arm while holding on to the stroller and signing the credit card return receipt with the other.

Once the return was finished, Sherrie, who by this point was drenched in sweat and nursing a sore arm, plopped her daughter back into the stroller and raced to the baby aisle. She puzzled over the various diaper options and finally picked one that looked reasonable. As she walked to the check-out area, she glanced longingly at the aisles she used to frequent (women's clothes, stationery, and office supplies—my god, the office supplies!) and quickly came to the disappointing conclusion that she did not have time to browse them. At the checkout, a woman behind her commented about how beautiful her baby was, and Sherrie was flooded with love and gratitude. When she returned home, she took her bags in the door and for a split sec-ond forgot that she had to go back for the baby. She felt a surge of guilt about this as she raced back to her car.

In a short trip to Target, Sherrie experienced frustration, anxiety, longing for her previous life, gratitude, love, and guilt. The "quick trip to Target"—a well-rehearsed staple of her previous life—had suddenly become an emotional minefield.

New motherhood is rife with emotional minefields. This explosion of emotions happens for a number of reasons: we undergo physical changes; we enter into brand-new environments (or have to learn to adapt to old environments); and we find that our emotional experiences may not be what we expected. Below, we'll discuss how physiological, environmental, and cognitive factors all play a significant role in shaping maternal emotional life.

Holy Hormones: Our Bodies and Our Emotions

As you may remember from adolescence, surges in hormones are usually accompanied by surges in emotions. Good or bad, the emotions come on fast, and with dramatic flourish. This is true of new motherhood as well, and in fact, one reproductive psychiatrist has been working to popularize a term—"matrescence"—to describe the emotional and self-identity changes that new mothers experience. She notes that as teenagers endure emotional upheaval, so too do mothers. I'm thinking about Lola, a brand-new mom who came to see me last week and confessed that she had spent the better part of a day the previous week crying, at times tears of joy, at times tears of sadness and loss, and at times a confusing mixture of both.

Aside from hormones, there are other physiological factors that contribute to the emotional lives of new moms. Sleep deprivation is the most obvious one; when we are low on sleep, we tend to have a shorter emotional fuse. This remains true for me to this day. If one of my sons wakes me up in the middle of the night, you can bet that I'll spend the better part of the next day ranting about something totally inconsequential ("How *dare* Netflix remove my *30 Rock* reruns?!?!"). Lack of exercise and poor eating can also leave us more vulnerable to emotional upheaval. Lola admitted that she "ate nothing but chocolate" during her lengthy crying jag. Which I understand—after all, what's more soothing than chocolate?—but which I think likely contributed to her mood swings. (We'll talk a lot about how to eat and sleep well in Chapter 6.) Also, many new moms experience issues with their physical health. This includes everything from prolonged birth/C-section recoveries to constant runny noses (a particular issue for moms with kids in day care). Needless to say, if we are feeling unwell, it can be difficult to meet both the physical and emotional challenges of having little ones.

"Hello, Uh . . . Where Am I?": Our Environments and Our Emotions

Along with changes in our bodies, changes in our environments can have a significant impact on our emotional lives as new moms. As adults, we've learned through experience how to navigate challenges in a variety of familiar environments. We know, for example, how to respond if we receive negative feedback at work or how to sidestep a gossipy neighbor. Yet when we become mothers, we find ourselves in a host of new environments, where we have no experience coping with the various challenges presented to us.

Take Asha, who had planned to be a stay-at-home mom after spending years in the corporate world. Once her son was born, her life was upended. One minute she was in a New York City skyscraper making deals and working until midnight, and the next she was at home in sweatpants watching Wendy Williams while walking loops around her apartment with her son strapped to her body. Asha felt confident in her ability to placate angry customers but had no faith in her ability to placate a screaming, colicky infant. Each day brought completely new experiences and corresponding new emotional responses.

Like Asha, Emma found herself thrust into an environment for which she was unprepared. Emma moved to the suburbs when her kids were 6 months and 4 years old and decided to join the PTO at her children's school, assuming it would help her meet new people. She was completely blindsided by the surprisingly political world of the PTO, where a few groups of aggressive parents attempted to exert outsize influence over school decisions. Emma had never been in an environment like this before, where, under the guise of advocating for kids, adults were so blatantly abusing power. She was confused, and angry, and didn't know how to respond effectively to the powers that be without alienating herself from the other parents.

Both Emma and Asha found themselves struggling to adapt to unfamiliar environments. Moms may also find that environments that were once familiar to them start to feel foreign when they experience them with kids in tow. Take Sherrie's Target run, for example. What used to be a quick, stress-free excursion turned into a stressful field trip once she started taking along (and shopping for) a small kid. Experiencing holidays with children is another interesting example of this. As you'll see in Chapter 12, celebrations that were formerly associated with relaxation and cherished memories often become associated with tears, tantrums, and stress eating once kids enter the picture. Moms have to expect that some previously manageable environments may start feeling totally unmanageable.

There's one other environmental change for new moms that deserves mention: the sudden immersion into an excessively judgmental culture. While we'll talk about this in much more detail in Chapters 7 and 8, I did want to bring it up here because the rampant mom-shaming to which we are all exposed has a significant impact on the emotions we experience.

Mothers are expected to mom perfectly and to deprioritize their own needs in the service of their children's. Of course, no one can mom perfectly, and we are judged all the time—by random strangers on social media, other moms, and even family members and friends—who don't agree with our parenting choices. Needless to say, our judgmental culture creates a breeding ground for anxiety, guilt, and self-criticism.

This Isn't What I Imagined: Our Expectations and Our Emotions

Chevonne liked to think she knew herself pretty well. She was one of those "calm, cool, and collected" people who tended to take things in stride and never really got worked up. At work, she was the one called upon to deal with difficult clients, as her calm demeanor helped put even the toughest customers at ease. Yet here was Chevonne with her 2-year-old, screaming her head off at him while trying to shove his writhing, tantruming body into his car seat. Chevonne felt frustrated, desperate, and totally out of control. How did this formerly cool customer become an emotional wreck?

By the time we become mothers, most of us, like Chevonne, feel like we know ourselves and our emotional reactions very well. We know what makes us laugh and cry, what makes us vulnerable and what makes us tick. Yet motherhood tends to elicit entirely new emotional responses, in large part because of the hormonal and environmental shifts we discussed above. Personally, I never knew what it felt like to be irritable until I had my kids. I have since been irritable on several (many) occasions, oftentimes for no discernible reason.

Many expectant moms think they know how they're going to feel when they become parents. And when they inevitably don't feel as they expected to, it can be disorienting at best and devastating at worst. Below, I share a few stories to illustrate some of the many ways our maternal emotions can defy our expectations.

The Mom Who Expected Sunshine and Flowers

Kate knew she wanted to be a mom from the time she was a little girl, providing her baby doll with love (and the occasional unfortunate haircut). She couldn't wait for the day that she could quit her day job and become a full-time mom. But after having her daughter, she found motherhood to be a lot less transcendent than she expected. There were moments of bliss, sure, but also many moments of sadness, and desperation, and exhaustion. Kate spent time looking at pictures of joyful moms and their sun-kissed babies on Instagram and wondered what she was missing. She believed that these moms were "naturals" at this parenthood thing, and she clearly wasn't.

Social media, with its highly curated (and generally inaccurate) portrayals of blissful motherhood, can throw moms like Kate for a loop. Often, when moms with high expectations don't end up feeling 100% happy and fulfilled like those Instagram moms seem to be, they feel as if they've failed, or that they're not getting motherhood right or they're not "naturals." Personally, I can't think of anything more *un*natural than a mother who always feels happy and thrilled to be a mom. (Much more on social media depictions of moms in Chapter 7.)

The Mom Who Expected the Ups and Downs (but Not the "In the Middles")

Mai felt absolutely prepared for the dramatic mood swings of motherhood. A frequent reader and commenter on a popular motherhood humor website, she related to memes like "I'm a hot mess mom" (complete with a picture of a clearly exhausted-looking mom with four kids in various stages of undress hanging all over her). She fully expected that motherhood would be heavenly one minute and punishing the next.

What she didn't expect, however, were the all-too-frequent "in the middles." Turns out that much of motherhood was not meme-worthy. There were those endless, boring days with an infant where literally nothing happened. There was the constant focus on seemingly mundane issues: Could she make it to the library after naptime but before the library closed for the night? When was OldNavy.com's baby sale again? Could she find a sitter so that she could attend her friend's birthday dinner?

Many of the moms with whom I work are surprised at how dull early motherhood can be. That's because the trivialities of parenting young kids aren't generally represented on mom blogs or on TV or in the movies. After all, it's not really entertaining to read about or watch moms going through the daily grind with little ones. Moms are usually depicted as stressed beyond all hope or awash in love and gratitude; rarely do you see anything in between. And the depictions tend to be totally unsubtle and wildly overgeneralized. (I'm thinking specifically about the endless posts and memes featuring overwhelmed moms downing huge glasses of wine. Are we assumed to be so lacking in coping skills that we need to rely on wine to get us through the day?)

The Mom Who Didn't Expect to Be "Feeling All the Feelings"

I always ignored those mom wine posts (and the super-flowery ones, too). I knew from my sister's experience that motherhood usually fell somewhere between exceptionally wonderful and soul-crushingly awful. What I did not expect, however, was that I would experience wildly conflicting but equally valid emotions about virtually every motherhood experience.

Take my story about being at the grocery store and feeling compelled to rush home and nurse Matty. While I was at the store, I felt both hopeless about the extent to which I was tethered to Matty *and* eager to get him back in my arms again. In the same moment, I was feeling upset about how much this kid had changed my life and completely in love with this kid who'd changed my life.

The more I work with moms, the more I realize that such contradictory emotions define the maternal experience: we often feel angry or frustrated with our kids at the same time as we feel totally in love with them. We may feel overcome with love when we see our partner with our child but also overcome with frustration about all the dishes left in the sink. We may be thankful that our parents watched our kid for the night but also furious when we return home and the kid is still awake, jumping up and down in his crib. During a particularly dramatic tantrum, Matty once confessed that he was "FEELING ALL THE FEELINGS!" I've always remembered that, as I think it's a particularly apt description of the emotional life of a new mother (and of a tantruming toddler, of course).

The Mom with the Illusion of Control

Remember "calm, cool, and collected" Chevonne? She found her coping skills were no match for a toddler who didn't feel like riding in his car seat. She was troubled by the fact that she often "lost it" with her son and felt like she could no longer control her emotional responses.

This expectation—that we should be able to keep our emotions "under control"—is by no means exclusive to mothers. How many of you, throughout the course of your life, have ever been told to "get over it" or "suck it up" when you were feeling upset or anxious or angry? Unfortunately, many of us are taught from a young age that we must control our bad feelings and do whatever we can to make them go away as quickly as possible.

But here's the thing: we humans are notoriously terrible at controlling how we feel. I'd argue that emotional control is even more of a challenge for moms, who are contending with the physiological, environmental, and cognitive challenges we discussed above. Once we become moms the volume of our emotions gets turned way up, making it that much more difficult to quiet them down. I once started to tear up after teenage environmental activists came to my door, thinking about how proud their parents must be that they're doing this work and fretting about the climate change problems that they and my sons will be inheriting. Had these activists come to my door before I had kids, I probably would have just been irritated that they'd interrupted me during dinner.

My fretting about climate change illustrates another unique feature of the maternal emotional experience. Many of us no longer feel able to tune out threatening information, because we recognize that our children's future is at stake. So many of my patients tell me that they now "obsess" about issues that they once felt able to take in stride, like climate change or political upheaval. And as we'll discuss in Chapter 4, news of events like school shootings and cataclysmic weather can become much harder to shake when you're fearful not only for your own safety but for the safety of your kids.

How Can I Be Feeling This Way?: Our Judgments and Our Emotions

As we've discussed, the maternal emotional roller-coaster ride is fueled by unmet expectations, new environments, and physiological changes. There is one additional feature of the maternal emotional experience that can make the ride even more perilous: negative self-judgment. Remember Kate, the mom who lamented that her life was nothing like the life of the Instagram moms she followed? In addition to feeling the hallmark negative emotions of new motherhood, like sadness, anxiety, boredom, and frustration, Kate judged herself for having these feelings. She believed that if she were truly a "natural" mom, she would be relishing her motherhood experience.

I cannot tell you how many moms have come to my office and expressed shame or guilt for feeling sad, or anxious, or for just kind of hating being a mom sometimes. Unfortunately, self-judgment adds another layer to an already complicated emotional picture. Think of it this way: it's bad enough having to experience anxiety, sadness, loneliness, or resentment. But if you're also judging yourself for these feelings, you're adding new negative emotions into the mix, like guilt and shame. It's as if you're punishing yourself for feeling bad feelings—kind of like kicking a dog when it's down.

We moms need to learn to accept our negative emotions, rather than judge them or try to control them. Our goal can't be to stop feeling a certain way; as we've discussed, we're terrible at controlling our feelings. Our goal instead must be to accept how we're feeling, and to consider options for responding.

Coping with the Maternal Emotional Experience

If there's one message I want you take away from this chapter, it's that it is *normal* for new moms to feel sad, bored, angry, resentful, and anxious (or all of these things at once). While it can be difficult to accept strong negative emotions, such acceptance is a critical first step in learning to cope with these emotions effectively. The way I see it, when we moms feel bad, we have a choice: we can spend time questioning our negative emotions, judging ourselves for them, and trying to get rid of them, resulting in frustration and wasted time and energy; or we can accept that we feel crummy, show ourselves some compassion, and focus our energy on figuring out how to respond to our feelings.

In the next several sections, we'll discuss a number of general strategies for accepting and responding to negative and complex emotions. You can start to use these strategies right away, regardless of the particular emotion (or combination of emotions) you're experiencing. Later in the book I'll share many other strategies designed to help you cope with the emotions common to specific maternal experiences, such as kid-related anxiety, perfectionism, social media comparison making, and relationship changes.

Monitor Your Moods and Figure Out Your Signals

Before you can respond to negative emotions, you need to be able to recognize them. Beth, mom of 4-year-old twins, likes to talk about her "hot face." When Beth gets frustrated with her kids or her partner, or feels generally stressed, her face gets flushed and sweaty ("Like I've just run a marathon, except I'm just, like, cutting up apples"). Like Beth, we all experience signals, sometimes in our bodies and sometimes in our minds, that let us know we're becoming overwhelmed by negative emotions. Common signals include sweating, upset stomach, repetitive thoughts, and Broadway song lyrics racing through your mind at an alarming pace (or is that just me?). For many of us, different negative emotions are associated with different signals; for example, we may get short of breath when we're anxious, tear up when we're sad, and tense up when we're frustrated.

It's important to figure out what our signals are, as they will serve as cues that we're becoming overwhelmed. Moms often tell me that they allow sadness, stress, frustration, and other negative emotions to build up until they are unable to cope and have an epic *Real Housewives*–style meltdown. There's a term for this in dialectical behavior therapy, actually: being in *emotion mind,* when we're so overcome with emotion that reason and logic fly out the window. If you're aware of your signals, you can, to paraphrase famed family therapist Dr. Irving Yalom, catch your emotions while they're young; that is, quickly recognize that you're starting to struggle and take effective corrective action before you hit that emotion mind "point of no return." I often wonder what would happen if someone took the time to teach the *Housewives* how to recognize their bad feelings. Surely fewer of them would end up with wine in their faces?

The best way to understand our signals and accompanying moods is to spend a few days monitoring them. Throughout the day, whenever you feel your emotions swinging (up, down, or back and forth!), take a minute to note the signals that are firing, and the emotions you suspect are behind these signals. Note also where you are and what you are doing during these times. You can use the notes section of your phone or a mood tracking app (see the Resources for some recommendations) for this purpose. Monitoring will help increase your awareness of your signals and negative emotions, and indicate when, where, and with whom you are most vulnerable to them.

Take an Adult Time-Out

Once you understand your signals and start to notice them firing, an effective next step is to give yourself an adult time-out. My patient Sarah joked that she had a "time-out" chair for her son and wished she had one for herself, where she could retreat when she needed some space. I told her that I loved the idea but didn't think she actually needed the chair. What she needed instead was to make a commitment to taking a short break when her emotions became too much for her to handle.

There are a number of different ways to take an adult time-out:

1. **Physically leave the room.** Sometimes it can help to get a change of scenery, even for just a few moments. Sarah, who had a 5-year-old son, had a screened-in porch that she described as the "zen place" in her house. She decided that she would go and spend a few moments in there when her emotional signals were firing. Sarah's son was old enough that he could be left unattended for a few moments (as long as there was an iPad at the ready, of course). For moms with kids who need to be watched at all times, I suggest taking the kids with you on your time-out, even if it's just a quick

walk around the block. One of the things I learned early on as a mom is that a change of scenery can often help stave off kid meltdowns. So taking a time-out with your kids can help chill them out, too. It's a two-for-one strategy!

2. **Try some muscle relaxation.** Progressive muscle relaxation (PMR) is a classic CBT technique that's extremely easy to implement. Starting with your head, and moving progressively down your body, tense and relax different muscle groups, holding the tension for 5–10 seconds before releasing. This obviously helps with physical tension but also serves as a mental time-out, enabling you to focus on your body and quiet your mind a bit. Ideally you'd sit or lie down while you're doing this, but there are also certain muscle groups (like the arms, hands, neck, or shoulders) that you can easily tense and release while walking around or standing up. I'm a personal fan of the stealth workplace PMR; on many occasions, I've put my hands under my desk and tensed and released them a bunch of times.

3. **Practice mindfulness.** Mindfulness activities are perfectly suited for adult time-outs. We'll be talking a lot more about honing your mindfulness skills in the next section.

In addition to ensuring that you get some time and space to process your emotions, adult time-outs help you model productive coping for toddlers and older kids. Your kids will come to see that "taking a break," rather than yelling or acting out, is an effective way to handle strong emotions in the moment.

Cultivate Mindfulness

Mindfulness has become wildly popular in recent years, as an antidote to stress, depression, and overstimulation. It has been incorporated into CBT work and is a prominent feature of several evidence-based treatments, including DBT and ACT. Many of my mom patients are intimidated by mindfulness work, believing that in order to be mindful you have to go on some extensive spiritual journey. But it turns out that mindfulness is super-easy to cultivate and thus perfectly suited for "adult time-outs." Mindfulness exercises allow us to quickly decompress, refresh, and refocus and are therefore a perfect coping strategy for those moments when we find ourselves awash in emotions.

When I use the term "mindfulness," all I'm referring to is focusing on one thing, in the present moment, without judging the moment or yourself and without trying to change the moment. By that definition, there are an infinite number of activities that qualify as mindfulness practice.

One such activity is the 3-Minute Breathing Space, a popular exercise from mindfulness-based cognitive therapy (MBCT). Each minute of the 3-minute breathing space is devoted to a different task; during the first, you observe your current circumstances (thoughts, emotions, physical sensations) as they are, without judging them; during the second, you focus on your breath; and during the third, you focus on your whole body and your surrounding environment. See the box below for a lengthier description of the 3-minute breathing space.

You can also easily incorporate mindfulness into your regular routine by choosing to mindfully focus on different daily activities. My favorite example of this came from Rosa, who loathed the drudgery of cleaning the 10,000 baby bottle parts (and who among us doesn't?), a task she slogged through several times a day. She decided to try mindfully focusing on bottle washing, switching up the aspect of the experience that she paid attention to: sometimes it was the feel of the warm, soapy water on her hands; sometimes it was the sight of the various nooks and crannies in those confusingly shaped bottle parts; and sometimes it was the sound of the water rushing out of the sink. By focusing mindfully on bottle washing, Rosa accomplished

---

The 3-Minute Breathing Space

- *Minute 1:* Try to take in the experience you're having right now, in this moment, without judging yourself. What is in your mind? What are you thinking? What are you feeling? Are you experiencing any sensations in your body, and if so, what are they? Observe and describe what you are experiencing.

- *Minute 2:* Narrow your focus to your breath. Turn your attention to your abdomen, or wherever you feel your breath in your body. Notice how your body expands with the in-breath and contracts with the out-breath. If your mind wanders, just bring your attention back to your breath. Do not judge or try to change your experience.

- *Minute 3:* Try to widen your focus to your body as a whole. Become aware of your entire body, from your head down to your feet. Gradually become aware of the environment around you, where you are and the space you are in. When the minute is over, open your eyes.

two goals: she made a mundane task palatable and she ensured that she had several opportunities to mentally refresh herself during the day.

Virtually any task can be the subject of a mindfulness exercise, like listening to music, taking a walk outside, or cooking dinner. Just make sure you're choosing one aspect of that task to focus on and not judging yourself or your experience. My personal favorite impromptu exercise is to focus on all of the Ugg boots I see while walking the streets of New York City in the winter. Don't worry if you can't focus 100% on the task at hand (and certainly don't judge yourself if you can't!). You're not aiming to make your mind go blank—you're aiming to give yourself a minute to regroup and refresh, which will hopefully enable you to cope more effectively with the stressor(s) at hand.

Approach Your Emotions Mindfully

The mindfulness activities I've described so far aim to help you take a "time-out" from your emotions. In these exercises you're encouraged to focus on something else for a few minutes until you feel more ready to return to the emotional issue of the day. There is another type of mindfulness activity that you can use during an "adult time-out," which asks you to deliberately focus on your negative feelings. Lest you think this sounds like an exercise in masochism, let me explain further. The most critical feature of these emotion-focused practices is that you *don't try to judge or change your feelings*. You simply sit with them, as they are. As you can imagine, these exercises are extremely helpful for those moms who judge themselves for their negative emotions.

Ramona is one of those moms. At each of our early sessions, she shared stories about feeling sad and anxious as a new mom, all of which ended with her berating herself for her feelings. A typical refrain was something like this: "My husband forgot to take out the recycling, and I freaked out. I was so mad and completely lost it on him. I couldn't stop yelling. I should have had been more understanding; after all, he's just as sleep deprived as I am. I feel so guilty."

I encouraged Ramona to cultivate mindfulness of her emotions by using imagery. This is very easy to do: just close your eyes and imagine your feelings and associated thoughts as leaves on a stream, or boxes on a conveyor belt, or bubbles floating up toward the sky. The key is just to notice what these feelings and thoughts are without judging them or trying to change them. The ultimate goal is to help you learn to accept your negative emotions in the moment, without pressuring yourself to make the feelings go away (which, as we discussed above, no one is really able to do). These exercises can also help reduce the strength and power of our emotions, a topic we'll discuss at length in Chapter 4.

Work on Your Self-Compassion (Even If You Feel Like a Mess)

One particularly important element of mindfulness for moms is self-compassion. Mindful self-compassion involves approaching yourself with kindness and an understanding that you, like all humans, are flawed. As moms are incredibly hard on themselves for, well, everything, practicing mindful self-compassion can help moms process guilt and other self-focused negative emotions.

A mindful self-compassion exercise I particularly like, from psychologists Kristin Neff and Christopher Germer, involves allowing yourself to be a "compassionate mess." This is especially useful during those times when you truly screwed up (as we all do). The idea is to take a mindful time-out to engage in a little self-talk, reminding yourself that yes, you made a mistake, but so does every mom at one point or another. You may be a complete mess at this moment, but you won't feel like this forever.

I once confused the dosage on a medication for Matty and inadvertently overdosed him. He ended up being fine (just very sleepy), but I was furious with myself, convinced that I was the world's most irresponsible parent. Instead of spending the day mentally self-flagellating, I wish I'd done some compassionate mess self-talk. If I had, it would have looked something like this: "I'm sorry that you're so angry with yourself, and it's understandable that you feel this way. But you won't always feel like this. You definitely screwed up, but you're a sleep-deprived mom, and you're not perfect, nor is any other mom, for that matter. Try, if you can, to be kinder and more forgiving toward yourself."

I know this may sound a little hokey, but I've found that there's something incredibly freeing about owning up to being a mess in the moment, trying to forgive yourself for it, and recognizing that you won't feel like a mess forever. It's almost like you're waving the white flag in surrender, instead of banging your head against the wall.

Engage in "Emotional Check-Ins"

Up to this point we've been talking about how we can respond when mom brain emotions threaten to overwhelm us. We can also preempt some of our emotion mind episodes by initiating mindful "check-ins" throughout the day, every day. It helps to do your "check-ins" at regular intervals, such as right before mealtimes or during certain points during the workday. All you need to do is stop for a minute and consider how you're feeling and what you're thinking about, and if there's anything you can do in the moment to help yourself cope. Think of it as taking your emotional blood pressure.

I started doing this myself a few years ago. At the time, weekdays in my house were divided into several distinct phases: getting everyone out the door in the morning; working; picking up the kids from school; getting dinner on the table; and doing the kids' bedtime routines. Each of these phases of the day were stressful, for different reasons. The morning routine was often a nightmare, as one of my two sons usually heavily protested going to school and at times had to literally be carried kicking and screaming to the car. I'd go to work already on edge, which made it more challenging for me to cope with the typical workday stressors. Still carrying the tension from the morning and from work, my husband and I would do pickup, dinner, and nighttime routines, all of which involved my kids in full Witching Hour mode. By the time I got my kids to sleep I'd be ready to blow.

I decided to implement a mindful check-in at the end of each phase of my day to take stock of my feelings and determine whether there was anything I could do to refresh myself. This sometimes resulted in my engaging in a mindfulness exercise . . . or a cross-town cookie run. Regardless of what I decided to do, I ended up in a better headspace for tackling the next phase of my day, which made it much more unlikely that I'd have a nighttime meltdown.

Before we wrap up our discussion of emotions, I want to spend some time focusing on the negative emotions we feel toward our kids. See the box below for more.

What to Do When You Kind of Hate Your Kids

They say that parenthood can really bite you on the ass. I always thought this was meant to be taken figuratively . . . until, that is, Sam, at 2½ years old, took a bite out of my butt while I was reaching into the fridge to grab him a yogurt. He didn't appear to be upset or angry with me; it wasn't as if I'd had the gall to turn off *Daniel Tiger's Neighborhood* midepisode or anything like that. He just really wanted to bite me.

I tried to laugh it off, but I couldn't. I was consumed with what mom writers have recently termed "mom rage." I thought about how much I'd sacrificed (time, energy, hobbies) to build a life for this kid and his brother. And this was how he chose to repay me?

Earlier in the chapter we talked in more general terms about the emotional highs and lows of early motherhood. However, there is a specific aspect of the maternal emotional experience, captured in my story about Sam, that I think deserves special attention: the all-too-common phenomenon of feeling negative emotions toward your babies and little kids.

My experience with Sam, while ridiculous, is in no way unique. Babies and little kids often do things that can truly anger and frustrate us. Little ones can also inspire significant resentment when we miss our old lives and recognize everything we've sacrificed (independence, spontaneity, sleep) to have them.

Generally, mothers are reluctant to admit (to themselves and to others) that they harbor negative feelings toward their own kids. They often worry that this means they are "bad mothers" who are unsuited for motherhood, and don't want others to find them out. This worry is often fueled by those social media depictions of blissful motherhood, which portray the love between mother and young child as universally positive, pure, and uncomplicated.

And yet, as I tell my patients, this notion of uncomplicated, pure love does not accord at all with what we know about relationships in general. Do you expect yourself to always feel immense love and extreme satisfaction in your relationship with your partner, say, or with your parents or siblings? Why then would you expect your relationship with your child to be 100% positive and uncomplicated? Especially because, as we'll discuss below, very small children do lots and lots of things (sometimes inadvertently, sometimes quite purposefully) to piss us off?

In the remainder of the chapter, I'll share several concepts that I think will help you better understand and accept your negative emotions toward your kids. These include mother–child "goodness of fit," the "toddlers are assholes" phenomenon, and the notion that thinking isn't doing.

When Moms and Kids Aren't a Good Fit

Stacey was a self-described "get up and go" kind of person. She talked fast and moved fast, and woke up each morning with an agenda already set for the day. Her 3-year-old son, James, however, seemed to be operating on a different frequency. He was a slow mover and a slow talker. He could stay inside all day long playing with blocks and doing puzzles. Getting James out of the house was a production; he spent time protesting, and when he eventually relented, it took what felt like hours to get him dressed. When they were out running errands, James always lagged behind Stacey, which was a source of immense frustration for her. By the time she returned home, agenda only half completed, she was often stressed out and angry with James. Why couldn't he get with the program?

Stacey's story illustrates a classic concept from developmental psychology: parent–child goodness of fit. Goodness of fit refers to the idea that it isn't a child's temperament that dictates whether she will thrive or struggle, but rather how well her temperament fits with her surrounding environment. One important feature of a child's environment is her parents, and specifically her parents' particular temperaments. Not surprisingly, parenting is less complicated when parent and child temperaments fit well together.

Like Stacey, you might struggle with your kid because your temperaments don't necessarily mesh. Which makes sense, right? As you might have difficulty navigating your relationship with an adult who is quite different from you, so too might you struggle with a kid whose style doesn't match yours. It's important to note that neither the parent nor the child is in the wrong in a situation like Stacey's. The conflict is no one's fault. It's just a product of two different personalities having correspondingly different agendas.

If your less-than-optimal fit with your little one inspires resentment and anger, try reminding yourself that these emotions are an understandable response to a poor fit. Consider approaching the situation with mindful self-talk. Can you take a step back (perhaps during an adult time-out) and try to mindfully observe and describe the situation in your head without judging yourself or your kid? Were Stacey to try this, she might come up with something like this:

"I hate being in the house and love moving quickly and burning through every item on my to-do list. James, on the other hand, moves slowly and only wants to be at home. This is why I am feeling so frustrated and angry with him right now—because I want to get up and go, and he's adamantly refusing to put on his shoes. We've clearly got two very different agendas here. My anger and frustration (as well as James's!) make sense, given the situation."

Taking a mindful approach to your fit issues will help you better accept the negative emotions that arise when your fit is poor. And once you are mindful of how your style differs from your child's (and how this impacts your interactions), you'll be better equipped to start thinking about adjustments you can make to better accommodate your kid. Stacey, for example, decided to set only one daily goal for her days at home with James, knowing that anything more ambitious would likely lead to frustration for both of them. She asked her partner to commit to watching James on Saturday mornings so she could tackle her agenda then (much more on setting goals and scheduling in Chapter 6).

It's also the case that parent–child fit can change as your child ages. As you probably surmised, Sam and I were not a good match when he was in his ass-biting phase. I've come to understand that I—someone who loathes chaos and loves to sit and chat—am a much, much better fit for older kids than I am for toddlers. It took having two kids to help me realize this. I'm sure you've heard different moms talk about favoring different stages of development: some love having babies, while others can't wait until their kids are mobile and talking; some find toddlers hilarious, while others, like me, just want their kids to stop throwing stuff at them all the time. Once again, it's important to show yourself some compassion and use mindfulness if you're getting frustrated or angry with your kid at this particular stage of the game. Try to remind yourself that kids change all the time and that later stages might be a better fit for you.

Acknowledge That, Yes, Little Ones Can Be Assholes

A few years ago the concept of "toddlers as assholes" became a thing in the mom blog-iverse. Parenting writers next took aim at 3-year-olds ("threenagers") and 4-year-olds ("fournados.") And while I'm not aware of any similar nicknames for babies, they are certainly not immune from criticism; parenting writers target them as well, noting how incredibly demanding they can be.

The truth is, little ones and even babies do things all the time that would be considered sociopathic in any civilized adult circles. Here is just a random collection of baby/toddler asshole behaviors I've heard about recently:

1. Toddler takes gourmet food lovingly prepared by mom and spits it in her face.
2. Baby decides he will only stop crying when Mom holds him, rendering Mom unable to do anything all day except hold him.

3. Four-year-old refuses to go to day care unless she's allowed to wear a sundress with no coat. It's 25 degrees outside.
4. Toddler opens bottle of baby powder, dumps it out all over his bedroom. (OK, so that one's personal. I walked into Sam's room to find him covered in white powder, looking like a drug kingpin surveying his stash.)

So yes, little ones and even babies can be assholes. And this asshole behavior can be really, really upsetting. I'll admit, I laughed when Sam dumped out the baby powder. But I didn't laugh when he bit me on the butt, nor when his brother had such a fit about going to day care one day that I had to physically push him out the door. I felt angry, and took their behavior personally. I was consumed with the idea that I was working so hard for these kids, and they were essentially flipping me the bird in return.

What I've come to understand, and now tell my patients, is that it makes sense that you might feel frustrated and even angry at your kids when they do this kind of stuff. Because it sucks to be hit or have things thrown at you or be screamed at. But it's also important to remember that kids at this age are not deliberately acting like assholes. Their behavior reflects where they are in their cognitive development. They are pretty much ruled by emotion (and therefore cannot be reasoned with) and have poor impulse control. They are all ego and do not have the mental hardware to take the perspective of anyone but themselves.

One of the traps I fell into was expecting logical and empathic behavior from my kids. Sam in particular did a lot of "threenager" stuff, and I would get so angry, literally asking him, "Why are you throwing this flashlight, Sam? Why would you throw a flashlight at someone?!?!" That's a fair question for an adult or an older kid, but not for a 3-year-old, who definitely does not have any idea why exactly he threw the flashlight. It was also unreasonable for me to expect an egocentric 3-year-old to praise me for my constant hard work on his behalf.

Along with working on some mindful self-talk as we discussed above, I encourage you to try laughing a little at the asshole behavior. It may help to tell the story to relatives and friends; they will most certainly find it funny, which will hopefully help you find some humor in it, too. Consider reframing your kid's asshole-ish incidents as family classics that you'll bring up at their rehearsal dinner one day. And if you're looking to read about some excellent strategies for responding to little-kid asshole behavior, see the "Parenting" section of the Resources.

Recognize That Thinking Isn't Doing

Rayna waited until the very end of her session with me to admit that she'd been having some "shameful" thoughts. The night before, her 2-year-old daughter was up for much of the night, refusing to go to sleep and literally laughing in her face when she pretended to fall asleep. Sometime around hour five of this nonsense, Rayna began fantasizing about throwing her daughter out the window. And what was worse, imagining this actually brought Rayna some peace. She was comforted by the idea that she could finally get a break from her kid. Rayna was sure that having these thoughts made her a "bad mother" and worried that maybe she would actually "snap" one day and throw her daughter out the window.

I've worked with lots of moms like Rayna who entertain intermittent, fleeting fantasies of somehow getting rid of their kids for a little while. Many of them feel ashamed and worried as a result. I wish moms would talk more openly about this, because they'd see that so many moms have borderline violent thoughts about their kids from time to time, often in response to the asshole behaviors we discussed above. I'm including myself here; one late-night fantasy involved throwing a relentlessly crying infant Matty off the balcony of our apartment.

Spoiler alert: I never threw Matty off the balcony. This is because fantasizing about doing something to get rid of your kid is *not* the same thing as actually doing it, despite what you might see in those Lifetime TV movies with titles like *Murderous Mommy's Deadly Secret*. The occasional violent thought about your child, born out of frustration or exhaustion, should not be taken as evidence that you will actually act violently.

It's important not to dismiss these thoughts, however, because they provide us with useful information. If we're fantasizing about getting rid of our kids, it probably means that we've reached our breaking point and need to find a way to get some relief. I encourage you to view your violent thoughts as helpful rather than shameful; let them serve as signals that you need to seek out support from loved ones or work on your self-care. Think of it this way: How would you rather use your limited mom brain space—to punish yourself for having violent thoughts, or to make an action plan for relieving your stress? In Chapter 6, you'll find a number of strategies for improving self-care and seeking out help when you need it.

One final note: I've been talking here about negative thoughts that are intermittent and fleeting. If these thoughts become more frequent and anxiety producing, they may be a symptom of a more serious issue, such as postpartum obsessive–compulsive disorder. See Chapter 5 for a more detailed discussion of this, including how to go about seeking help.

3

"Who Am I Now That I'm a Mom?"

Redefining Who You Are and How You Work

All women are aware that motherhood is going to change their lives. We know that having kids makes it more challenging to focus on work and spend time with friends and pursue hobbies. But what I don't think most women are aware of (or at least I wasn't) is how motherhood fundamentally changes your sense of who you are.

Here are a few examples:

• *"Who is this lady crying at ASPCA ads?"* As we discussed in Chapter 2, motherhood brings with it a completely new set of emotions, many of them foreign to us. We often feel surprised when we experience emotional responses that we don't recognize as our own. After having my sons, I, someone who formerly regarded animals with ambivalence at best and antipathy at worst, started crying at those Sarah McLachlan ASPCA commercials, believing for whatever reason that the puppy at the end looked like Sam. Suddenly, it was Sam who was left in the cold, starving, with a half-bitten-off ear. Through my tears, I wondered, *How the hell did I become one of those people who cry at animal rescue commercials?*

• *"Why can't I think straight?"* We talked in Chapter 1 about mom brain, how the issue is less that we actually lose cognitive capabilities and more that we suddenly have so many more things begging for our cognitive attention (remember my pre- vs. post-kid pie charts?). Faced with such cognitive overwhelm, we may lose our ability to approach something with single-minded focus and feel far less sharp as a result. Jada, a patient of mine, remarked that she had previously viewed herself as a smart, informed person. But when she became a mother, she could not keep up with the news or pop culture, to the point where she confused a well-known political candidate with a television actor. When a friend pointed out her mistake, she was horrified (and mortified).

• *"What happened to my body?"* If you became a mom by giving birth, you may feel like you don't recognize yourself in the mirror and your once-familiar body doesn't feel or work like it used to. Whether you gave birth or not, it's incredibly difficult to find time to do the things you once did to maintain your body and appearance, like exercise, eat healthy, and, well, shower. And when you spend most of the day with kids draped all over you, it's hard to feel like your body is truly your own. All of these factors can impact both your satisfaction with your appearance and your desire to be intimate with your partner.

• *"Where did the athlete/singer/party girl/partner/helper go?"* Many of us stop playing our familiar roles once we become parents. This makes sense, of course; new moms simply don't have the time and emotional resources to devote to sports or partying or helping. But—are we still the athlete/singer/social butterfly/consummate romantic partner/family helper at heart? And if not, who are we, other than Mom?

• *"Why doesn't anyone know me for who I really am? And why don't they seem to care who I really am?"* Laura was a veterinarian, a job well known for sparking the curiosity of others. When she started carting a baby around with her, however, people seemed to lose interest in her job and instead just wanted to know about her kid. She was embarrassed to admit that she at times purposely wore scrubs to day-care dropoff in the hopes that someone would engage her in a discussion of her career. But it never seemed to happen. Nobody seemed to care about her life outside of her son.

• *"Where's my gold star?"* Before I became a mother, I was used to earning praise and thanks for my hard work as a psychologist and employee and friend. But once I had Matty, I was rarely if ever praised for my parenting. In fact, the opposite was often the case: as babies or toddlers my sons seemed to give me feedback only when I did something not to their liking. Sam once told me he was going to "throw [me] in the dumpster" because I insisted he eat the slow-cooked oatmeal I'd made for him instead of a cheese stick for breakfast. In the face of nothing but negative feedback, I couldn't help but think that I was no longer the competent, effective person I'd once been.

- "*What should I do about work?*" Pre-kids, work is what moms devote most of their time and energy to. Post-kids, moms have to adjust their working lives to accommodate the little people they're now devoting most of their time and energy to. Many struggle to decide whether to work at all—assuming they have a choice. Moms are understandably frustrated that dads don't seem to have to make any of these decisions; even today, no one assumes that fathers' careers will change one iota once they have children.

Clearly, our identities as mothers are challenged on a number of fronts. We're forced to adapt to our new mom emotions, brains, and bodies and have to figure out where work and our former passions fit into our new lives. I so wish that someone had warned me about the profound identity shifts and lack of validation that accompany new motherhood. Had I expected it, I might have spent less time puzzling over why I didn't feel like myself anymore and more time trying to adapt to my new identity.

Now when I talk to moms about maternal identity, I often bring up one of the central tenets of DBT: that it is important both to accept the things we cannot change and work to change the things we can (basically the serenity prayer, in therapy form). In this chapter, we'll discuss how both acceptance and change can help you successfully craft your new mom identity. At the end of the chapter, we'll focus specifically on work–life identity in a special section devoted to the topic.

New Mom Identity: A Lesson in Acceptance

Accepting that aspects of who you are as a person have fundamentally changed can be extremely difficult. Fortunately, it turns out that some of these identity changes can have unexpected positive consequences. And even when certain identity shifts don't seem at all positive, you can generally find ways to respond effectively to the change. Much of this can be accomplished through values-based goal setting, which we'll be discussing at length in the second part of the chapter.

Yes, You're Now That Person Who Cries at Animal Rescue Ads

If you've read Chapter 2, you pretty much know what I'm going to say here. It's important that you accept the new emotions that come with motherhood, even if they do not fit with your pre-mom self-image. I'll remind you of what I said in Chapter 2 about confusing emotions: You can either spend your time trying to figure out why you feel a certain emotion and/or trying to make an unfamiliar emotion go away, or you can mindfully focus on the emotion (perhaps using an exercise for this purpose, like leaves on a stream), approach it with curiosity instead of criticism, and figure out how it fits with your new sense of self.

For me, this involved consciously changing my thinking from "Why the hell am I crying at ASPCA commercials?" to "Hmm, I guess I'm now one of those people who cry at ASPCA commercials." What this has meant, practically speaking, is that I am much quicker to defend helpless victims, be they animals or people, than I was before I had kids. I'm much more sensitive to perceived injustices. I've spent a considerable amount of time calling my elected officials about issues like immigration and gun safety, something I don't think I would have done before I had children. And I honestly consider my newfound sensitivity to be an important part of the person I am now.

Prepare to Lose Your Edge (Temporarily)

In Chapter 1, we talked about the many ways in which our brains change once we become parents. At any given time, there are a million thoughts and concerns in our heads, competing for our attention. Our kids take up a lot of space in our mom brains, often crowding out other topics. For moms who previously identified themselves as being well organized and focused, this can be a particularly distressing development.

This was certainly the case for me. When I returned from maternity leave after having Sam, I had a number of brand-new patients scheduled to start therapy with me. I've always prided myself on being able to remember details about each and every person I work with, but during those early months I was horrified to discover that I'd confuse the specifics of some of my patients' stories. Someone would bring up her daughter and I'd realize I had been confusing her with another new patient who had two sons. I didn't understand what had happened to my once sharp mind.

We unfortunately need to resign ourselves to the fact that perhaps we won't be as cognitively sharp, or be able to focus quite as successfully, when our kids are small. As we discussed in Chapter 1, this is less due to cognitive deficits and more due to cognitive overload. Plus, as we know, lack of sleep can certainly contribute to mental fuzziness. However, I can personally attest to the fact that these focus and attention issues definitely improve with time as your kids age and you start sleeping again. In the meantime, however, the box on the facing page offers a few quick tips that can help.

Quick Tips for Improving Focus and Attention

1. **Use memory aids.** I worked with a mom who persistently misplaced her cell phone, and together we discussed her creating a "home base" on her kitchen counter where she could put things like this whenever she was done with them. Another mom who was always forgetting certain things her kids needed for dropoff made a morning checklist for herself, listing every item she needed to pack for her three children before leaving the house. I used a memory aid to solve my patient confusion issue: I made a list of all of my new patients with bullet points containing the important information I needed to remember about each of them. I'd consult this list before my sessions to make sure I was getting everyone's stories straight. However your mental fuzziness tends to manifest itself, consider using a memory aid to help.

2. **Put the phone away!** You don't need me to tell you that the phone is a constant source of distraction. If you're feeling mentally overloaded, consider turning your phone off or placing it in another room or even just turning off notifications. Quieting your phone, even temporarily, can be a great way to quiet your mind. We'll talk a lot more about managing your phone time in Chapter 7.

3. **Set timers.** This is another strategy we'll elaborate on in Chapter 7, but I think it's worth mentioning here. I used this strategy with Ana, who couldn't focus at work because she was always browsing the pictures of her twins that her husband frequently uploaded to their new family blog. Ana and I decided that she would check the blog once an hour on the hour and would set a timer for 5 minutes. Once the timer went off, she knew she had to close the blog and resume working.

4. **Use mindfulness.** If you're struggling to pay attention to the task at hand, whether at work or at home, consider taking an "adult time-out" and practicing a mindfulness focusing exercise. Mindful breathing or progressive muscle relaxation are both great for this purpose. After completing such an exercise, you'll be in a more focused, centered headspace, which will improve your ability to fully engage in whatever you need to be doing in the present moment.

Acknowledge All of the Changes Happening to Your Body (Nonpuberty Edition)

So this is a complicated one. Accepting that you can't look or feel like you once did can be incredibly difficult, especially because it isn't just about your appearance; it's also about feeling uncomfortable in your own skin and the intimacy issues that can result. Fortunately, there are a number of helpful strategies to help you manage your body image and self-care issues, which we will discuss at length in Chapter 6. We'll also delve into feelings about sex in Chapter 9. In the meantime, you can start setting values-based self-care goals when you tackle the values worksheet at the back of the book.

"Mom": The Role of a Lifetime

Moms often lament that the role of "mom" swiftly replaces all the other roles they once played. While it's certainly true that motherhood leaves you with less time and brain space to be the party girl or the family helper or the elite athlete, you can learn to play modified versions of these roles that fit better with your current circumstances. You can adapt what it means to "party," organizing get-togethers at a nearby bar that start at 6 and end by 9. You can teach your parents how to call you on FaceTime whenever their computer "breaks" and they desperately need your assistance. You can decide to train for a 5k instead of a marathon. By getting creative, you can find new ways of playing old roles. Our discussion below about setting values-based goals will help you do this (as will our discussions about self-care in Chapter 6 and navigating relationships with partners, family, and friends in Chapters 9–11).

Recognize That "Momversation" Will Be Your Daily Vernacular

Remember Laura? She wondered why no one seemed to care about her career as a vet or anything besides the fact that she had a kid. I wish I could say that this gets better, but it doesn't, at least not for a while. As a mom of a 6- and 9-year-old, I still find myself talking primarily about my kids anytime I'm with other parents at school or playdates. If anyone does find out that I'm a psychologist who works with stressed moms, they'll usually say something like "Man, I could really use your help!" and then totally drop it.

For better or worse, moms of young children tend to speak the language of kids (a phenomenon I've heard referred to as "momversation"). This is because kids are our common ground; whatever our differences, we are all raising kids, and kids are always a socially acceptable topic of polite conversation. I don't know whether the mom I see at dropoff has any interest in psychology, but I can guarantee she'll want to chat with me about the stomach virus that ripped through our children's school. In addition, as we've discussed, moms are always on cognitive overload and just may not have the space in their mom brains to think about anything other than their kids.

So you need to accept that lots of moms will only engage you in momversation and will not ask much about your job or anything else about you. But here's what you can do: deliberately nurture friendships with people who are interested in talking about topics other than kids. These might be friends from work, or from college, or even fellow moms of young kids who seem to want to engage in deeper conversations. At a birthday party a few years ago I saw a mom in a *Hamilton* T-shirt and pounced. I was thrilled to have a 10-minute conversation in which kids were not mentioned at all.

In Chapter 11, I'll share specific skills for effectively finding and reaching out to like-minded moms. In the meantime, you can start thinking about friendship goals when you complete the friends section of the values worksheet.

If You Want a Gold Star Sticker, You'll Have to Buy It Yourself

I had a patient once who shared that she got regular performance reviews at work and wished she could get regular parental performance reviews. I would absolutely be in favor of that idea. (Although who would provide such a review? Your nonverbal baby? Your irrational toddler?) The idea that there could be regular opportunities for other people to praise our efforts and provide us with constructive criticism is extremely appealing.

In the absence of such reviews, however, there are a few ways you can seek out validation. For starters, try to adopt a "proof is in the pudding" mindset. Your kids might not tell you that you're doing a great job, but you can sometimes see the results of your hard work by observing their behavior. This is easier to witness with older kids who are verbal and social: you can see how the things you've taught them play out in the way they treat other kids and handle stress and make decisions. But you can even sometimes recognize the fruits of your efforts with babies and toddlers, such as when you sleep-train your baby and it actually works or when you notice your toddler sharing toys.

Also, partners and like-minded mom friends can be great sources of validation, especially if you're willing to ask them for it. We'll be talking about how you can go about doing this when we delve into couples issues (Chapter 9) and friendships (Chapter 11).

Crafting Your New Mom Identity by Focusing on Your Values

It's clear that there are many aspects of the maternal identity shift that we have to accept. But as we discussed, even as we're accepting our altered circumstances, we can consciously make changes that enable us to retain at least some of the identities we used to inhabit. Many of these changes can be accomplished by pursuing values-based goals.

Values work is a prominent feature of ACT. Dr. Steven Hayes, the founder of ACT, describes values as "chosen life directions," noting that values are meant to guide us as we make choices in different areas of our lives, such as intimate relationships, work, and friendships. I think values work is extremely helpful for new moms, who, because of all the issues we discussed above, cannot possibly live their lives the way they once did. You need to be able to focus on what's really important to you and make time for those people and things that are truly meaningful. Using your stated values as your guide, you can start to make informed decisions about how you want to live your life each day. Values work can also help you think through how you want to approach parenting.

Remember What Really Matters

The first step in living according to your values is articulating what your values are. To do this, you must consider different critical domains in your life (e.g., relationship with your partner, parenting, work, and self-care) and think about how you want to live your life within these domains. Take parenting, for example. Say you decide that parenting is an important value domain for you (which I'm assuming it is, if you're reading this book!). How do you want to be as a parent? How do you want your kids to regard you? Do you want to emphasize structure or spontaneity? Discipline or permissiveness? Acknowledging your parenting values, and then making decisions based on these values, will help you become the type of parent you'd like to be.

To help you think through all of your values, I've created a comprehensive values worksheet, located at the back of the book. The worksheet includes 12 valued domains: relationship with partner; parenting; extended family; friendships; work/career; health/self-care; education/learning; recreation/leisure/passions; spirituality; community engagement/activism; holidays/special events; and family vacations.

Within each domain, I include a series of possible values. Take some time to determine whether you hold any of the values listed and add any additional values you may deem important. Next I present a number of values-based statements, which reflect how you want to live according to your particular values. Place a check next to those statements that apply to you and add any additional statements that further reflect your chosen values.

To help you with your values worksheet, I've included an excerpt from a values worksheet completed by Joy, the stay-at-home mom of a 2-year-old and a 5-year-old. See the box below for a sample of Joy's values and corresponding values-based statements. I chose to highlight three of the valued domains that Joy reported were most important to her: relationship with partner, parenting, and recreation/leisure/passions.

A few things to note as you're completing your values worksheet. First, you will not necessarily care about all 12 domains. If continuing your education, say, is not important to you, you probably won't check any of the values or the values-based statements in the education/learning domain. Second,

---

An Excerpt from Joy's Values Worksheet

Domain: *Relationship with partner*
- Values: *Communication, Connection, Humor, Intimacy, Supportiveness*
- Values statements: *I value communicating openly with my partner, sharing my feelings and perspectives and listening to my partner's feelings and perspectives; I value having the time to work on my relationship with my partner; I value having the opportunity to pursue kid-free social and recreational activities with my partner*

Domain: *Parenting*
- Values: *Adventure, Authenticity, Caring, Fun, Role Modeling*
- Values statements: *I value exposing my children to unique experiences; I value engaging in "fun" activities with my kids; I value imparting my own values to my kids; I value being a source of emotional support for my children, who they can turn to in times of need*

Domain: *Recreation/leisure/passions (Joy's passion was doing "craftsy stuff")*
- Values: *Accomplishment, Challenge, Community, Creativity, Fun, Ritual*
- Values statements: *I value being able to engage with my passion on a regular basis; I value the stress relief/mental break that comes with pursuing my passion; I value pursuing my passion by myself; I value repeatedly setting and reaching goals*

within the domains that are important to you, you'll find that only some of the sample values and statements reflect how you want to approach that domain. It is only those values and statements that you'll place a check next to.

You also may find that you endorse a large number of the sample values in a given domain (especially in the domains focused on relationships). If that's the case, I encourage you to prioritize, noting your top three or four values and values-based statements. This will make things easier for you when you start to think about values-based goals.

Finally, it's useful to think about how your values may have shifted since having children. Some moms find that their values change entirely. Others continue to hold the same values but think differently about how they can enact those values in their daily lives. And some end up reprioritizing the things they value, with family becoming more of a priority than, say, leisure pursuits. Consider how your values may have changed and try to capture any of these changes in your worksheet.

You can (and should!) use the values worksheet as a reference throughout the rest of this book. As we discuss specific issues like maternal anxiety and relationship changes, I'll be continually referring you back to the worksheet. Note that you do not need to complete the worksheet in one sitting; in fact, you might wish to tackle certain sections as you're reading the chapters that correspond with those sections. This would mean, for example, holding off on completing the section on partners until right before you start Chapter 9.

Use Your Values to Set Goals

Now that you've articulated your values, try setting a few attainable, short-term, values-based goals for yourself. To start, look at your worksheet and choose two or three values to focus on. In selecting values, there are two things you should consider. The first is feasibility: what is reasonable for you to work on right now, given your current circumstances and the age of your kids? For example, I love musicals and very much value performing in shows. But community theater companies rehearse for several hours each week, often on weeknights, which is when I'm done with work and able to focus on my kids and husband. I therefore decided to hold off on honoring my musical theater value until my kids are older and I have more flexibility.

You should also aim to select values that are particularly meaningful for your own self-definition. Paula, for example, always considered herself to be the "helper" in her family. She prided herself on her close relationships with her parents and her uncanny ability to fix their frequent computer problems by turning the power off, then back on again. Because she appreciated her role as a "helper" and wanted to retain that part of her identity, she prioritized the extended family value. This resulted in her setting several values-based goals regarding her family relationships, including scheduling regular FaceTime "dates" with her parents and allotting a certain number of days per month to take her baby to see them.

Once you've decided which valued domains to focus on, write down one goal for living your life within this domain. This goal should be small, specific, and easily achievable in the short term. As we moms often can't think much beyond the present hour, it makes sense to start working on small, short-term goals. Once you've met these smaller goals, you can start to think about experimenting with larger ones. If I and the moms with whom I work are any indication, larger goals become easier to pursue as your kids get older and your life falls into a somewhat more predictable routine.

When trying to set goals, it may help you to think about how you acted on each of your important values before you had children. For example, if you're someone who's always valued activism, what sorts of social justice organizations were you involved with before you had children? Would it be possible, even in a limited way, to recommit to these organizations? Do you have friends who still work in the community who might be able to help you become active again?

Here are the three valued domains Joy chose to focus on, along with a small goal associated with each of them.

Domain: *Relationship with partner*
- Values: *Communication, Connection, Humor, Intimacy, Supportiveness*
- Goal: *Set aside Sunday night, post-kids' bedtime, as "date night at home." Both of us need to put our phones away. Each week we can decide what we want to do during this couple's time.*

Domain: *Parenting*
- Values: *Adventure, Authenticity, Caring, Fun, Role-Modeling*
- Goal: *Plan one "adventurous" activity per month, involving taking the kids someplace different and modeling enthusiasm and exploration for them.*

Domain: *Recreation/leisure/passions (Joy's passion: doing "craftsy stuff")*
- Values: *Accomplishment, Challenge, Community, Creativity, Fun, Ritual*
- Goal: *Go to Michael's and buy craft supplies for new projects. Work*

on projects while watching TV after the kids are asleep or while
they're napping.

As you can see, Joy's goals are very concrete and specific. If she had
set vague goals, like "get more alone time with husband" or "do some more
crafting," there's very little chance that she'd achieve them. Make sure the
goals you set are well defined, so you know exactly what it is that you'll be
working to accomplish.

Also note that Joy's goals are small and attainable. Take the parenting
goal, for example. Joy realizes that she can't realistically take her kids on
daily "adventures," as these entail commitments of time and money that Joy
does not have. But she can plan a monthly excursion, giving herself the several weeks before to determine where she wants to go and what she'll need
to do to get her family there.

Take some time to set a few small values-based goals for yourself. Once
you've decided what your goals will be, you can start figuring out how to
incorporate them into your daily routine. It's important to note that we'll be
discussing goal setting throughout the book. So consider this to be your first
pass at goal setting; you'll continue to hone and refine your goals as you read
more about specific issues like self-care and relationships.

Get Creative—and Get Ready to Compromise

Setting values-based goals may necessitate some creativity on your part.
Let's take Joy's "date night at home" goal, for example. She told me that her
value of going out alone with her husband conflicted with other values she
held; specifically, she valued saving money, and she did not feel comfortable
leaving her kids for the night. She and I put our heads together and came
up with the idea of scheduling date nights at home with her husband, when
they would commit to ditching their phones and spending time engaging
in activities both of them valued, like watching classic movies and cooking elaborate meals together. This allowed Joy to honor several seemingly
conflicting values.

Like Joy, many of my mom patients have had to get creative with their
goals. Take the mom who loved cosmetics but didn't have the kid-free time
or the money for regular trips to the makeup counter: she committed to
devoting one of her son's naptimes per week to watching YouTube makeup
tutorials and doing her own makeup while she watched. Or the mom who
valued involving her children in activities but recognized that getting her
little ones to and from these activities was stressful for her (thus conflicting

with her value of prioritizing her self-care) and expensive (thus conflicting with her value of frugality): she decided to choose one activity per season for each of her kids. With enough creativity, you can find a way to work toward all of your meaningful values-based goals.

Schedules and Routines: They're Not Just for Kids!

You know how kids are said to thrive on routine and predictability? The same is true of parents! As far as I'm concerned, there is nothing scarier than staring down a completely unscheduled day with your child. Setting a schedule for yourself in advance, even if it includes totally arbitrary tasks (like taking walks or returning stuff at the mall) will reduce the anxiety and boredom that come with an empty day with a little one(s).

Anxiety/boredom reduction is only one of the many potential advantages of setting a daily schedule for yourself. Most relevant to what we've been discussing, setting a schedule will help ensure that your values-driven goals are met. If you're establishing a schedule for yourself ahead of time, you can include those activities that will help you stay true to your values.

How you set up your schedule is up to you. You can establish a schedule each night that you'll follow the next day. You can also set a schedule on Sunday evening for the coming week. You can keep the schedule on a sheet of paper or put it into the calendar on your phone (my personal preference). You can determine what you will be doing on an hour-by-hour basis, or you can think of your day in terms of what you'll be doing in the morning, afternoon, and evening. It honestly doesn't matter what you put on your schedule for any given day, so long as you're making progress toward at least one values-driven goal.

You can also use your schedule to help you break more overwhelming goals into smaller pieces. Say you value order and organization and cringe every time you see the many large boxes of infant clothes and toys in your basement. You know you need to sort through these boxes but don't feel you have the time. Why not schedule yourself to do a little bit of cleaning/ sorting every week? Break the large task into smaller chunks and schedule yourself time each week to tackle a specific chunk. Bigger values-based tasks become far less overwhelming when they're divided into manageable parts.

In the box at the top of the next page you'll see Joy's schedule, and at the bottom of the page you'll see a schedule for Kayla, who's a working mom with a 2-year-old. Let's start with Joy's schedule. As you can see, there's nothing ambitious here. She's not trying to reorganize her closets or teach her kids to speak Italian. Instead, she aims to engage in one of

Joy's Schedule

Pre-nap: Take kids to park
Nap time: Throw laundry in, work on knitting
Post-nap: Grocery store
6–8: Dinner, bedtime routine, bed

her values-based activities, working on a knitting project. She also plans to devote some time to taking her kids to the park and some time to stopping at the food store. She chose one major activity for pre-nap, a second for nap time, and a third for post-nap. This is a reasonable schedule that she can likely adhere to, which will help her feel like she's accomplished something.

Turning to Kayla's Monday schedule, you can see that she doesn't have too many slots to fill outside of her 9-to-5 workday. She decided that she wanted to focus on her self-care values of reading, exercising, and doing mindfulness work, all of which would help her manage the stresses of a long workday and commute. She thought about waking up early to exercise, but that turned out to be incredibly punishing. She also attempted to read after she put her daughter Sadie to bed but ended up passing out with an open book on her face. She decided to schedule reading and/or mindfulness practice for her train commute and to try to take a walk every day during her lunch hour. Although she missed the lunchtime gripe sessions with coworkers and just watching the scenery slip by on the train, she was pleased that she was able to squeeze some self-care time into her workday.

But what if Kayla or Joy is unable to adhere to her schedule? What if

Kayla's Schedule

7:30 a.m.: Drop Sadie off at school
8–9 a.m.: Train commute—read book, do mindfulness app
9–12: Work
12–1: Lunch hour, walk (with or without coworkers)
1–5: Work
5–6: Train commute—read book, do mindfulness app
6 p.m.: Pick up Sadie
6–8: Dinner, bedtime routine, bed

even a short trip to the food store or a walk during lunch proves too ambitious? It's critical to remember that not following through on your schedule does **not** make you a failure. We all know how unpredictable life with young kids is, and so, despite our best efforts to prepare, we often can't follow through on daily goals. One kid's diaper blowout can cause your daily routine to, well, blow up. So go easy on yourself if you've spent an entire day doing nothing but cleaning poop and watching YouTube; or if you barely made it to work and passed out as soon as your kids fell asleep. The next day will be a fresh opportunity for you to meet a values-driven goal.

Finally, note that the values-driven goals you may set for yourself now might be very different from the goals you set 6 months from now, and certainly a year or 2 years or 5 years from now. You should aim to revisit your values worksheet on a regular basis, noting whether and how your values and priorities have changed, and setting new goals consistent with these changes.

How to Navigate Your Work Identity

If you don't work or don't consider work a priority, feel free to skip this section entirely. If you are one of the many moms for whom work–life identity questions are prominent and stressful, please read on.

I've heard a wide variety of work–life stories over the years. I've worked with moms who choose not to work but who later regret that choice; moms who are forced to work because they need the money but who would much prefer to be at home; and moms who think a part-time work plan is the way to go, only to find that they are always expected to be on call both at work and at home. Most of these moms experience guilt of some kind and believe that their work and home lives aren't "balanced." At the same time, they are exposed to countless blog posts and advertisements and articles asserting that they in fact can "have it all!" and that leaning in or leaning out will somehow solve their work–life angst.

There is so much that's unfair for us working moms. Most of us do not have paid maternity leave. We're expected to pay equal attention to our work and home lives, but there are not enough hours in the day (nor stores of energy, even for the most organized, together mom) to make this possible. We're told that achieving a work–life balance is a real possibility, even though our government does not provide us with any of the resources that would enable us to achieve such a balance. And of course, no one ever even talks about the work–life balance when it comes to dads. It's assumed that dads can continue pursuing their careers while we moms work *and* pick up the parenting slack.

I hope at some point our government will start advocating for working mothers. I hope by the time my sons are fathers, parental leave will be widely available, and fathers, like mothers, will be expected to honor both home and work commitments. But unfortunately, we're not there yet. In the meantime, you need to think carefully about what you're willing to sacrifice (and ensure that your partner does the same; much more on equitable parenting in Chapter 9).

Work–life issues are exceedingly complicated for American moms, and my goal here isn't to try and simplify what remains an incredibly complex problem. Instead, I want to share some CBT and ACT skills that will help you make thoughtful, reasoned decisions about how you want your work and home life to look. Make sure you have your values sheet in front of you; it will serve as a helpful guide as you set your priorities.

Use Your Imagination

We often use imagery in CBT—to help people think through how they will approach a scary situation, as a means by which we can expose ourselves to anxiety-provoking thoughts, and/or as a form of mindfulness or relaxation. When my mom patients come to me with lots of career angst but literally no idea about how to proceed, I generally encourage them to engage in an imagery exercise. I simply ask them to close their eyes and envision themselves as working women. Where are they? What are they doing? Who are they with? I encourage moms to let their guards down and see where their minds take them. See the box on the facing page for an imagery script.

I purposely don't ask moms to consider their kids when they do this exercise, although obviously their kids and their child care situation will be a prominent feature of their workday. Again, I just want moms to be able to think completely freely for a few minutes, and considering kids and care issues tends to limit their ability to do this.

I'm aware that such a visualization exercise might sound a little hippy-dippy. However, doing imagery work can provide a rare opportunity for you to allow your mind to roam without being bogged down by worries or practical considerations. Some moms end up being surprised by what they see themselves doing. One mom told me that she literally could not picture herself working, which she took as a sign that staying at home

---

Work–Life Imagery Script

Try to imagine yourself at home, preparing to start your workday. What are you wearing? Are you dressed formally? Are you in jeans? Are you in workout clothes? Are you carrying anything with you? Take some time to consider how you're dressed, from head to toe.

How do you get to work? Are you getting into your car and driving? Walking? Taking the train? Or are you just traveling to an office space in your own home?

So now you arrive at work. Where are you? At home? Somewhere outdoors? A big office building, where you have to take the elevator to get to your floor? A smaller office building? A school? Some sort of performance studio? A store? Take some time to take in your surroundings.

What are you doing? This doesn't have to be anything specific; you may just see yourself sitting at a computer in a cubicle or working in your own home, or sitting in a conference room in a meeting, or doing some work outdoors, or walking around on a sales floor.

Who's with you while you're working? Are you by yourself? With one or two others? With a group of colleagues? Surrounded by people on all sides?

Once you've gotten a general picture of your work environment, give yourself some time just to imagine yourself there.

---

was the right move for her. If you find career planning to be overwhelming, consider starting off with an imagery exercise. It can help spark your thinking about how you should proceed.

Use Your Values to Prioritize

Next, take a look at the work section of your values worksheet. Which of the values statements did you place check marks in front of? Rank all of your checked values statements in order of how important they are to you. The top three or four statements represent your most significant work-related values and should therefore serve to guide your thinking about your career.

Below I provide a number of examples of moms who used their values sheets to make work–life decisions. I note their top-ranked work values statements and explain the choices they made based on these values. As you can see, all of them prioritized very different things and as a result ended up on very different career trajectories.

Ruby: "I need to talk to some adults"

Ruby's top-ranked values statements

1. I want to get out of the house and interact with other adults.
2. I want a job/career that gives me flexibility.
3. I want to help people/make a difference with my work.

Ruby didn't want to climb the corporate ladder, nor did she have any desire to return to her pre-kid career. She just wanted to engage her mom brain in some non-kid-related topics and get out of the house for a few hours each day. She also wanted to have some flexibility in her schedule so that she didn't have to work when she didn't want to. She decided to take a part-time job working the front desk at a yoga studio in town owned by one of her friends. This gave her the opportunity to engage with other adults and even take free classes, which fulfilled her self-care value of regular exercise.

Ruby lamented that she didn't make more money—and in fact, her entire salary went directly toward paying the babysitter who was watching her kids while she worked. She also acknowledged that this job didn't necessarily allow her to make a big difference in the world. But she ultimately decided that she would have to sacrifice her last value in the service of her first two.

Soraya: "I want to make partner"

Soraya's top-ranked values statements

1. I want to rise to the top of my field.
2. I want to make as much money as possible.
3. I want to use my brain for something intellectually challenging.

Prior to having her son, Soraya was on the partner track at her law firm. Making a good living and earning a prestigious partner position were very important to her. She knew that she would have to sacrifice flexibility and availability for her son, but she decided that her career was worth sacrificing for. So she found a very reliable nanny and continued on the partner track. She struggled off and on with mom guilt, which was ultimately the reason she sought help from me. We talked often about how she could compensate for missing out on her son's milestones, which typically involved having her nanny take lots of videos of her son. But Soraya often just had to come to a place of acceptance: her commitment to work meant that she would miss some things at home.

Eva: "I want to make money"

Eva's top-ranked values statements

1. *I want to make as much money as possible.*
2. *I want a job/career that gives me flexibility.*
3. *I want to use my mom brain for something intellectually challenging.*

Eva needed a full-time salary and had no choice but to work full-time. Despite this, she longed for a career that would provide her with some flexibility so that if one of her children got sick or had an event at school, she could be there. In order to satisfy her dual desires to make as much money as possible and be as flexible as possible, she chose to work in an office that allowed employees to occasionally leave work early or work from home. Unfortunately, she found her job to be boring: she had to sit in a cubicle and stare at a computer all day and didn't have many opportunities to think creatively. Eva had to sacrifice her third value, using her brain for something intellectually challenging, in order to honor her first two values.

While these three moms pursued very different paths, they were all forced to make choices and to accept the sacrifices that came with these choices. None of them achieved any sort of perfect "balance," and none were 100% satisfied with their situations. Each of them came up with the best solution for their particular needs and circumstances.

Like these moms, you probably won't achieve the elusive "work–life balance." And at some point (or more likely, many, many points) you will probably feel guilty for the sacrifices you're making, as when you "phone it in" at work so you can get home for your kid's holiday sing-along or when you miss your kid's holiday sing-along because you have to work late. (In

Chapter 8 we'll discuss strategies for coping with the guilt that comes with not being able to do everything perfectly.) But by focusing on your values, you'll at least ensure that you're pursuing a career that reflects what matters to you at this particular stage of your life (and your kids' lives).

P.S. It's OK to Prioritize Your Work!

In a viral *New York Times* opinion piece titled "I've Picked My Job over My Kids," an accomplished lawyer and mom wrote candidly about how she routinely prioritizes her work over her children. She notes: "My choice is more than a financial imperative. I prioritize my work because I'm ambitious and because I believe it's important. If I didn't write and teach and litigate, a part of me would feel empty."

Not surprisingly, this article was met with a storm of criticism. (One comment on the piece included the following: "I'm not buying it. There are thousands of highly competent lawyers out there—some would say a glut. Everyone has only one Mom." I should note that this comment was written by a man.) But I responded to the article with vigorous head nodding and some subtle fist pumping. This is because it underscores a point I've been making to my mom patients for years—that it is OK to want to work and to find work a welcome respite from the drudgery of child care. Feeling this way does not make you a bad mother, despite what Jeremy from NJ says.

If you love working, and you love your kids, commit to your job and to finding a child care situation that works for you and your kids (see below for details on this). And try your best to ignore the Jeremys of the world—they don't know you, and they don't know what you need to function well as a person (and as a mother)!

Remember That Work Priorities Will Change

When Rena's children were small, she prioritized being at home. She had absolutely no space in her mom brain to even consider returning to her elementary school teaching career. When her kids hit the toddler years, she found that she wanted to do something to engage her brain and started blogging about strategies parents could use to help their children learn to read. Her stint as a blogger eventually led to her becoming a reading tutor, working one on one with local kids. The older her children got, the more hours she was able to devote to the blog and tutoring. By the time her kids were school-age, she had somewhat accidentally turned her blogging experience into a full-fledged career.

Rena's story illustrates two important concepts. First, the work decisions you make while your kids are small are by no means permanent. I can't tell you the number of moms I know who have made significant career changes at various points in their children's lives. One of my sister's best friends, who'd stayed at home with her four children when they were small, started law school when she was 40 years old. A patient of mine who jumped off the corporate track when she had her first child got her real estate license and is now a realtor with a large clientele. A friend of mine went back to work after having her first and second child, but after having her third decided that she wanted to be home full-time and quit working entirely. These women's careers all took dramatic turns as their children got older.

Second, smaller jobs and side projects or even volunteer positions can turn into more high-powered careers once you have more time and mom brain space to devote to them. I think a lot of moms, myself included, assume that if we are making the commitment to going back to work after having kids, we have to hit the ground running the second we're back in the office. But in many careers, that's simply not true. I fell into this trap: when I started working after my maternity leaves, it took a while for me to build up my clientele. While things were slow I was very down on myself, believing that my career was a "joke." I only now realize that I would not have been able to mentally handle a full caseload at that point, and that I was working at exactly the right pace for me at that time. Now, 6 years later, I can (and do!) handle a lot more.

So yes, be very thoughtful about your work–life mix now but also recognize that your feelings on the matter will likely change. And that's a good thing! You don't need to commit yourself now to a set of work–life values that you will need to adhere to for the rest of your life. If you're looking for further guidance on work–life issues, please see the Resources, where I list several excellent books and articles to help guide your thinking.

Coping with the Child Care Nightmare

I didn't want to end a section on working motherhood without talking about the child care decision. Maternal anxiety about child care starts immediately after our children are born (or even way before that for some moms, who are forced to put their unborn children on school wait lists). Those who are lucky enough to have a choice about their child's care face an array of confusing options (see the Resources for more on the significant inequities in American child care).

I remember talking to an older relative at a family party when Matty was 6 months old. At the time he was in a day care center we loved. This family member somehow got on the topic of neighborhood parents he knew who sent their infant to day care. He was shocked that they did not see their baby all day and deemed them "irresponsible." I was tempted to tell him that my husband and I were similarly "irresponsible," but for the sake of politeness kept my mouth shut.

As with all issues involving parenting, there is so much judgment around child care decisions from all sides. There are those who, like my relative, think day care is akin to torture, and there are those who believe that day care is the only way to properly socialize children. There are those who praise nannies as a godsend and those who criticize nannies for always being on their cell phones. Believe me: there is no child care situation that goes uncriticized. (Criticism of moms—a theme we'll be returning to often!)

If you're agonizing over which care situation to adopt, stop and answer these two questions:

1. Is your child being well cared for in this care situation?
2. Is this care situation working for *you*?

If your answer to both of these questions is "yes," then you've found the right care situation for you and your family.

Regarding question #1: I truly do not think it matters who is caring for your child, as long as your child is well cared for. My children's day care providers loved them (shout out to Ms. Kelly of the Cuddly Clouds!) and treated them like their own children or grandchildren. Being loved is what matters. There is no one right person to care for your child. It can be a day care teacher, or a nanny, or a relative.

Regarding question #2: Being a mother of young children is hard as it is. Burdening yourself with an untenable child care situation makes it infinitely harder. Take my former patient Callie, for example. At her last session with me she explained that her son, who was in kindergarten, complained so much about the aftercare program at his school that she pulled him out of it. Because Callie works, she had to find a nanny for her son, a near impossibility in the middle of the school year. So she cobbled together an arrangement with two different nannies who worked on different days and switched her work schedule around so she could pick up the slack. As a result she no longer had time for therapy.

As you can see, Callie was only considering the needs of her son. The aftercare switch was incredibly burdensome for her. She had to pay more for the nannies than she did for aftercare, which was a financial burden for her; she was forced to rearrange her work schedule; and she no longer had time for much-needed therapy sessions.

You absolutely need to consider yourself when making care decisions. Pick the situation that works best for everyone involved, even if it isn't your child's (or your judgy relative's) top choice. And once you've made your decision, give yourself (and your kid) time to adjust to the new child care situation. I don't need to tell you that little kids tend to struggle mightily when they first start in a new care situation (I can still remember 18-month-old Sam sobbing as I left him at a new day care), only to adjust fairly quickly to their new routine. The same tends to be true of mothers. By the end of Sam's first week at his new day care, I, like him, had pretty much fully adjusted and had stopped crying at dropoff.

Hopefully, with time, you'll end up feeling good about your child care situation. Keep in mind, though, that your answers to the two questions I posed above might change as your child grows. If they do, you'll need to make a change in care. I know of many, many moms (myself included) who switched day cares or nannies at some point. I also know a number of moms who switched from "Grandma day care" to a real day care once their kids hit the preschool stage. If you're starting to feel inordinately stressed about your child's care situation, ask yourself the two questions again and reevaluate. Your main objective should be to ensure that both your child *and you* are well cared for. See the Resources for more information about child care options.

4

"Why Can't I Stop Worrying?"

How to Cope When You Sweat the Small Stuff (and Big Stuff)

Jane came to my office during her daughter's first week of kindergarten. I asked if she'd experienced the classic parental response to that first dropoff (a dramatic mix of happiness, pride, and utter despair). She confessed that she hadn't, because she was too busy "obsessing" about her daughter's class placement. While her daughter knew a number of other kindergartners at her school, none of them were in her class. Jane could not stop ruminating about the possibility that her daughter would "have no friends." She admitted being so "stuck in her own head" that she barely paid attention as her daughter lined up to go into her classroom.

Shanice's son was 1 year old when he first had a severe allergic reaction to peanuts and tree nuts. Initially, Shanice found it easy to control what her son ate, as she prepared most of his meals at home. But as her son grew older, Shanice's terror about inadvertent exposure to nuts grew. She struggled with her anxiety and the resulting impulse to keep her son home as much as possible. She recognized that avoiding leaving the house would not benefit her son (or the rest of her family) but at the same time did not want her son to face the potential dangers of any outside environment that was not completely under her control.

I was sitting at my computer, working on an early draft of my outline for this book, when the news of a tragic school shooting came across my Facebook feed. The more I read, the more I cried, picturing, of course, something similar happening at my sons' schools. I started to worry actively about their safety at school, something that is always in the back of my mind but moves to the foreground whenever I hear news of another shooting. When I finally got back to my outline, I wondered what I would be able to say to my readers about coping with things like school shootings and other horrific national or world events. How could I possibly console other moms when I was unable to console myself?

Moms: The "Designated Worriers"

In 2015, a popular *New York Times* opinion piece proclaimed mothers to be the "designated worriers" in the family. This notion has evidence to support it; studies show that mothers are less happy, more stressed, and more fatigued than fathers. It's also the case that women in general are more prone to developing anxiety. I'm not saying that dads don't worry, but there's no disputing that we moms are pretty much experts at it.

If my clinical and personal experience is any indication, the types of things that moms worry about can vary widely. Sometimes, like Jane, we worry about "small stuff"; that is, we ruminate about relatively mundane daily issues. We might worry about how well our kids are faring at after-school activities or whether we've made a good impression on the cool mom we just met or how on earth we're going to host Thanksgiving dinner when our son throws food like it's an Olympic sport.

Other times, as was the case for me and for Shanice, we worry about "big stuff." The big stuff can be personal, like coping with a life-threatening allergy, or a mentally or physically ill loved one, or a job loss or a divorce. The big stuff can also be news of scary national or international events, like school shootings or other types of violence, terrorism, pandemics, or cataclysmic weather. Unfortunately, there has been an influx of this type of big stuff recently, with catastrophic news coming across our feeds virtually every day.

Some moms also find themselves obsessively worrying about things that they know rationally are not likely to happen. Such worries often center around their own or their children's health and well-being. I'm thinking here, for example, of those moms who are terrified that their children will become gravely ill or injured, or who are convinced that their children will die of SIDS, or who think a slight pain in their body is a sign of cancer. Many of these moms engage in frequent checking (including persistent Internet searching), constant reassurance seeking from loved ones, and/or avoidance of perceived threats.

Because managing anxiety is so critically important for moms, I am devoting two chapters to it. This chapter will focus on small-stuff and big-stuff worries. Chapter 5 will focus on obsessive thoughts about injury, illness, and other threats.

Anxiety and Worry:
What They Are and When They Become a Problem

Before we begin, I want to clarify what I mean when I use the terms "anxiety" and "worry." When I discuss *anxiety*, I'm describing a general emotional state that is comprised of several different components: cognitive (what you're thinking); emotional (what you're feeling, e.g., nervousness or dread), physiological (accompanying bodily sensations, such as upset stomach, tight chest, headache, rapid heartbeat, or shortness of breath), and behavioral (what you're doing, such as trying to escape or avoid a situation).

When I talk about *worry*, I'm referring to the cognitive component of anxiety. Worry thoughts often take the form of "What if . . . ?" questions, as in "What if my daughter doesn't make friends at school?" or "What if the whole family gets that nasty stomach bug?" In this chapter, I use the term "worry" often, as I discuss many strategies designed to target the cognitive component of anxiety.

It is perfectly normal for new moms to have anxiety and to worry. Research has shown that new mothers demonstrate anxiety about their babies and a preoccupation with their well-being (although do we really need studies to tell us that?), which hits an all-time high during the first weeks postpartum. Of course, this worry and anxiety persists throughout our children's formative years (we *are* the designated worriers, after all). As we discussed in Chapter 2, having kids tends to turn the volume of our worry way up because in addition to worrying about our own safety and well-being we start to worry about the safety and well-being of our kids. And in fact, it's *our job* to protect our kids.

So having *some* anxiety and worry is a good thing, because it helps motivate us to do what we need to do to keep our kids well. Sasha, for example, was anxious about her son, who was extremely resistant to leaving for day care each morning. Her worry prompted her to set up a meeting with the day care director in order to discover what she and the school could do to make his morning transition easier. Sasha's worry was helpful; it inspired her to get in contact with the school director, who helped her formulate a plan to remedy the situation. In CBT, we would call Sasha's worry a "productive worry," in that it led directly to helpful problem solving.

However, there is a very slippery slope between helpful anxiety and problematic anxiety. Again, some anxiety is a good thing for us, and frankly is necessary, as it prompts us to advocate for our children, as Sasha did. That's why it can be so tricky to determine when anxiety becomes a problem. We can all understand Sasha's situation: her son was very obviously miserable every morning, she was appropriately worried, and she addressed her worry by meeting with the school director. But what if Sasha found that her mom brain was still consumed with worry even after this meeting occurred, and even after her son told her that things had gotten better? What if she started focusing on every one of her son's preschool complaints, like the one kid he didn't really like, or the fact that he didn't want to nap at nap time, and found herself contacting the director on a regular basis with her growing list of concerns? You can see how worrying can easily change from productive to unproductive very quickly.

If you're worried that you're worrying too much, here are some signs that you should be working on your anxiety:

1. Trouble sleeping due to anxiety
2. Physical symptoms of anxiety: headaches, stomachaches, nausea, dizziness, shortness of breath, rapid heartbeat
3. Difficulty concentrating or focusing due to worrying
4. Feeling like you have a 24/7 anxiety script running in your head, with topics varying widely
5. Often thinking in terms of "What if . . . ?"
6. Worrying about worry; fearing that your worry will become so overpowering/unmanageable that you will no longer be able to enjoy your life and/or that you'll "go crazy"
7. Worrying about the physical symptoms of anxiety, believing that they might be dangerous
8. Noticing that anxiety/worry is the predominant theme of your mood monitoring
9. Often making decisions consistent with your anxiety, not with your values (e.g., when a mom who wishes to make better social connections decides not to attend a school parent event for fear of social rejection)

If you're finding yourself sweating the small stuff, or big stuff, or anything in between, there's some good news: CBT, DBT, and ACT have a wealth of strategies to help you manage.

Before sharing these strategies with you, I want to remind you of a point I made in Chapter 1: that while some of these strategies may seem at odds with each other, you can choose which ones work best for you, which may differ depending on the situation. For example, there may be times when you want to challenge your worry thoughts using evidence and other times when you want to just observe your thoughts using mindfulness. The important thing is to *use what works for you.*

Recognize Your Thinking Traps (a.k.a. Know Your Enemy)

The first step in managing your mom brain worries is to become familiar with your worry patterns, or what we call "thinking traps" in CBT. The way I see it, you've got to know your enemy to confront it effectively. You've probably noticed that you worry in predictable ways and that your worries all tend to follow a certain form (or forms), even if what you worry about varies from day to day.

When I worry, I tend to be a hard-core catastrophizer. I go big, always assuming that catastrophic outcomes will ensue. For example, when Sam spiked a fever on the first day of our summer vacation, I spent the whole day fretting that we would all get sick and it would ruin our vacation (we didn't, and it didn't). When we heard that Matty's good buddy was moving out of state, I worried that he would be completely devastated (he wasn't, although I was, since this friend's mom had become one of my go-to mom friends).

Catastrophizing is a very common thinking trap. Here are some of the others I hear about most often from moms:

1. *Overgeneralizing:* Drawing a broad conclusion based on a single piece of information or limited information. "My daughter got in trouble for throwing a shoe at preschool today. What if this means she's going to have significant behavior problems in grade school?"
2. *Black-and-white thinking:* Believing that if things are not 100% perfect, they are abjectly terrible. "It's supposed to snow right at the time that Ava's birthday party is starting. What if some of the kids can't make it? It would be a disaster."
3. *Comparison making:* Looking at other moms and kids and worrying that you don't quite measure up. "Shayna's son just listed the names of all the U.S. presidents in order while my son ate dirt. Why isn't my son gifted like hers?" (Lots more on this in Chapter 7.)
4. *Discounting positives/negative filtering:* Ignoring any positive information about yourself or others and focusing only on the negative.

"Sure, I just worked a full day, got my kids fed and bathed, sent out 100 holiday cards, and decked my house out to look like a winter wonderland, but I can't figure out how to make this Pinterest-inspired pinecone Santa for my kid's preschool holiday party, so clearly I am failing at this mom thing."

5. *Mind reading:* Assuming you know what other people are thinking without asking them. "I can just tell that my boss is upset with me for leaving early for Allie's school play yesterday."

6. *Personalizing:* Blaming yourself for things and assuming that things are about you when they likely aren't. "I just saw Pam at dropoff and she looked really upset. Did I do something to upset her?"

7. *Shoulds:* Worrying about things you feel you should have done but didn't do: "I should have signed Ryan up for travel soccer this year. What if he's at a major disadvantage when he tries to play next year?"

It can be helpful to spend several days monitoring your worry thoughts. As I noted in our discussion of mood monitoring in Chapter 2, I recommend using the notes section of your phone or a mood monitoring app (see the Resources) for this purpose. Pay attention to the types of thoughts that come through your mom brain when you're feeling anxious. Are you more of a comparison maker or a mind reader? A black-and-white thinker or a discounter of positives? Or all of the above? This can be a great activity for a mindful "adult time-out."

How Not to Sweat the Small Stuff

Once you've monitored for a few days, you'll be an expert on your own worry. You'll know what types of thinking patterns you generally fall into and whether you tend to be a small-stuff or big-stuff worrier (or both). I'm going to start by presenting strategies tailored to small-stuff worries. Later on I'll focus on the big stuff.

Use the Evidence

One of CBT's favorite (and most research-supported) methods for managing worry involves looking at the facts. Ask yourself, "Is there any evidence to suggest that what I'm worried about will actually occur?" and "Is there any evidence to suggest that what I'm worried about won't occur?" You need to consider real evidence, not opinions, conjectures, or feelings. Just because you feel anxious about something doesn't mean it's necessarily going to happen, because (and this is a big, important point) **feelings aren't facts.**

Jane recognized that she was catastrophizing when she worried so much about her daughter not making any friends at school that she could not appreciate her daughter's first day. I challenged Jane to answer these two questions: "What evidence exists to support your worry thought that Chloe is not going to make any friends?" and "What evidence exists to refute your worry thought?"

Here's what Jane came up with:

Evidence that Chloe is not going to make any friends
- *Chloe is shy and quiet.*
- *Chloe was very nervous about the first day of school.*

Evidence that Chloe is going to make friends
- *She is a quiet kid, yes, but she did well in preschool and made several friends.*
- *All of my friends' kids were nervous about the first day too, and all the kids looked vaguely terrified at the first dropoff. I didn't assume that just because these kids looked scared, they wouldn't be able to make friends. I only made that assumption with Chloe.*
- *At the kindergarten orientation the teachers said that they make socialization a priority during the first months of school.*
- *There is a "buddy bench" on the playground for kids who don't have friends to play with at recess. The students at the school know to approach anyone they see on the bench and ask them to play.*
- *I can invite other kids over to our house to play so that Chloe can get to know them in a more comfortable setting, thereby making it more likely that she'll engage with them at school.*

As you can see, Jane had considerably more evidence to refute her worry thought than to support it. Considering the evidence for and against her worry helped her to see that her fears were unfounded and that it was her anxiety talking, rather than the facts.

Sometimes it can be tricky to come up with facts that refute your worry thought. In the box on the facing page you'll find some questions that can help you generate evidence.

Questions to Help You Refute Your Worry Thought

- "When I have worried about things like this in the past, what has the outcome ultimately been?"
- "If a friend had this same worry, what would I say to reassure my friend?"
- "Am I taking responsibility for something that is at least partly out of my control?"
- "If I was not feeling this way, would I think about things any differently?"
- "Am I ignoring any positive aspects of myself or the situation?"
- "How will I look at this situation several weeks/months/years from now?"

As helpful as examining the evidence can be, moms sometimes tell me they don't feel 100% better after doing it. They remain anxious and assume that this means the strategy didn't work. I tell these moms that rapid anxiety reduction is not the goal of this strategy (although it can happen). Rather, the idea is to get you to consider that what you are worrying about might be a product of your anxiety rather than reflective of the truth. This will sow some seeds of doubt in your mind, which will help you move on from the worry more quickly and effectively.

Consider the Worst-Case Scenario

Once you've considered the evidence, you will hopefully conclude that the outcome you're afraid of is not very likely. However, "not very likely" doesn't mean "definitely out of the question." And of course, there will be times when you find that there is, in fact, some evidence for your worry thought. So what if the feared outcome does come to pass?

Try talking yourself through your anxious prediction by asking yourself these questions:

1. "What is the worst-case scenario?"
2. "What is a more realistic (based on the evidence) scenario?"
3. "If the worst-case scenario does come to pass, could I manage it? What would I do to manage it?"

To illustrate, consider Jessie, who is consumed with worry about her daughter's schedule. After almost 2 years, Jessie's daughter is finally sleeping through the night, napping well, and following a somewhat more predictable routine. However, her daughter is about to start day care, and Jessie is panicked that the change will wreak havoc on her schedule, disrupting her naps (and therefore her nighttime sleep). Here's Jessie, answering the three questions I posed above:

1. *Worst-case scenario:* Sienna starts day care and is confused by her new environment. She refuses to go down for her nap at day care and passes out in the car on the way home. This late nap affects her nighttime sleep; she starts waking in the middle of the night again and her whole schedule is disrupted. She is extremely cranky as a result.

2. *More realistic scenario:* Sienna may be confused and may have to spend some time adjusting. It will probably be like when we went on vacation last month; she was out of sorts for a few days, then resumed somewhat reasonable naps and bedtimes (just in time for us to go home, of course).

3. *Managing the worst-case scenario:* If Sienna's schedule does get totally out of whack when she starts day care, we'll just have to sleep train her again. It was a miserable experience the first time around, but we did it, which means we know how to do it. In the meantime Jill and I will just have to resume the nighttime schedule that we adopted before Sienna was sleep-trained, where I'm on call the first half of the night and Jill's on call the second. I will also reach out to day care to ask if there's anything they or we can do to encourage Sienna to nap there.

To summarize: If Sienna is thrown by the transition, Jessie and her wife can put a plan in place to ensure that Sienna gets back on track as soon as possible. And in the meantime, they can resume the schedule they used before Sienna was sleeping through the night.

One important note: moms sometimes get confused when I present this technique, believing considering the worst-case scenario to be the same thing as catastrophizing. It isn't, because in addition to imagining the catastrophic outcome you're *imagining what you would do to cope with it.* You're adding a problem-solving component to your catastrophizing, which makes a big difference. Often when you're able to entertain several viable solutions, worst-case scenarios don't seem nearly as catastrophic as they once did.

Sing a Song of Your Worry (and Other Tools for Taking Your Anxiety Down a Few Pegs)

This next set of tools comes from ACT, which takes a different approach to worries than CBT does. Instead of aiming to challenge worry thoughts, ACT strategies aim to change the *relationship* we have to our thoughts. ACT stresses the importance of seeing our worry thoughts as they are—as merely collections of words and temporary products of our own mind—rather than as truths. This takes much of the power away from our worry thoughts, rendering our worries much less threatening. Think of it this way: What sounds scarier to you—the thought "I'm a terrible mother!" or the thought "**I am having the thought that** I am a terrible mother!"?

Bethany, mom to three kids under the age of 5 (a hero, we can all agree!), loved using ACT strategies to respond to her worry thoughts. Bethany struggled with anxiety about her middle child, Jake, fearing (thanks to those ubiquitous—but inaccurate—mom blog pieces about the "middle child syndrome") that because he was in the middle he was not getting enough love and attention. She did a lot of personalizing, in that she considered it solely her responsibility to provide Jake with all the love he needed, despite the fact that he had a dad and tons of loving relatives. She also discounted the positives; there were many encouraging signs that Jake did indeed feel loved, but Bethany ignored these, choosing instead to focus on the few comments Jake made when he was frustrated about being ignored (and what kid, birth order aside, doesn't sometimes get frustrated about being ignored?).

While Bethany was able to consider the evidence that Jake was doing just fine, she preferred instead to reduce the power of her worry thoughts by using ACT strategies. These are the strategies I encouraged her to use:

- Sing your worry thought (yes, I'm serious).
- Repeat your worry thought ad nauseam.
- Say your worry thought very slowly.
- Say your worry thought out loud using a silly voice.
- Tack "I am having the thought that . . . " in front of your worry thought.
- Give your worry thought a silly name—of a celebrity, perhaps, or fictional or "real-life" person you don't care for. (For some reason a number of my patients have selected the name of a particularly strict elementary school teacher.) Every time you have a worry thought, exclaim, "There goes Mrs. Jones again, telling me that [insert worry thought here]."

Here's what Bethany came up with:

Singing her worry: "My Jake is getting ignored, and he is suffering!" sung to the tune of "Poker Face" by Lady Gaga: "My Jake is! My Jake is! Getting ignored and he is suf-fer-ing . . . " Singing this made her laugh, which immediately helped her take her worry less seriously.

Repeating: "My Jake is getting ignored, and he is suffering" over and over again, or saying it super-slowly. After repeating her thought and saying it super-slowly, the words started sounding strange to Bethany and basically lost their meaning.

Tacking "I am having the thought that . . . " in front of her worry: "I am having the thought that my Jake is getting ignored and he is suffering." This clarified that what Bethany had in her mind was a thought, rather than a truth.

Naming her worry (Bethany went with "Bellatrix," in a nod to one of the villains in the Harry Potter series): "Well, there goes Bellatrix again, telling me that my Jake is getting ignored and he is suffering!" This helped Bethany see her worry as something external to her, rather than reflective of a fundamental truth.

All of these techniques will give you perspective on your worry, hopefully enabling you to realize that your worry thoughts are just collections of words and not representative of reality.

There are certain types of worries that are particularly well suited to ACT strategies. Many moms who worry a lot confess that they are scared of their anxiety. Some find their worry thoughts to be threatening, believing that they might worry so much that they will one day "lose control" or "go crazy." Others believe that certain physiological anxiety symptoms (like sweating, shortness of breath, or stomach upset) are dangerous and could lead to significant problems.

In addition to asking moms to consider the evidence for these worries ("Have you ever actually gone crazy or lost control?" "What would it even look like for you to 'go crazy?'" "When you've been anxious in the past and experienced rapid heartbeat, did it ever lead to a heart attack?"), I encourage moms to use ACT strategies to manage their anxiety about their worry and bodily symptoms. To illustrate, compare the thought "This rapid heartbeat is a sign of an impending heart attack" to "I am having the thought that this rapid heartbeat is a sign of an impending heart attack"; and the thought "My worry is making me 'go crazy'" to "I am having the thought that my worry is making me 'go crazy.'" ACT strategies expose worries about worry and worries about physical symptoms for what they really are: brief mental events, not signs of impending catastrophe. (More on coping with the physiological symptoms of anxiety and "worry about worry" in Chapter 5—stay tuned.)

Schedule Worry Time

Jasmine, working mom of an 8-month-old, was extremely frustrated with how worry disrupted her day. She always had a tendency to worry but felt able to manage it when she was in the middle of work or doing something else important. Since having her daughter, however, she found that the volume of her worry was turned way up, and she could no longer brush her anxiety aside. She would catch herself losing focus during an important meeting, distracted by worries about how her daughter was adjusting to her new nanny or whether her daughter's poops were the right color.

Jasmine benefited from using the CBT strategy of scheduling worry time. I asked her to find a time during the day when she had a few minutes to herself and could engage in "worry time." For her, it was at 7:30 P.M., right after her daughter went to bed but not within an hour of her own bedtime, which could interfere with her sleep. Whenever she encountered worry thoughts during the day, she wrote them down and promised herself that she would think through them carefully during her worry time. She often left long meetings at work with a note page full of phrases like "When should Sophie start seeing a dentist?" and "Grinding noise from breast pump this morning."

What Jasmine found, and what many moms find, is that when she finally made it to worry time, a bunch of the things she had fretted over earlier no longer stressed her out. During the hours between writing the worries down and worry time, the worries often lost their power, or the things she worried about got resolved. She realized she could save herself a bunch of time (and space in her mom brain) by putting off her hard-core worrying until 7:30. She often found herself using her worry time to focus on productive worries, devising effective plans for addressing these concerns.

An important note about scheduling worry time: the goal of saving worries for worry time is *not* to be able to push a worry thought out of your mind in the moment. As you'll recall from Chapter 2, we're no good at controlling our emotions and making ourselves stop feeling and thinking something. Instead, worry time is about giving yourself permission not to focus on or try to problem-solve a worry at a particular moment. Recognize that you have this worry but that you don't have time to think it through, so you'll save it for your designated worry time.

Many moms tell me that their default worry time is nighttime, when their brains, no longer occupied with the tasks of the day, go into worry overdrive. In the box on the facing page, I share some strategies for managing nighttime worry, taken from CBT-I, the extremely effective CBT treatment for insomnia.

How to Manage Your Big-Stuff Worries

When I first had the idea to write this book, I was seeing a lot of moms struggling with daily small-stuff worries. By the time I actually started writing the book, however, the world had completely changed. Our country had become a much scarier place, with news of potential threats (nuclear war, gun violence, cataclysmic climate issues) coming across our feeds at an exceedingly rapid pace. This change affected me as well as my patients. As I mentioned, when I heard about events like school shootings, I wondered how I could possibly help moms through such big-stuff events because I was paralyzed with worry too.

In addition to big-stuff worries about our country and world, moms come to me for help with personal big stuff, like coping with an illness in the family or life transitions like job loss or divorce. These worries, too, are of a very different sort than those about, say, your kid refusing to eat vegetables or inexplicably feuding with your neighbor's toddler.

I've found that some of the strategies that work well for small-stuff worries aren't necessarily as effective for the big stuff. For example, I talked earlier about considering the facts in order to highlight the lack of real evidence for your worry thought. This strategy doesn't work terribly well for big-stuff worries, as there is often ample evidence to support these concerns. Take Shanice, whose son has severe nut allergies. There is in fact evidence that if her son is exposed to nuts, he could die.

Unfortunately, many big-stuff worries do have evidence to support them. However, even when there is evidence for your worry, there are still a number of strategies you can use to cope, which I'll discuss below. A quick note before we move on: The COVID-19 pandemic certainly qualifies as a big-stuff worry, but I address germ fears in Chapter 5 rather than here.

How to Manage Nighttime Worries

Are you one of those moms who, as my grandma used to put it, "does her best worrying at night"? Here are some strategies for managing nighttime worry, adapted from Drs. Colleen Carney and Rachel Manber's excellent CBT-I (CBT for insomnia) manual.

1. Take time to revisit your day: Sometime before bed, revisit and process the events of your day. Journaling or doing a mindfulness activity or talking to a loved one can be very helpful for this purpose. Also consider scheduling your "worry time" at this time, which will enable you to think through and problem-solve the worries of the day. Make sure you finish revisiting your day at least an hour before your bedtime.

2. Ensure that the hour before bedtime is restful: During the hour before you plan to go to bed, do things that are relaxing and not connected with the stressors of the day. This might include mindfulness activities, progressive muscle relaxation, watching TV, or reading.

3. Get out of bed: This is the most important strategy: if you're in bed and worrying and it's clear you won't be able to turn down the volume on your worries, leave the bedroom. Go do something relaxing and nontaxing (progressive muscle relaxation, reading a frothy novel) until you feel tired and ready to go back to your bedroom again. The worst thing you can do is remain in bed worrying; this will cause your brain to start associating your bed with wakefulness and brain activity.

4. Try distraction: Distraction is not a great long-term strategy. However, you don't want to engage in CBT worry management strategies like considering the evidence in the middle of the night, when using such tools will serve to further activate your brain. For the middle of the night, distraction is a far better alternative. Drs. Carney and Manber recommend trying to think through the plot of a book, TV show, or movie you love (but that isn't too stimulating).

5. Remind yourself that nighttime worry will not serve you well: If you hit the pillow and immediately start to worry, remind yourself that your mom brain is not at its best when you're tired. You'll have more opportunities to work through your worry tomorrow, at a time when your brain will once again be more alert.

Show Yourself Some Mindful Self-Compassion

We talked in Chapter 2 about the importance of mindful self-compassion; that is, of recognizing that you are feeling a certain way and accepting these feelings without judgment. Mindfulness and acceptance are perhaps nowhere more necessary than in the case of big-stuff worries, because these worries do often have evidence to support them, and they are objectively very scary.

Mala, for example, struggled to mother her 3-year-old son while coping with her father's cancer diagnosis and rapidly declining health. She came to me because she believed that she had to stop crying so much so she could appear "strong for her son." She did not want her son to witness her suffering.

The first thing Mala and I discussed was the importance of changing her initial therapeutic goal from "stopping the crying" and "being strong" to accepting her (very understandable) worry and sadness. How could she possibly expect herself to control her feelings when her father was dying? (And who says that "being strong" means hiding your emotions? Personally, I can't think of a more powerful demonstration of strength than acknowledging your feelings and actively employing skills to cope with them.)

I ask similar questions of myself and other moms who are struggling to understand horrible news on a national or global level. How can any of us expect that we will hear news of, say, a school shooting and be able to swiftly put it out of our minds? I am still struggling to process the Sandy Hook shooting, and it happened years ago. When you have kids and you contemplate any threats to their safety, your mom brain goes into overdrive.

We talked in Chapter 2 about mindfulness exercises aimed specifically at thoughts and feelings, like seeing your feelings and accompanying thoughts as leaves on a stream, or clouds in the sky, or boxes on a conveyor belt. The idea with these exercises is not to try to push your feelings and thoughts away, or change them in any way, but just to see them in your mind's eye and accept them.

This type of mindfulness exercise can be extremely helpful when you are consumed by a big-stuff worry and, like Mala, are trying desperately to put it out of your mind. Just allow yourself to have the worry, noting that it's going to be there (at least for a little while) whether you like it or not. Engaging in exercises like this will not make the worry disappear nor help you feel more relaxed. However, they will prevent you from doing things that make the worry worse, like pressuring yourself to stop worrying or judging yourself negatively for worrying.

A related strategy comes from compassion-focused therapy (CFT), a type of treatment whose main objective is to help us learn to be more compassionate and understanding toward ourselves. A former colleague of mine and expert CFT practitioner, Dr. Dennis Tirch, recommends responding to your anxious thoughts by considering what the most compassionate and kind version of yourself might say. To illustrate, consider Rose, who started "obsessing" about the dangers of climate change every time she heard about a severe weather event. For a few days she would be unable to think of much else, and she grew frustrated at her inability to stop focusing on her thoughts.

What if, instead of responding to her "obsessions" with frustration, Rose attempted to respond with kindness? A more compassionate version of Rose might tell herself something like this: "It's understandable that you're worried about climate change. It's scary and all over the news. Keep volunteering for the environmental organization you're working with and try to move about your day despite the fear that you carry with you."

It can also be helpful to think about what you would say to a close friend in your situation. What kind of compassionate response would you give her? Generally we are kinder to others than we are to ourselves, so considering what we would tell a friend can help us cultivate self-compassion more effectively. We'll come back to this strategy in Chapter 7.

Once we can be mindful and accepting of our big-stuff worries, we are in a better position to start problem solving.

Consider the Odds

As I noted above, cognitive strategies aren't always my go-to for big-stuff worries. After all, examining the evidence is a central feature of cognitive work and many big-stuff worries do in fact have ample evidence to support them. However, I do think there are some cognitive errors worth working through when we have big-stuff concerns. For global worries, overgeneralizing is a big one. Social psychology research shows that we tend to overestimate the likelihood of things we can easily bring to mind. Due to the substantial amount of news coverage about, say, hurricanes, we can easily picture vivid details of such hurricanes in our minds, and because of this, we assume that they are more commonplace than they actually are. We confuse the frequency of this coverage with the frequency with which such events actually occur. But mass catastrophes are typically highly unlikely; the odds of, say, death by mass shooting are substantially lower than the odds of dying by choking or bike riding.

I spent a lot of time talking with Lana about overestimating threat. Lana vividly remembered news coverage of a movie theater shooting, and when her son started asking her to take him to the movies, she always refused. Lana admitted that she felt bad about depriving her son of the fun of seeing movies in a theater, which she had so enjoyed as a child; she considered attending movies with her son to be something she valued. But because she was convinced that movie theaters were dangerous, she vowed never to step into one again.

Obviously it's no big deal to avoid movie theaters, but as there is seemingly no end to venues where violence can occur, there is no end to places you can theoretically avoid. I worried that Lana's avoidance of movie theaters would lead to avoidance of other places, too. Lana eventually decided that she needed to start taking her son to the movies because she did not want her life choices (and the choices she made for her son) to be dictated by her anxiety; she wanted instead to make choices consistent with her values. Together we devised a plan to help Lana meet this values-consistent goal by approaching it gradually (using a technique called exposure; we will discuss exposure and values-consistent action in much greater detail in Chapter 5).

I like to think of it this way: we play the odds every day. Every time we walk out our door or get into our car or take our kids to one of those disgusting birthday party hellscapes, we are risking our safety. Yet we take these risks, because we need to exist in the world and live our lives. And so do our kids!

We have to play the odds when it comes to scary world news, too. When you are bombarded by coverage of some awful event, absolutely feel worried and sad and angry, and whatever else you might be feeling. But also try to temper your anxiety with the knowledge that such an event is exceedingly uncommon, and that avoidance will only serve to limit how you and your kids can live your lives.

Consider the Worst-Case Scenario, Take Two

When I'm working with patients dealing with personal big-stuff issues, I often talk with them about catastrophizing. I am very much aware that any kind of difficult personal situation, like an ill loved one or a divorce or a job loss, is already in itself catastrophic. But what moms often don't see in the face of such a catastrophe is that things may not be quite as cataclysmically awful as they fear.

Consider my patient Eliza, who was going through a miserable (and, from her perspective, unwanted) divorce from her husband. She was understandably devastated by this and consumed with worry about what the future held for her. I acknowledged that much of Eliza's future was uncertain but challenged her to consider whether there was any aspect of life as a divorced woman that excited her.

After spending time considering what her future might look like, Eliza was eventually able to recognize that having partial custody of her daughter would leave her with more time for pursuing her long-held dream of trying to launch her own business. Clearly this information didn't automatically make Eliza feel better; she remained anxious about her future and devastated by the divorce. However, she was able to take some small comfort in the fact that at least one area of her life might improve after the divorce.

At this point, you might be thinking: Sure, I can see how someone could see a few upsides of something like a divorce, but what about something like a loved one's serious illness? I am aware that it can be very difficult to make any lemonade out of a lemon like that. But if you can possibly challenge yourself to decatastrophize even a small aspect of a terrible experience, it might temper your anxiety about the future. Below, we'll talk about the importance of taking action where you can, a behavioral strategy that can help you cope with even the worst of catastrophes.

Figure Out What You Can Control, Consider Your Values, and Make It Happen

Even during a seemingly out-of-control catastrophe, you may be able to exert some control over certain aspects of the situation. One of the most common things I hear from moms dealing with big-stuff worries is that they feel completely helpless. I've found that the best antidote to this helplessness is taking values-consistent action.

Start by consulting your values worksheet and noting the values that relate to the big-stuff worry you're experiencing. Then, following the guidelines we discussed in Chapter 3, set some values-based goals that you believe are achievable and make specific plans for how you'll meet these goals. Below, we'll talk about how to do this, for both personal and global big-stuff worries.

Take Action with Personal Big-Stuff Worries

Taking action helped Gabriela cope with her anxiety about an impending cross-country move. After her husband was offered a rare job opportunity, he and Gabriela decided to move, despite the fact that they both felt connected to their community and Gabriela liked her job. Initially, Gabriela felt completely helpless; she was being forced to make a move she did not want to make, away from her family and friends and the life she'd known for many years. She worried about what her life would be like and feared that her 5-year-old son would have difficulty adjusting. She also felt overwhelmed by all of the things she needed to do in advance of the move.

After several evenings of excessive HGTV watching (a reasonable coping strategy, we can all agree), Gabriela decided to take stock of the things she could control in her situation. No, she could not control the fact that she was moving and leaving loved ones and heading out into the unknown. But she could make several values-based decisions in several areas, including:

1. The house she moved to
2. The new job she found
3. The school she selected for her son
4. The activities she selected for her son

In true lemonade-out-of-lemons fashion, Gabriela also recognized that she actually appreciated the opportunity to make some changes. For example, she had never loved her house; now she had the opportunity to find a new one that was more in line with her tastes. She had also been thinking about making a career change, and a geographic move would facilitate this process.

So Gabriela took action. She broke each of the four tasks listed above into small, manageable pieces that she could start working through immediately. Here's an example, from Gabriela's plan for her new house search:

1. *Week 1: Contact friend of friend who lives in* [the new city]; *ask for a description of different neighborhoods and local realtor recommendations*
2. *Week 2: Search real estate websites to get a feel for available houses; do more online research on neighborhoods*
3. *Week 3: Contact realtor; talk to Paul about finding a weekend to house hunt*
4. *Week 4: Contact realtor with dates of house hunting trip, share ideas about types of houses you'd like to look at*

Gabriela also decided to involve her son in her planning, in an effort to help him manage his own feelings of helplessness about the move. They went online together and selected a new tae kwon do studio for him, and signed him up for classes. They did a search of kid-friendly activities in their new city and talked about all of the cool new places they would visit together. Gabriela was surprised to hear her son express excitement about the move for the first time.

Taking values-based action didn't make Gabriela feel any less sad about her impending move. She still wanted to stay where she was. But it did help her manage her anxiety and restored her sense of control.

Now let's consider those worries concerning truly catastrophic personal big-stuff issues, like a loved one's serious health problems. While you can't necessarily do anything to impact your loved one's situation, you can still find ways to take values-based action and feel less helpless. Shanice, whose son was severely allergic to nuts, decided to become involved in a nonprofit group that advocated for individuals with nut allergies. She raised money for research and helped raise awareness about allergies in her community. Shanice also worked with her son's doctor to develop a plan for navigating birthday parties, restaurants, and other places where nuts could be present. Shanice continued to fear for her son's well-being but felt confident that she was doing everything she could to take control of the situation.

Another example comes from a friend of mine whose father had a terminal illness. She decided to plan a big trip for her entire extended family, so that her father could enjoy his children and grandchildren all together while he was still well enough to do so. Of course my friend remained anxious and sad about her father's prognosis. But she appreciated having the opportunity to focus on something positive that she could control. She also took comfort in the fact that she was doing something that would bring her father joy and give her family the opportunity to celebrate him.

Take Action with Global Big-Stuff Worries

Taking action can also help you manage your global big-stuff worries. I can personally attest to this, as I used this strategy to help myself cope with my own anxiety around the seemingly constant news of mass shootings. Needless to say, I knew I couldn't personally control the epidemic of gun violence in our country. But I realized that I could take values-consistent action by helping elect a gun-sense candidate to the House of Representatives. Using the goal-setting and scheduling guidelines I laid out in Chapter 3, I planned to carve out time each weekend during the weeks leading up to a big election when I could go door to door in my neighborhood and share my enthusiasm for our candidate who believed in commonsense gun laws.

My candidate won—which, I won't lie, was awesome. But even if she hadn't, I would have felt that I'd done something to effect change and control what felt like a completely out-of-control situation. Which was such a better plan than just staring at my social media feeds, worrying that my family members would be the next victims. I still have these worries, but at least I am tempering them with action, which truly helps me feel empowered.

I encourage all moms who feel powerless about the news to take stock of their values and commit to some sort of action. It doesn't need to be canvassing door to door, which I'm aware is not everyone's cup of tea. It could be raising money for a charity or reaching out to elected officials—whatever helps you feel like you are taking some control over the situation.

What If You Just Don't Have It in You to Take Action Right Now?

Some of the moms I've worked with don't feel like they have the bandwidth to take action. They are so overwhelmed by the demands of their kids and/or jobs that they don't have space in their mom brains for calling their elected officials or canvassing door to door. They acknowledge that taking action sounds good theoretically, but they simply can't make it happen at the moment.

For these moms, I change my tune and prescribe good old-fashioned denial.

OK, OK—before you judge me for being a CBT therapist who recommends denial, let me explain. There will be times when you are so overwhelmed with your personal stuff that you don't have the energy to consider the global stuff. And during those times, it is OK to stop watching the news and poring over Facebook posts. It's also fine if you need to delete news or social media apps from your phone. Obviously denial is not a great long-term strategy. However, when it's strategically employed it can help you get through your day (or week, or month, or however long you need).

It is perfectly acceptable to read nothing and do nothing, if that's what you need to do to keep yourself feeling mentally healthy. I am certain that there will be plenty of opportunities for you to take action in the future, should some more space become available in your mom brain. In the meantime, practicing a little denial might be what you need to do to effectively navigate the myriad stressors of the day. We'll talk more about the importance of tuning out in Chapter 7.

5

"Why Don't I Feel Safe?"

Managing Fears about Injury, Illness, and Other Threats

When her daughter was a newborn, Sofia, like many moms, feared that the baby might stop breathing. She carried her video baby monitor around with her whenever her daughter was asleep, and by the time her daughter was 8 months old, Sofia was checking the monitor so often that she felt like she was "binge-watching the baby show." She acknowledged that this checking was interfering with her life; it made it impossible for her to unwind after her baby finally went to sleep. But she believed that she had to do it to keep her daughter safe.

Before she became a mother, Katie saw a Facebook post about a friend of a friend whose toddler son fell off a slide and was seriously hurt. When she later had a son of her own, Katie worried about taking him places where he could get similarly injured, like playgrounds and kid gyms. As a result, she sometimes avoided these places. When she did decide to go, she spent her time following her son up and down the kid-sized gym equipment, which made it impossible for her to socialize with the other parents.

My first weeks of nursing Matty were incredibly anxiety provoking. I never knew whether he was getting enough milk and nursed him for hours. I saw a lactation consultant, who told me, on two separate occasions, that his supposed "tongue tie" was impeding his ability to eat, and that he was "gaining too much weight" (which meant that he was eating too much). I believed it was my responsibility to crack the case on Matty's nursing, and I worried that I was not doing the right things to ensure he was properly nourished.

If you are a new mom and find your mom brain awash in worry about harm coming to your baby (or to you, especially as it relates to your ability

85

to care for your baby), you are not alone. All of us—Sofia, Katie, and I, and every new mom I've ever met—experience these worries. As we've discussed, once our babies are born we suddenly find ourselves in the position of having to keep them alive. That's a heady responsibility, to be sure.

Research shows that new mothers often experience obsessive thoughts about their baby's well-being that result in compulsive actions, such as constantly checking that the baby is breathing. These obsessive thoughts and compulsions resemble the symptoms of obsessive–compulsive disorder (OCD) and tend to occur most often during the first few weeks of an infant's life. They generally become less frequent as babies age.

However, there are many moms, like Sofia and Katie, who continue to "obsess" about harm even as their babies mature. Among these moms, worry topics tend to vary widely. Some stress out about the rickety climber at the park but don't give a thought to the nutritional content of their children's meals. Others spend tons of time reading food labels in an effort to avoid serving their kids any potentially harmful processed foods and yet don't think twice about the structural integrity of playground equipment. What we worry about can be based on our own personal experiences, as when a mom who got sick once from eating shellfish refuses to let her kids eat shellfish for fear that they'll get sick, too. We may also worry after hearing warnings or disaster stories from other people, either in person or on social media.

As we discussed in Chapter 4, some worry about our well-being and our children's well-being is helpful, in that it inspires us to take actions that keep us and our children safe. But once again, there's a slippery slope between worrying productively and worrying obsessively. It's reasonable for Sofia to check in on her daughter periodically to make sure her baby is safe. But if her checking is interfering with her ability to live her life, she needs to address it.

Here are some signs that you might need to work on your harm-related anxiety:

1. Any of signs 1–8 discussed in Chapter 4 (see page 67)
2. Persistently seeking reassurance, either from family members or from the Internet, that you (or your child) are safe
3. Repeatedly checking your own or your child's body for illness or injury
4. Researching symptoms or "disaster scenarios" on the Internet
5. Avoiding certain situations, people, or environments for fear that they will expose you and/or your child to harm

6. Frequently visiting your doctor or your children's doctor despite the fact that you are usually given a clean bill of health
7. Worrying that you might harm your own child (this is a special type of harm-related anxiety, which we will discuss below)

Many of the concepts we discussed in Chapter 4 apply to harm-related worries too. These worries fall into the same categories as the big and little stuff worries do (catastrophizing, overgeneralizing, etc.) and can also be managed using the cognitive and mindfulness techniques you've learned. However, there are some additional strategies that are particularly effective for these types of worries, which are described below. In turn, you'll find that these additional strategies might help you with the types of worries we discussed in Chapter 4.

Before we continue, I should note that a certain type of harm-related worry—about kids being exposed to germs—has become complicated in light of our experience with COVID-19. At the end of the chapter, we'll discuss how to approach germ worries in a post-COVID world.

Recognize That You Don't Have Control by Eating a Slice of Pie

If you're a mom who worries excessively about your own or your kids' health and well-being, the first thing you need to acknowledge is that you have limited control over it. I know what you're thinking: You monster! How could you be telling me this? This is just making me more anxious! I get that—but stay with me. I think that recognizing that you don't have total control will ultimately help you better manage your anxiety.

Let's take the example of my experience with Matty's nursing. I felt anxious that he was not receiving enough nourishment. Much of my anxiety stemmed from my misperception that whether or not each feeding was a "slam dunk" was entirely under my control. But in truth, there were many factors outside of my control that influenced how well he nursed at any given time.

An effective exercise for helping you determine how much control you have over a given harm-related situation is called the pie chart technique, a staple of CBT. I'll use the example of my nursing anxiety to illustrate. We're going to pretend I was smart enough to complete this exercise in the moment, when in reality I'm just doing it now for the first time and Matty is 9 years old. Just go with it.

First, I listed all of the factors that could affect the situation in question, which in my case was Matty's ability to nurse successfully. Then I drew a circle (a "pie") representing Matty's total nursing experience. I considered each of the factors to be pieces of this pie. I then estimated the percentage of the pie accounted for by each of the factors. I assigned a greater percentage to those factors that I felt had a greater impact on Matty's nursing.

The pie that I definitely created 9 years ago looked like the one below. Considering the pie as a whole, it occurred to me that many of the factors that influenced how well a given nursing session went were entirely out of my control. This included Matty's supposed tongue-tie (which was never actually confirmed, by the way), how tired he happened to be in that moment, how well he'd nursed earlier, and whether I'd had to pump that day. I recognized that even if I had done an absolutely perfect job with the slices of the pie that I did have control over (like following expert advice for how to best "set the stage" for breastfeeding and eating lots of foods that supposedly encourage milk production), I could not have guaranteed a successful feeding session.

I honestly wish I'd completed this exercise during those early weeks of nursing. Perhaps realizing how many factors were completely out of my control would have enabled me to give myself a break. This is why acknowledging our limited control over health and safety, while anxiety provoking at first, can ultimately be freeing for us. Knowing how little we can truly do gives us permission to relax a little. It helps us relieve ourselves of the burden of going to extreme, exhausting lengths to protect our kids from harm and focuses us on those aspects of our environment and our kids' environments that we truly do have some control over.

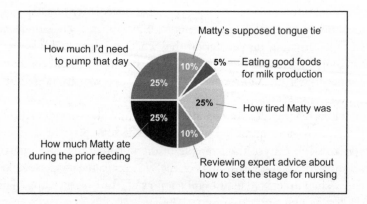

Factors contributing to Matty's nursing

Expose Yourself to Exposure Therapy

The most widely used CBT strategy for managing harm-related anxiety is exposure. What exposure entails is purposely facing the situations you fear without doing anything to give yourself a false sense of security, like over-stuffing your stroller with supplies for the apocalypse or continually asking a loved one for reassurance that everything is going to be OK.

None of us likes to feel anxious, so our initial impulse is to avoid things that make us worried. This works in the short term but becomes a problem in the long term. If we continually avoid a situation, we never have the opportunity to learn whether we can manage our anxiety and effectively navigate that situation (hint: we pretty much always can). And of course, by avoiding certain people, places, and things we limit what we (and, by extension, our kids) can do.

Uncertainty is pretty much a given where our health and well-being are concerned. Short of committing to living our lives in bubbles, we can never guarantee our safety. So the goal of exposure is *not* to convince yourself that you or your kids will always be safe all the time, nor is the goal to stop worrying about harm. The goal is to recognize that you can tolerate anxiety and uncertainty, on your own, without having to avoid certain situations or rely on things like reassurance from others or doomsday-prepped strollers.

You can engage in exposure in three different ways: in real life, via your imagination, and by bringing on a symptom you fear.

Try Exposures IRL

Remember Katie, who preferred to stay in her house rather than expose her son to potentially perilous kid play spaces? Katie recognized that by staying in her house she was missing out on opportunities for her and her son to socialize. Because she valued exposing her son to new situations, her avoidance was interfering with her ability to take values-consistent actions.

Katie decided to try exposure in real life (IRL; also called "in vivo"). Katie's exposure plan involved leaving the house every day and visiting places and attending events she formerly avoided, like the "big kid" playground in town and her friend's daughter's birthday party at a local kid gym. She also challenged herself not to follow her son up and down the gym equipment, but to watch him from a reasonable distance, as the other parents seemed to do. While her son played, she tasked herself with making small talk with the other parents, even though she remained somewhat preoccupied with her son's jumping and sliding. In the section "Set the Stage for Exposure," we'll talk about how to structure your exposure practices and how to choose which situations to face at which times.

The good news about exposure IRL is that you don't always have to go out of your way to find exposure opportunities. Of course, you can (and should) commit yourself to planning out exposures and taking your family to places you find threatening (and for which there is little evidence of actual threat). But you can also decide to face challenges that present themselves over the course of your day—for example, deciding to keep your plans to drive an hour to your friend's house despite a stormy forecast. It helps to adopt an "exposure mentality," where, in addition to completing planned exposures, you're prepared to face exposure challenges as they arise.

Remember that the goal of exposure is *not* to stop worrying about safety or to convince yourself that everything is going to be fine. This means that you might feel anxious or grossed out every time you encounter a certain threatening situation, regardless of how many times you've already encountered it. But you'll learn that you can tolerate your anxiety in the situation and therefore don't need to avoid it. Katie, for example, continued to worry when she took her son to "dangerous-looking" kid spaces, even after exposing herself and her son to many of them. But she grew confident in her ability to tolerate her anxiety, which meant that she could honor her value of exposing her son to a variety of new environments (no matter how "dangerous").

Imagine Yourself Doing Exposures

Imaginal exposure entails writing out a detailed description of your feared scenario, using the first person, present tense (as if you are experiencing the scenario at the current moment). You can write a "worst-case scenario" narrative, in which the thing you're most fearful of actually comes true (e.g., you or your child has sustained a serious injury). You can also write an uncertainty narrative, in which you're consumed with uncertainty about the future (e.g., you're awaiting a report on the severity of your kid's injury).

Imaginal exposures can be used at any time but are especially good for those situations where you cannot do a "real-life" exposure. For example, you would not deliberately send your child on a playdate with a friend who you know is home from nursery school with the stomach flu. You could, however, imagine a scenario in which your son has played with a kid you later learned had the flu and you're waiting to determine whether or not your son got it. (More on imaginal exposures for germ fears at the end of the chapter.) You can also use imaginal exposure as the "lead-up" to a more challenging exposure. Andrea, who feared that her daughter would choke on solid foods, first wrote an imaginal exposure scenario in which her daughter started coughing while eating grapes. Later, she started actually serving her daughter grapes.

Once you've composed your imaginal scenario, read it again and again, as many times as you can. To make it even more powerful, record yourself reading it aloud (smartphones are great for this purpose) and listen to it over and over, while closing your eyes and imagining the scenario in your head. After reading or listening to your imaginal exposure script ad nauseam, what does the feared scenario sound like to you? Does it feel as real and frightening as it once did, or does it start to sound almost "boring"?

If it becomes "boring," that's good; it means that the feared scenario no longer sounds as threatening to you. Moms often report that after repeated listening their scenarios lose their punch, kind of like what happens after you see a horror movie several times and you no longer feel afraid of it. Moms also tell me that their feared scenario starts to sound ridiculous or implausible. Others are able to recognize that while the situation sounds very scary, they can identify and think through methods for coping with it.

See the box below for an example of an imaginal exposure script written by Grace, who traveled often for business and had always been a nervous flier. After she had her daughter, her anxiety about her business trips hit a fever pitch as she worried she would die while traveling for work and leave her daughter all alone.

Grace's What If? Work Trip Scenario

I get on a plane to California and already miss Millie so much. I can't stop looking at pictures of her on my phone. Sometime during the flight, the cabin starts to shake, first slowly, then violently. Eventually the lights in the cabin start flashing and the engine starts sputtering audibly and something starts beeping. I look at the other passengers, who all appear panic-stricken. The pilot gets on the loudspeaker and shares that we've had an engine malfunction and that all emergency measures are being taken. People in the plane start screaming, and the oxygen masks drop down. The lights continue to flash and the noise continues and I think, "This plane is going down. I am going to be leaving Millie motherless." Clinging to my seat, I scroll through her pictures, knowing that this is likely the end.

Grace's scenario likely sounds a little extreme to you. But that's kind of the point. After listening to her recording several times, Grace reported that the narrative she'd written sounded like the plot of a movie and didn't really feel like something that was likely to happen to her in "real life." As a result, the scenario lost its punch, and Grace started to feel at least somewhat better about flying (I believe she said something like "I've downgraded myself from 'terrified' to 'scared'"). We were then able to concentrate on other behavioral strategies to help her manage her anxiety about flying (e.g., doing mindfulness work while waiting to board).

Imaginal exposure also works well for "worry about worry." As I mentioned in Chapter 4, some moms worry that their anxiety will somehow overtake them, causing them to "lose control" or "go crazy." I encourage moms who worry like this to write an imaginal exposure script in which they describe in detail how they eventually lose control of themselves. Moms often report back that they have trouble even writing such a scenario— because it seems "ridiculous" to them, and/or because they can't even describe what "losing control" would actually look like. Some moms even laugh at the mental image of themselves coming unhinged, which instantly helps reduce some of their anxiety about it.

Fearful of a Body Symptom? Bring It On!

In Chapter 4, I noted that some moms worry about the physiological symptoms of anxiety. They believe that these symptoms are dangerous or could result in catastrophic outcomes. This type of anxiety can be managed effectively by engaging in symptom exposures, where you deliberately bring on bodily sensations that are part of the anxiety experience, like shortness of breath, hyperventilation, dizziness, or sweating. Symptom exposures help moms recognize that their physiological symptoms, while perhaps unpleasant, are not dangerous.

There are a number of easy ways to induce your feared physical sensations, which are detailed in the box on the facing page. Note that you might need to get creative here: if the exercises listed don't elicit your particular brand of physical anxiety sensations, you may need to come up with exercises that do. Also it's important to make sure that you continue the exercises long enough for the symptoms you fear to actually occur.

Maya tended to become short of breath when she was very worried about something. When she noticed this, she began to worry that this shortness of breath was a sign that she was truly in danger. This compounded her worry significantly. Maya tried a symptom exposure with a thin straw,

---

Sample Symptom Exposures

1. **Shortness of breath:** Pinch your nose closed and breathe into a thin straw for 1–2 minutes.

2. **Hyperventilation:** Take quick, deep breaths through your mouth for 1 minute.

3. **Dizziness:** Spin in a swivel chair for 1 minute.

4. **Sweating:** There are lots of options for inducing sweating, including running up and down stairs, wearing several layers of clothing in a warm room, or just carrying your toddler around the house!

5. **Feelings of unreality:** Stare at a strange picture/pattern for several minutes.

---

where she breathed through it for 2 minutes. At the end of it, she recognized that she was able to make it through without any danger to herself (other than some discomfort). She repeated this exposure a number of times, all of which yielded the same outcome: she felt uncomfortable but did not "have a heart attack." Following her exposure practices, her episodes of shortness of breath no longer felt threatening to her.

Symptom exposures can also help you if you tend to worry about your own health. Gayle, for example, often scanned her body for any potential problems, most often focusing on perceived feelings of dizziness (more on body scanning when we discuss checking below). She assumed that this dizziness was very problematic and a sign that she was seriously ill. So Gayle practiced chair spinning, which helped her recognize that she could manage her dizziness and that dizziness didn't necessarily portend significant danger.

I should note that some physical symptoms of anxiety (the one that immediately comes to mind is hives) cannot be reproduced easily; and in that case, doing an imaginal exposure about the feared symptom occurring is probably the better strategy to use. Also, some moms report that they don't always fear the symptoms from symptom exposures. This is because they know they are creating these symptoms themselves, as opposed to these symptoms coming on out of the blue or unexpectedly. If this is the case for you, it's OK—you can still benefit from practicing with these symptoms and showing yourself that you can manage them.

Set the Stage for Exposure

Now that we've discussed the three types of exposure, let's talk about how to effectively set up and carry out exposure practices. First, to identify potential targets for exposure, think about any people, places, situations, or physical sensations you typically try to avoid (or endure with much discomfort) and make a plan to face these people, places, or situations, either in real life or in your imagination.

You can also benefit from taking a look at your values worksheet. Are there any values-consistent activities you're avoiding because of harm-related anxiety? For example, perhaps you value cultivating a neighborhood "village" for your child but avoid playdates with neighbors for fear that your kid will get injured or catch other kids' colds? If so, committing to attending neighborhood play groups would be an effective exposure for you, as well as a values-consistent action.

How you structure your exposure practice really depends on you. We used to recommend systematically facing fears by starting with a situation or symptom that was moderately scary (maybe a 50 out of 100 on your anxiety scale) and moving to scarier ones as you conquered the less scary ones. You repeatedly exposed yourself to each situation or symptom until you recognized that the outcome was not as catastrophic as you expected (and/or that you could handle the outcome better than you expected to be able to), and that you could successfully tolerate your anxiety.

Recently, however, research has shown that exposure does not have to be gradual to be effective. In other words, if you're ready to face a fear, go ahead and face it, even if it's a 90/100 on your anxiety scale. You may decide to focus your exposure practices on those fears that are immediately relevant to your daily life, regardless of how anxiety provoking they are. For example, Andrea was afraid both of taking her daughter on plane flights and of letting her eat solids. As she did not have to fly anywhere immediately, she chose instead to focus on her daughter's eating for her exposure practice.

However you choose to conduct exposure, it's important to set goals for yourself and make specific plans for how you will carry out your exposure. It's also important to take stock of each exposure practice once you've completed it. The easiest way to do this is to monitor yourself before and after the exposure. Before the exposure, ask yourself what you are expecting will happen. Afterward, consider what actually did happen and whether you were able to get through the experience. Think about what feelings you had and whether you were able to tolerate them effectively (I'm guessing you could). Again, you should repeat a specific exposure until you're able to recognize that the outcome was not as catastrophic as you expected and/or that you could handle the outcome better than you expected you would be able to and successfully tolerate your anxiety.

Exposure can also be used to manage small-stuff or big-stuff worries, such as Lana's fear of movie theater shootings (Chapter 4), and it can work really well for socially focused small-stuff worries, like those of a mom who avoids outings with other moms for fear that she'll be judged. Exposure for this mom would involve challenging herself to attend different mom events.

Exposure Dos and Don'ts

All three types of exposure are extremely effective for managing anxiety, provided you approach them correctly. Here are some recommendations for making exposure work.

Do:

1. **Be goal directed and specific.** I mentioned this above, but it's worth repeating. Before starting exposure practices, think carefully about what fears you want to face and develop a specific plan for how you will do this. Roz was fearful of driving on the highway with her kids in the car. She made a plan that entailed taking her kids with her while she drove on highways, starting with smaller ones and moving on to larger/busier ones. Roz made specific plans each week for which highways she would tackle and on what days.

2. **Stick to repeated practice.** Roz, for example, had to drive on a specific highway near her house several times before it no longer intimidated her as much and she felt like she could move on to the next highway on her list.

3. **Practice in as many different contexts as you can.** The more exposure you can get to a specific stressor, the better. So, for example, if Katie avoids kid gyms, she should visit lots of different kid gyms. If she visits only one kid gym repeatedly, she may come to believe that she can deal with that particular gym but no others. She'll therefore have trouble when her son starts getting invited to birthday parties at different gyms all over her area. Varying the context is a surefire way of making an exposure practice more powerful.

4. **Combine different types of exposures.** If you really want to get the most bang for your buck, consider combining different types of exposures. For example, Andrea tended to become short of breath when she

was worried about her daughter's eating. She decided to keep a straw in her kitchen and practice straw breathing while watching her daughter eat grapes and other solid foods, thereby combining a real-life exposure with a symptom exposure. Grace tried listening to her business travel imaginal exposure recording while spinning in a chair and thus was able to effectively add a feared symptom (dizziness) to her imaginal exposure practice. The more things you can expose yourself to at once, the better!

Here are a few ways to ensure exposures *won't* work.

Don't:

1. **Try to manage your anxiety beforehand.** The goal of exposure is to get you to face your fears head-on so you can realize that you can tolerate them. That means that when you're doing an exposure, you don't want to do anything that makes the situation less scary for you. Trying out other anxiety management strategies, like considering the evidence for and against a worry, is not helpful right before an exposure; these strategies will bring down your anxiety, ensuring that you are not confronting the situation in all its anxiety-provoking glory.

2. **Practice inconsistently.** If you practice exposures only occasionally, with long stretches of avoidance in between, you won't see any benefit.

3. **Make it too easy.** If exposures aren't making you feel anxious, you're not doing the right exposures. Say Roz, the mom who feared highway driving with her kids, stuck to one local highway and kept taking it over and over, even after it ceased to scare her. She would be doing herself a disservice, as she wouldn't truly be facing her fears. Needless to say, if Roz were tasked at some point with driving on a bigger highway, she'd likely still refuse to do it.

4. **Engage in checking and/or reassurance seeking.** These are two very popular and very ineffective coping strategies for managing harm-related anxiety. They render exposure practices ineffective and also serve to maintain anxiety in the long term. Because they can be such a big problem for moms, I've devoted the next two sections to discussing them.

Check It Out: The Problem with Constant Checking

Remember Sofia, who couldn't stop watching "the baby show" on her baby monitor? She was anxious about the possibility that her baby would stop breathing and tried to manage this worry through frequent checking. Checking can come in lots of different forms, such as keeping your eyes glued to your baby monitor, sleeping on the floor of your child's nursery to ensure that nothing bad happens to her during the night, or constantly taking your child's (or your) temperature.

Another popular form of checking among moms is body checking, where you scan your own body, or your children's bodies, for signs of illness or injury. Keiko, for example, noticed that her 7-month-old son was rocking back and forth a little and became fearful that this might be a sign of some sort of developmental delay, even though her pediatrician assured her that nothing was amiss. She started tracking her son's rocking, constantly scanning him for signs of rocking instead of enjoying his giggles or marveling at his crawling.

Christine was more apt to check herself than her child. Every time she noticed something unusual in her body, she feared it was a sign of something serious. She recognized that staying healthy was so much more important now that she had a child in her care, and the idea of leaving her son motherless filled her with anxiety. When Christine noticed a lump under her arm, she became consumed with worry that this lump was a tumor, even after a visit to the doctor confirmed that it was merely a lymph node that tended to swell in response to hormone changes. Despite the doctor's reassurances, Christine remained convinced that the swollen lymph node could be a tumor and spent time each day feeling it, trying to ascertain if it had grown in size and therefore worsened.

Like Christine and Keiko, lots of moms use checking to alleviate their anxiety about harm coming to their children or themselves. But here's the problem: **checking doesn't work.** There are a number of reasons checking is totally ineffective:

1. **If you check it, it will come.** Typically, if you are looking for something, you will find it. For example, if you're watching the baby show on the baby monitor all night long, you'll see at least one thing that looks superweird. I remember once seeing Sam wake up at 10:00 P.M., pull himself up to a standing position in his crib (an impressive feat, considering he was bound up in one of those swaddle blankets), survey the scene around him, then fall back down on his mattress with a thump and immediately resume sleeping.

The notion that you'll find something if you're looking for it is particularly true in the case of body checking. As Jonathan Abramowitz, an expert in CBT for anxiety, likes to say, we all have "noisy bodies" and can easily misinterpret noisy body symptoms in ourselves or our kids (like stomach

upset, muscle aches, and exhaustion) as signs of something much more serious. Also, if you're scanning your kids' bodies for any fine or gross motor
issues, you'll likely find something that looks strange. Who hasn't witnessed
a 3-year-old writhing around like one of those Cirque du Soleil contortion-
ists?

2. **Checking can make a body symptom worse.** Remember Christine, who kept pressing on her lymph node each day? The constant pressure
seemed to actually cause an increase in pain, which made it that much more
noticeable and scary.

3. **Checking just leads to more checking.** I remember Sofia talking about how addictive watching her baby monitor became. Checking the
monitor had become so routine for her that at a certain point she stopped
even realizing she was doing it.

4. **Checking keeps whatever you are anxious about at the forefront
of your mind.** If you are constantly checking yourself or your kid for a feared
problem, then you are constantly thinking about that feared problem.

I hope I've made it clear that checking is ineffective at best and harmful
at worst. However, it can be tricky to determine whether you are checking
too much, as some amount of checking is important to ensuring your own
and your child's safety. Certainly you don't want to ignore signs of trouble in
yourself or your children, and of course you want to visit the doctor if you
fear that something is not right.

To determine if you are spending too much time checking, think about
whether your checking is getting in the way of other things you want to
be doing. Sofia, for example, had a DVR that was 90% filled with seasons
full of shows she wanted to watch. She regarded TV as her escape from the
monotony of caring for a baby and her reward for momming so hard every
day. But because of her constant monitor checking, Sofia couldn't pay attention to any of her shows. As I said to her, it's hard enough to have to spend
your whole day focusing your attention on one small baby. Forcing yourself
to continue focusing on your baby even after she's gone to bed and you
finally have some time to yourself? That's just masochistic.

Another way to determine whether your checking is unreasonable is to
challenge yourself to examine the evidence. Is there evidence to suggest that
the problem you're obsessively looking for is likely to occur? Christine, for
example, asked herself whether there were any facts supporting the idea that
her swollen lymph node was a sign of something much more serious. Turns

out there weren't, other than some post she'd read on Facebook about a friend of a friend who'd recently been diagnosed with cancer. And of course, this wasn't actually evidence, but rather an example of overgeneralizing, hearing about one isolated incident and assuming it would likely also happen to her. There was ample evidence against Christine's worry, such as the report from her doctor and the fact that her cyst became more pronounced before her period (confirming the hormone hypothesis).

How to Check Yourself When You're Checking

The first step in eliminating checking is noticing that you're doing it. Try monitoring yourself for a few days. Are there certain times of day/situations that make it more likely that you'll check? Do you check only in response to anxiety (like Keiko, who started focusing on her son's rocking only when she was worrying about it), or has your checking become so automatic that you do it without thinking about it (like Sofia with her monitor)?

If your checking involves repeated physical actions, like looking at a monitor, feeling a bump on your body, or taking your child's temperature, make a plan to cut back on or eliminate these behaviors. For example, I've had several patients like Sofia, each of whom handled her monitor in a slightly different way. Sofia decided to gradually lengthen the amount of time she had to wait between monitor views (while keeping her monitor sound on, which would alert her to any immediate problems). First she looked every 5 minutes, then every 7, until eventually she reached a checking frequency that did not interfere with her nighttime relaxation routine.

Another patient gave the monitor to her wife, and they agreed on a reasonable number of times for her to check it during the night. This mom noted that giving the monitor away was initially very scary but ultimately very freeing; she was able to relieve herself of the responsibility (and burden) of constant vigilance.

If your checking is more of the body scanning variety, consider using mindfulness to cope. Keiko decided that whenever she noticed herself checking her son's rocking she would instead try to mindfully focus on one unrelated feature of her present experience: the sound of her son's coos, for example, or the different colors she saw in his nursery. A mindful shift away from focusing on the rocking helped her temporarily shift her brain to something other than harm-related thoughts. When Keiko found herself returning to focusing on the rocking, she'd once again focus on another aspect of her environment. Interrupting checking behaviors in this way can be a helpful way of managing the checking and is especially useful for checking behaviors that are difficult to stop entirely (as was the case for Keiko; if she was looking at her son, and he happened to be rocking, there was no way she wouldn't notice the rocking).

Giving up on checking can be anxiety provoking, especially if your urge to check is very strong. That's why it can be helpful to think of some other activities you can engage in when you feel the urge to check. I recommend trying the DBT strategy of choosing three alternative activities to move through systematically. When Sofia struggled not to check her monitor, she first tried watching TV. If that wasn't distracting enough, she read a gossip magazine. And if that didn't do it for her, she called a friend. Typically, by the time Sofia made it through those activities, her urge to check wasn't nearly as strong as it had been.

Let Me Reassure You: You'll Never Feel Reassured

Another ineffective strategy that moms often use to manage their harm-related anxiety is reassurance seeking, whereby they look for reassurance that they or their children will be OK. This reassurance seeking usually comes in one of two forms. The first occurs when moms repeatedly ask other people (typically loved ones, and usually the same person over and over again) to reassure them. Irena's husband, for example, grew so tired of her asking, "Are you sure Bailey doesn't have X?" (X being whatever rare childhood malady Irena happened to read about on social media that day) that he often wound up yelling at her in response.

The other form of reassurance seeking involves consulting the Internet to research what a certain symptom means or ascertain whether your child is on track developmentally. I'm not talking here about occasionally looking at a reputable pediatric or medical website if you have a health-related concern. I'm talking about constantly checking the Internet in search of answers about your kids or yourself. Generally moms who use the Internet for reassurance don't rely exclusively on reputable websites but read anything and everything available to them. This includes posts by nonexperts in random mom chat rooms and message boards. I can't tell you the number of moms I work with who sheepishly admit that they rely on "Dr. Google" far more than they should.

I'm discussing Internet searching as a form of reassurance seeking, but I think it can be considered a form of checking as well, in that moms are checking to see if they or their children have certain symptoms. Moms often profess that they are going online to reassure themselves that certain symptoms are benign. However, I find that they often seem to settle on the most deadly possible explanation for the symptoms in question. I mean sure, fatigue, heartburn, and indigestion are possible symptoms of stomach cancer, but they are also possible symptoms of stress, a condition that pretty much all moms have in spades.

Whether you get your reassurance from a loved one or from the Internet, I can promise you it will not help you effectively manage your anxiety. This is because:

1. **The person from whom you're seeking reassurance might not be qualified to give it to you.** Irena's husband is not a pediatrician, so how can he know for sure that their daughter doesn't have the pediatric illness du jour? In addition, so many moms put too much stock in Internet posts written by nonexperts. I'll never forget Kelly, who rushed into my office in a panic about having received confirmation online that her son definitely had a significant speech problem. "Who confirmed this?" I asked. "Sarah," she reluctantly admitted. Sarah, it turns out, was an anonymous mom on some website who swore that Kelly's son's issues completely mirrored those of her daughter, who did turn out to have a speech problem. No offense to Sarah, but I'm pretty sure her testimony is not enough to hang a diagnosis on. (More on questioning the validity of online posts in Chapter 7.)

2. **In many cases, immediate reassurance is not possible.** Unless you have doctors/bodyguards following you around 24/7, how can you know for sure that you or your child is healthy or safe at any given time? (If this makes you anxious, see my earlier tip about recognizing how little control you have.)

3. **When you seek reassurance from others, you are relying on these people, rather than yourself, to manage your anxiety.** A major goal of CBT is to build people's confidence that they can help themselves, using a variety of evidence-based strategies. If you're relying on others for help, you're sending yourself the message that you are not capable of helping yourself. As a result, you'll be far less likely to attempt to use effective strategies and will probably end up feeling demoralized.

4. **Reassurance seeking keeps worry at the forefront of your mind.** As with checking, the more time you spend online or asking other people for reassurance, the more time you spend focused on the thing you feel anxious about.

5. **Reassurance seeking is ineffective.** If you're someone who relies on reassurance seeking, you probably already know this to be true. Irena,

for example, asked her husband for reassurance, felt reassured for about 30 minutes to an hour after he provided it, then started to doubt things again and returned to him for more reassurance. Worry has a way of coming back stronger after reassurance is provided, rendering the reassurance unhelpful.

Stop the Cycle of Reassurance Seeking

Eliminating reassurance seeking is in some ways easier when the Internet is the source of your reassurance, because you can physically close your computer or turn off your phone to stop yourself from checking the Internet. Raquel, for example, often found herself going online during her daughter's nap looking for information about what other kids seemed to be doing at her daughter's developmental stage. Every time she read about a kid her daughter's age doing something her daughter couldn't do yet she started to panic.

Raquel agreed that she would check her email one time after her daughter went down for her nap, then physically close her computer and turn the Wi-Fi off on her phone so she could not go on message boards. Raquel had a very difficult time resisting the urge to go online (a predicament with which we are all familiar). So she came up with a list of three alternative activities in which she could engage while her daughter napped, none of which involved a computer. I think the two-pronged approach to minimizing Internet searching that Raquel used—removing your devices and/or turning off Wi-Fi, and coming up with viable alternative activities— is the way to go.

Working on reassurance seeking from loved ones requires some cooperation from them. It's typically hard for loved ones not to provide you with reassurance, as they love you and want to do whatever they can to help you feel better. Of course, as we discussed above, providing reassurance doesn't actually help you, but many loved ones don't know that. And sometimes, even if they do, they want so much to make you feel better that they'll reassure you all the same, because they know it's what you want from them.

I recommend sitting down with your reassurer and devising a phrase that he or she can say in response to your bids for reassurance. This phrase should not be reassuring but should be encouraging and supportive, perhaps even reminding you that reassurance seeking is not helpful or urging you to try alternative activities. Examples include: "I love you, so I'm not going to reassure you" and "What can you do now, instead of asking me for reassurance?"

Once you hear a statement like this from your reassurer, it should be a cue for you to stop asking for reassurance and start actively trying to cope.

Again, I recommend that you come up with a list of three alternative activities and try making your way through this list.

You may find that the alternative activities that work best for you vary according to the particular reassurance-seeking situation. If you're asking for reassurance at nighttime when you're chatting with your partner, trying a distracting TV show might be the way to go. If you're texting your mom in the middle of a birthday party for reassurance that your kid won't be mowed down by the older kids in attendance, a quick mindfulness imagery activity (maybe leaves on a stream) might be most helpful. Try out different activities in different situations and see which are the most effective for you.

A Different Kind of Harm Anxiety: Worry about Harming Your Child

Up to this point we've been focused on anxiety about something terrible happening to you or your child. There's an additional harm-related type of anxiety that some new moms have, where they fear that they will be the one to cause harm to their child. There are two varieties of this type of anxiety. The first involves fearing that your own inexperience or incompetence will cause you to inadvertently harm your child. As you'll see from Deirdre's example below, this type of anxiety can be addressed fairly easily by cultivating acceptance of anxiety and considering the facts. The second variety involves obsessive, violent thoughts about harming your child. This can be a more serious issue that I'll be discussing in the next section, "When Is It Time to Seek Professional Help?"

Deirdre was one of those moms who worried about her own cluelessness and didn't think she should be trusted with a baby. She had no younger siblings, had spent very little time with kids, and before her son was born actually thought that an Ergo was a type of coffee machine. She worried that she would accidentally do something, like drop her son or press too hard on the soft spot on his head, that would land him in the hospital.

The first thing I did with Deirdre was validate her anxiety. Of course she felt anxious—after all, she'd never done any of this child-rearing stuff before. What I told Deirdre, and what I will tell you, is that until you actually have some experience with your own children, who are your sole responsibility and live with you 24/7, you will not feel at all competent to be a parent. Sure, I get it, your friend Elizabeth believes that her summer spent at the shore nannying for three kids under the age of 4 will prepare her for motherhood. To her I say: Just wait until the 2:00 A.M. vomit-poop-rage explosion or the random bottle refusal hunger strike. No number of trips to the beach with someone else's kids can prepare you for that.

It's clichéd, but true: the only thing that will decrease your feelings of incompetence and increase your confidence is experience. Anyone who's had more than one kid will tell you that it is so much easier navigating those early years the second time around, because you actually feel like you know what you're doing. In the meantime, consider the evidence for your thought that your incompetence will endanger your kid. What are the facts suggesting that you're doing a great job with your kid? And what are the facts suggesting you aren't? More on constantly feeling like a motherhood amateur in Chapter 8; stay tuned.

When Is It Time to Seek Professional Help?

Most moms have at least occasional anxiety about inadvertently doing something to harm their children. Some moms also experience obsessive thoughts about deliberately doing something to injure or kill their kids. We talked in Chapter 2 about moms getting so frustrated with their kids that they fantasize about, say, throwing them out the window. I'm not talking about that here. Instead, I'm referring to moms who have frequent, obsessive thoughts that they will lose control and commit an act of violence toward their child (even though they genuinely do not wish to ever harm their child).

Juanita, for example, had a persistent vision of herself cutting her son with her kitchen knife. It horrified and terrified her. She didn't believe she actually wanted to harm her son, but she couldn't get the image of the knife out of her head, and she worried that she might "go crazy" and actually do something. She repeatedly checked her kitchen knives throughout the day to make sure they remained where she had left them and frequently checked her son's body for signs of knife wounds.

Juanita, I assure you, is not a monster. She is suffering from postpartum OCD, with obsessions about harming her son (a very common form of postpartum OCD) and compulsive checking behaviors. These harm-related obsessions and compulsions can be debilitating for moms like Juanita.

If you have such harm-related thoughts, you need to know that thinking about doing these things does not mean you're going to do them, nor that you want to do them. The moms with whom I've worked who have these fears are extremely caring, attentive mothers who are horrified by the thoughts passing through their minds.

Fortunately, exposure work is extremely effective for OCD symptoms like this. While you can certainly try to craft your own exposures related to harming your child, I strongly recommend seeking out a mental health professional who can guide you. Exposures relating to harming your children can engender significant anxiety (not surprisingly) and are much easier to carry out when you have ongoing therapeutic support. See the Resources section for more information about accessing relevant support.

I've been focusing on harm-related OCD here, but I want to emphasize that it isn't only worries about harming your child that might warrant a consultation with a mental health professional. **If any kind of anxiety—be it about you or your kids getting ill, big stuff, or small stuff—is so severe or overwhelming that the strategies I've presented in this chapter and in Chapter 4 are not effectively addressing it, it's imperative that you seek professional help.** Again, the Resources section in the back of the book includes information about how to access mental health professionals who can help you.

The Case of COVID-19:
Lessons Learned While Helping Moms through a Pandemic

For many of my patients, COVID-19 was a hybrid of a Chapter 4 big-stuff worry and a Chapter 5 health/safety worry. Because of course, as with all big-stuff worry topics, there was ample evidence to suggest that COVID-19 was a real threat to health and safety. But, as is often the case with the types of worries we discussed earlier in this chapter, many of my patients engaged in frequent avoidance, checking, reassurance seeking, and sanitizing. In trying to protect their (and their kids') physical health, they jeopardized their mental health.

To help my mom patients with the big-stuff aspects of COVID-19, I leaned heavily on strategies from Chapter 4. I recommended mindfulness to foster acceptance of the (many) things they couldn't control and encouraged them to set values-consistent goals to target the things they could control. This of course included taking appropriate safety precautions to keep themselves and their kids safe and protected. Also, many of my patients benefited from getting active, helping with virus mitigation efforts in their communities.

I also constantly reminded moms to be compassionate toward themselves during what was an (exceedingly) challenging time to be a parent and suggested keeping to a daily schedule (with time set aside for "worry time" and self-care and limits on time spent watching the news/scrolling through social media). Finally, I encouraged moms to choose one reputable website to rely on for evidence-based virus information and reminded them of the thinking traps (overgeneralizing in particular) that were clouding their judgment of risk. I had many, many conversations about using the evidence to make decisions and the importance of considering both the physical and mental health implications of certain choices (e.g., whether or not to send a child to day camp if he was clearly struggling at home). I constantly reminded moms that there were no "right answers" and that their decisions needed to be based on the evidence, as well as their own particular kids and circumstances.

Helping moms who were clearly going overboard with avoidance, sanitizing, reassurance seeking, and checking was tricky. I could not in good conscience ask them to do the types of exposures I would have assigned them in the past, such as going to a doctor's office and touching everything in the waiting room.

Here are the coping strategies these moms and I ultimately found most effective:

1. Designing IRL exposures that, based on the evidence, were not high risk from a health perspective; for example, challenging a mom who was petrified to leave her house to attempt a series of progressively more stressful "social distancing exposures" (starting with taking a short walk around the block, progressing to attending a neighborhood backyard barbecue wearing a mask).

2. Writing/recording imaginal exposures featuring "disaster scenarios," such as the whole family contracting COVID-19.

3. Setting safety "ground rules." Again, based on evidence, I asked moms to make decisions about what environments they were and were not comfortable with. I had moms draw up detailed (and reasonable) plans for the specific steps they would take to sanitize/clean and encouraged them to set firm limits on their washing/cleaning.

4. Targeting checking and reassurance seeking. This was a particular problem during COVID-19, and we approached it just as we would have under normal circumstances.

Our experience with COVID-19 has forever changed our attitudes about infectious disease risk and safety. For the foreseeable future (and maybe forever), we will have to treat germ anxiety as a big stuff/health stuff hybrid issue and respond to it accordingly.

6

"How Can I Possibly Find Time to Shower When I Have to Take My Toddler to Her French Lessons?"

Taking Care of Yourself
While You're Taking Care of Your Kids

It was 7:30 P.M. Joanie breathed a sigh of relief as she said good night to her twin toddlers and closed their bedroom door. She had been racing around nonstop since arriving home from work at 5:30, getting the kids settled, fed, and bathed. She was about to plop down on her couch when she remembered that despite having fed her kids she had not eaten dinner herself. Nor lunch, for that matter; she was so busy trying to finish a task in time to get her kids from day care that she had worked through her lunch hour. All she'd had to eat between the hours of 9:00 A.M. and 7:30 P.M. was a cereal bar, a piece of a coworker's birthday cake, and some popcorn from the vending machine. She knew she should fix herself some dinner but couldn't muster the energy to get up off the couch and do it.

Sunita, a stay-at-home mom of two, ages 1 and 3, was burned out. She marveled at the fact that her days managed to feel both action packed and boring at the same time. She had very little downtime and sometimes felt trapped at home. A friend suggested that she hire a high school student to watch her kids for an hour on weekday afternoons so she could get errands done and spend some time by herself. But Sunita believed that hiring a sitter would be selfish, since sitters, in her mind, were for working mothers. If she chose to be home, she reasoned, she should be home. Being a mom was her full-time job, and hiring a sitter would be an indulgence.

One of the more thoughtful gifts I received after Matty was born was a gift certificate for a massage. I could not wait to use that thing. It required a lot of advance planning, including securing Grandma as my babysitter and choosing a time that would fall between Matty's typical nursing times. But I got it planned and practically floated to the massage place. Unfortunately, as soon as I positioned myself face down on the massage table, my swollen boobs started to hurt. I spent the duration of the massage worrying about said boobs and feeling like I needed to get home to nurse Matty ASAP. As soon as the massage was over, I raced home, only to find a screaming baby and a frazzled Grandma. By the time I finished nursing Matty, I was exhausted and hungry. I honestly couldn't even remember having had the massage.

During pregnancy everyone—doctors, partners, family members, and even random people on the street—focuses on mom. Moms are treated like delicate flowers, encouraged to eat well and rest and ask for help. But once the baby arrives, those delicate flowers are left to wilt, while all the available resources, all the sunshine and water, are directed at the new seedlings.

There's no question that caring for yourself is much, much harder once you become a mother. For starters, young kids require nearly all of your time, energy, and effort, leaving you with little for yourself. And, perhaps more significantly, many moms seem to believe that it is their duty to sacrifice their own happiness and well-being for the sake of their children. Lots of people have talked and written about the concept of mother-as-martyr, or what Judith Warner, author of *Perfect Madness: Motherhood in the Age of Anxiety,* terms the "sacrificial mother." "Sacrificial mothers" often feel extreme guilt if they are doing anything that isn't 100% for their kids. They believe their kids should be at the forefront of their mom brains 24 hours a day.

But what "sacrificial mothers" fail to understand is that proper self-care is critical for moms; more critical, in fact, than it was before the kids came along. We've got to be in good shape, both mentally and physically, if we're going to be able to care for our kids effectively. Further, as we discussed in Chapter 3, pursuing what is personally meaningful to us allows us to hold on to some critical aspects of our identity. It also provides us with a non-kid-related outlet, which can do wonders for our mood and stress level.

Recently mom blogger types have been writing about how good self-care means a lot more than just getting mani-pedis. This is an important message, since self-care for women has historically been associated with trips to the nail salon. To me, self-care is about regularly scheduling breaks for yourself and focusing on things that will replenish your body and mom brain, like getting enough exercise and sleep and pursuing your passions. It's about letting your kids watch screens so that you can have a minute to yourself and accepting help when you need it and saying no sometimes. Further, as I learned, self-care is not a one-time thing. You can't just get a massage and expect to feel rejuvenated. You've got to make self-care a regular part of your schedule and commit to it on a daily basis.

The First Step in Self-Care: Dispense with the "Selfish" Self-Talk

Sunita believed that hiring a babysitter would be "selfish" of her. Many other "sacrificial mothers" tell me they can't possibly ask for help or start an exercise regimen or take up a hobby. Didn't they sign on to this parenthood thing with the understanding that it would be a 24/7 commitment, regardless of their mood or stress level?

When I hear moms engage in this "selfish" self-talk, I remind them that there is a big difference between taking care of yourself and being selfish. Unfortunately, many women fail to see this difference. To my mind, hiring a babysitter for an hour on the weekdays is an effective method for ensuring that a stay-at-home mom like Sunita gets the mom brain break she needs to return to her kids refreshed and ready for the next parenting challenge. Sunita felt that she needed to be a working parent in order to justify hiring a babysitter. The truth is, **you never need to justify doing anything that you think will improve your mental or physical health.**

The Second Step in Self-Care: Break Out That Schedule

This is a good time to take out your values worksheet and the schedule you created while reading Chapter 3. I'm hoping you're already scheduling in small values-based goals. In this chapter we'll be discussing a number of other things you can add to your daily schedule, such as exercising, eating, and leisure activities. As mentioned in Chapter 3, setting routines for each day will increase your chances of successfully meeting your self-care goals, providing a framework for your day and enabling you to prioritize yourself and the things that matter to you.

Care for Your Body

Remember how diligent you were about getting proper nutrition, eating, and sleeping when you were pregnant? You need to be equally diligent about those things now. You'll need all your energy and physical strength to meet the responsibility of providing nourishment, comfort, and safety for your little one.

Good Sleeping and Eating: It's Not Just for Kids!

I want you to think for a minute about the substantial amount of time, effort, and even money you've invested to ensure that your little one sleeps and eats well. Perhaps you've purchased 50 different white noise machines in the hopes of finding the one that will successfully lull your kid to sleep. Maybe you spend hours making fruit and vegetable concoctions using all organic produce. Or maybe you and your partner have spent hours talking about how you can possibly get your kid to stop howling at 4:00 A.M.

Why put in all this work? Because pediatricians tell us that establishing good eating and sleeping habits is important for a child's growth and development. And because we can all agree that a kid who hasn't slept or eaten well is like one of those White Walkers from *Game of Thrones,* whose sole aim is to crush you (or at least your spirit).

And guess what? Adults who don't eat and sleep are monsters, too. You don't need me to convince you of the psychological toll that a lack of sleep and poor eating takes on moms. If we're running on Cheez-Its and three hours' sleep, the volume on our already heightened emotions gets turned up even higher. We're more prone to anxiety, mom guilt, and feelings of sadness and overwhelm. And we're not as cognitively sharp, making it far less likely that we'll be able to use our coping skills to effectively manage these emotions.

I'm not suggesting that you prioritize your own sleep and eating over your kids' sleep and eating. I am suggesting, however, that you at least put sleep and eating *somewhere* on your priority list. To help you accomplish this, I've listed some strategies for maximizing your chances of eating and sleeping well (see the boxes on pages 111 and 112).

Note that I said "maximizing your chances." As we know, kids are so unpredictable (especially in their sleeping) that even the best-laid plans for a decent meal or a solid night's sleep can be curtailed by a baby who's flinging her food everywhere or a toddler who decides to confer with his stuffed animals at 2:00 A.M. Still, if you're committed to making good sleep and eating

Quick Tips for a Good Night's Sleep

I am fortunate to have a friend in the sleep business, Dr. Shelby Harris, author of *The Women's Guide to Overcoming Insomnia*. She shared some ideas for how new moms can get some rest. For more on sleep, see the Resources.

1. **Sleep when the baby sleeps.** If you have a newborn, sleep when the baby sleeps. Really. Even if you can't actually fall asleep, try to quiet your mom brain by resting in a calm, relaxing environment (read: do not use the time to catch up on texts).

2. **Divide up the night.** If you have a partner, make a plan to divide up the nighttime responsibilities. Maybe you cover one half of the night and your partner covers the other. Even if you're nursing, make sure your partner is doing other things (like changing the baby and bringing the baby to you) to help minimize the amount of time each of you is awake.

3. **Make sleep a priority.** Yes, your kids' sleep time might be your only alone time, but you will be doing yourself a huge disservice if you stay up late falling down Instagram rabbit holes. Choose regular sleep and wake times for yourself and aim to adhere to them, even if kid-related disruptions often interfere.

4. **Ask for help.** If your baby is 6 months or older and still not sleeping well through the night, consider consulting with your pediatrician or a sleep specialist. The sooner you can get your baby's sleep on track, the better.

a regular part of your schedule, you'll at least ensure that you sleep well and eat well on some days, which is certainly better than nothing!

Get Moving!

Thea, mom of a baby and a toddler, was an occasional exerciser before she had her children. But since having kids, she's been unable to get herself

Quick Tips for Eating Well

Here are some ideas for prioritizing healthy eating. For more on eating well, see the Resources.

1. **Make sure you are actually eating.** If you're one of those moms who skip meals, consider setting a daily eating plan, which you can add to your daily schedule. I recommend that you aim to eat three meals and two to three snacks each day, a guideline I've borrowed from my years of doing CBT for eating disorders (CBT-E).

2. **Have healthy, quick options around.** If all you have in your house are mashed-up baby vegetables and potato chips, you'll be unable to feed yourself effectively. Put together a list of quick, reasonably healthy foods and make sure your house is always stocked with them.

3. **Make your food while you're making your kid's food.** If you're spending time preparing food for your kids, why not plan to make your own food at the same time? If you've got fruit and vegetables out already, just cut up some more for yourself.

4. **Do not plan to eat with the goal of losing baby weight.** Your aim with eating post-baby should be to keep yourself nourished and energized, not to restrict your calories in the hopes of weight loss. This is especially true if you are nursing and desperately need the calories. If you're struggling with your post-baby body image and feel the need to restrict what you're eating as a result, see the section starting on page 113.

moving. For starters, she's always exhausted. She also relishes her rare free moments and doesn't want to waste them exercising, which she honestly doesn't really enjoy. She has no exercise equipment at home or a gym membership. And even if she did belong to a gym, she doubts she'd ever make it there. If even getting up off the couch is a chore, how would she motivate herself to drive across town to get on a treadmill?

As Thea's case illustrates, unless they really love to work out, new moms often struggle to prioritize exercise. But of course, as you know, exercise is great for you, for all kinds of reasons. It benefits your heart and gives you energy. Especially relevant for our purposes, studies have indicated that regular exercise can improve mood and relieve anxiety and stress. And as we discussed in Chapter 3, achieving a values-driven exercise goal can be deeply satisfying and validating.

In the box on the next page I share some quick tips for incorporating exercise into your routine. Obviously these are not for those of you who are posting photos of yourself bench-pressing your 6-month-old twins. They're for those of you who value exercise and would like to do more of it but can't seem to make it happen.

What to Do If You're Obsessing about Your Post-Baby Body

Gossip magazines and even some mom blogs and parenting websites talk about losing baby weight as if it's a competitive sport. This is a huge problem for a number of reasons: First, it makes moms think they have to drop weight right away, which is exceedingly difficult to do, given the time and energy constraints on new mothers. Second, it sends the message to new moms that they are not attractive if they're holding on to post-baby weight, and that if they only worked a little harder, they could get this "problem" under control. And most important, it inspires some mothers to engage in unhealthy dieting and obsessive exercising, which is obviously detrimental to both their physical and mental health.

I've tried to point out to moms that their bodies have done something amazing and encourage them to focus on that rather than on the weight they've gained. I've also tried showing them images of "real-life" post-baby bodies on Instagram. But I honestly haven't found this to be very helpful. Yes, moms are thrilled that their bodies enabled them to carry a baby, but they also want to go back to looking and feeling the way they used to. Seeing pictures of Meghan Markle looking like a supermodel at 3 weeks postpartum only amplifies their anxiety and their desire to lose the baby weight.

Clearly female body image—during every stage of a woman's life, not just in the postpartum period—is a fraught, complicated topic. Unfortunately there aren't any handy CBT strategies for swiftly changing societal standards of beauty or convincing moms that it's what's on the inside that counts. There are, however, a number of things you can do to turn down the volume on body image concerns. Below, see my "Dos" and "Don'ts" of post-baby body image.

Let's start with the *don'ts*:

Quick Tips for Getting Some Exercise

1. **Figure out what you can do at home.** There are numerous apps and websites that guide you through brief home-based exercise routines. See the Resources for some recommendations.

2. **Walk when you can.** Forget the elliptical machine—perhaps the most valuable piece of exercise equipment for new moms is the baby stroller. Walking is great exercise for you and also gets both you and your kid out of the house for some air and a change of scenery.

3. **Aim to get some lifestyle exercise.** "Lifestyle exercise" involves looking for opportunities to get in some exercise while you're doing other things. Examples include parking farther away from your destination so that you have to walk there, taking the stairs instead of the elevator (that is, if you don't have a kid in a stroller with you), or even challenging yourself to carry heavy kid equipment.

4. **Exercise with friends.** Need someone to help motivate you to exercise? Consider making a plan to exercise with a friend. Added bonus: If you value socializing with friends, you'll be able to honor two values with one activity!

5. **Remember that any amount and any type of exercise is good exercise.** Like her posts indicate, that Instagram mom bench-pressing her twin babies is #crushingit. You don't need to #crushit. Just get your body moving, in whatever way is comfortable and feasible for you.

6. **Use your schedule:** To ensure that any exercise, even a quick 7-minute workout, will happen consistently, include it in your daily schedule and plan for it in advance. Otherwise you may get pulled away by the looming piles of laundry or the siren song of marathons on Bravo TV.

1. **Don't obsessively check pictures of yourself.** If you want your mom brain to be consumed with negative thoughts about your body (regardless of whether you've experienced pregnancy or not), take time out of your day to stare obsessively at your recent selfies. For bonus points, be sure to

continually check the photos of you posted by friends and family on social media. When we discussed body checking in Chapter 5, I noted that if you check your body for a health-related symptom, you will find it. This is true for body imperfections as well. If you stare at pictures, convinced that you will find evidence of your fat thighs or stomach rolls or crow's feet, then you will indeed find this evidence.

2. **Don't check your actual body.** What I said about checking yourself in pictures also applies to staring at your post-baby body in the mirror. Again, if you look for a protruding stomach, or for dimpled thighs, or for anything else thought to be undesirable on the female body, you will find it. As discussed in the CBT treatment for eating issues and body image (CBT-E), the more time you spend meticulously scrutinizing a perceived bodily flaw, the worse that flaw is going to look. (Anyone who's ever had a blemish and stared at it in the mirror knows this to be true. By the time you're done staring, it looks like the zit is going to swallow up your whole face.)

3. **Don't try to squeeze yourself into old clothes.** If I had a dime for every time a new mom complained about not being able to fit into her old expensive jeans . . . I'd be able to go out and buy myself multiple pairs of those expensive jeans. Continually trying on old clothing and finding that it doesn't fit is demoralizing and depressing. As is squeezing yourself into old clothes and insisting on wearing them. Wearing tight clothes ensures that your attention will be constantly drawn to how uncomfortable you are. You might as well set off an alarm every 5 seconds that blares: "You are too big for these clothes that used to fit you!"

4. **Don't keep stepping on the scale.** This is another thing I hear about all the time—moms obsessively stepping on the scale, looking to see how much (if any) baby weight they've lost. Constant weighing serves to keep your mind focused on how much you weigh. Eating disorders experts recommend that you weigh yourself once a week; this helps you get an idea of what your weight is doing without causing you to hyperfocus on it.

Now, here are some *dos:*

1. **Do eat well and get moderate exercise** (see above for details on this).

2. **Do purchase a few new things to wear.** Trying to fit into pre-baby clothes is demoralizing, and so is continuing to wear maternity clothes when you are no longer pregnant. Who wants all that itchy elastic fabric around

her waist? Consider going out and buying a few comfortable, reasonably stylish items that you can wear at this very moment, not when you've lost 10 or 20 pounds. You will feel so much better about how you look if you're wearing comfortable, flattering clothing.

3. **Do focus on what you can control.** As we've discussed, it can be very difficult to control your postpartum body shape and weight. It is far easier to control other aspects of your appearance, like your hair and makeup. Now I know some moms could care less about how put together they appear in public and are proud to rock the unshowered/messy bun/yoga pants look. But if you are someone for whom looking presentable on the outside is essential for feeling good on the inside, consider adding some grooming to your daily schedule. Take stock of the things that are important to you (e.g., blow-drying your hair, putting a little makeup on, taking regular trips to get your nails done) and schedule them in.

4. **Do try some mirror exposure work.** Mirror exposure is a strategy used in CBT for eating disorders and body image issues. It involves looking at yourself in the mirror, in whatever state of undress is comfortable for you, and attempting to describe each of your body parts in nonjudgmental terms, as you might to someone who can't see you. Describe yourself from head to toe, so that you are focusing on your whole body, rather than on "trouble spots" like your stomach or thighs. When looking at different body parts, consider things like shape, length, width, color, proportion (how different parts of your body look in proportion with other parts), and function (what that body part is designed to do). Don't spend too much or too little time on any one part; just give equal attention to each part as you move down your body.

The goal here is to view your body more holistically and to change the way you regard your "trouble spots." This might mean replacing your description of your thighs as "fat-tree trunks" with a more nonjudgmental description like "thick and muscular thighs that at one time helped me run in the state track finals." A "fat" stomach could instead be described as "a stomach with rolls and stretch marks, a product of having recently had a baby." Throughout the process, be mindful of your feelings and judgments. Don't try to distract yourself from them; just experience them as they are.

You'd be surprised at how effective mirror exposure can be. I've found it to be a lot more helpful than those inspirational body-positive memes you often find posted on mom blogs and websites (usually featuring an undoctored photo of a newly post-baby body and some inspirational phrase like "Those stretch marks are a sign of your super-hard work, you amazing Mama!").

5. **Do question your comparisons.** Those endless articles and posts about losing baby weight are often accompanied by pictures of celebrities who look outrageously great at, like, 2 weeks postpartum. You may find that you're comparing yourself to these celebrities, or to random moms you see on social media or even people in your day-to-day life. But oftentimes these comparisons are incredibly unfair. Sure, that lady on Instagram or the mom across the street might be looking svelte after she just pushed out a baby. But do you know what it takes, and what she might be sacrificing, to look that way? Is it possible that these women (especially the celebrities!) have access to resources you do not (like a personal trainer, or someone to watch their kid so they can exercise, or a personal chef) to help them shed weight quickly?

If you are mired in comparisons and feeling anxious and body conscious as a result, be sure to question these comparisons. For much more on dealing with comparisons, see Chapter 7.

6. **Do seek further help if you feel you need it.** If you are experiencing significant or persistent problems with your body image, including related issues with your eating or exercise, I urge you to seek help from a professional who specializes in these problems. See the Resources for more information about accessing help.

Make Your Bed

In a 2014 commencement speech that went viral, retired U.S. Navy admiral William H. McRaven famously extolled the virtues of bed making. Making your bed, the admiral remarked, ensures that you start off your day having accomplished one goal, which will set you on a course to accomplish more goals throughout your day. You can't expect yourself to conquer large jobs, he reasoned, if you can't first conquer small ones. And if your day turns out to be miserable, well, at least you'll have a neat bed to go home to.

I remember reading about this speech while on maternity leave with Sam. It instantly resonated with me, no doubt in part because I spent eight summers at sleep-away camp endeavoring to make the perfect hospital-cornered bed. But I also recognized that making one's bed (and doing other small, seemingly trivial chores) could be really important for me and other new mothers, for all the reasons Admiral McRaven describes, of course—to help moms feel accomplished and start off the day on the right foot and ensure that they have a haven to come back to at night. I also think bed making and other chores can help you cut through some the chaos of those early years of parenting.

When you have young children, there are so many things you can't control, like whether your kids are eating or sleeping well (see Chapter 8 for more on this). Needless to say, losing control of things tends to send our anxiety into overdrive. But you *can* control whether your bed is made. And, at least for me, seeing a made bed was (and is!) a reminder that I did have mastery over some things in my life, and that order, at least in my bedroom, could prevail. If Sophie the giraffe and her animal pals were going to be strewn all over my floor, at least I could look to my bed as an island of calm in a sea of chaos.

You may be thinking: Is this crazy lady really encouraging me to do chores as a means of self-care? Please know that I'm not telling you to do anything super time-consuming, like vacuuming the whole house or cleaning the bathroom every day or (God forbid) tackling the pile of thank-you cards that you've been meaning to write since your child was born. I'm simply suggesting that you follow through on really small household tasks, like making your bed, that will help you feel accomplished and in control and hopefully set the stage for a productive day. And if your day is not productive, at least you'll have a really neat, inviting surface to pass out on when it's all over.

When Screens for Kids Mean Peace for You

As a mom of little ones you've no doubt read a slew of articles about the perils of screen time for young children. Screens will rot their brains! Screens will make them into zombies! Screens will make them antisocial! I read all of those articles too and as a result decided that Matty would be allowed to watch no more than one hour of educational TV each day. I shared this idea with my friends, all of whom had different opinions about how much screen time was too much for their kids. But I felt confident in my decision.

I remained confident for about 8 months, until the cold New Jersey winter forced me and Matty to spend many days alone in the house. On numerous occasions, I'd find myself stuck with a cranky kid who'd already watched his hour of *Sesame Street*. I knew another hour of *Sesame Street* would save my sanity but felt such extreme guilt at the harm such TV might cause that I resisted turning it on. This issue became even more fraught with Sam, who did not like *Sesame Street* and was only entertained by YouTube videos of adults playing with toys (a bizarre form of entertainment that my husband and I have termed "freaky toy videos"). What kind of mother was I if I let him watch random videos with zero educational value?

Thinking back now, I am so regretful that I didn't let my sons watch more TV during those epic, cold, tantrum-filled days—because, preachy articles be damned, I'm sure it would have done them no damage, but would have helped me so, so much. A free hour would have enabled me to take a much-needed adult time-out when I could have done mindfulness work or exercised or done any number of other things to quiet the noise in my mom brain.

Now, when I see moms who have arbitrary screen time rules like mine, I urge them to be more flexible. I share my recommendation for *strategic screen time*—that is, using screens strategically, when they will serve to soothe kids or their parents (or both!). If my experience as a parent is any indication, screens can be a lifesaving last resort when you and/or your kid have reached an emotional breaking point.

Use Your Values to Pursue Your Passions

In Chapter 3, we talked at length about articulating your values and scheduling in values-based actions. I think it's important to remind you about that here, as pursuing activities you're passionate about, be they sports or traveling or knitting, can be a critical aspect of self-care as well as an important way to maintain your sense of self.

You'll recall that I stressed the importance of being creative when it comes to making plans for values-based actions. This is especially true when it comes to pursuing passions, as things like crafting and singing don't necessarily rank high on a new mom's must-do list. To illustrate how you can creatively engage with your passions, consider the case of my patient Marla. Marla was an absolute travel fanatic, so much so that she wasn't sure she even wanted to have a baby. Marla struggled when she was home on maternity leave; not only was she not traveling anywhere interesting, she wasn't traveling anywhere at all.

Marla and I discussed how she could indulge her love of exploring in smaller, more feasible ways. She created a list of drivable parks in her area and set out to visit as many of these parks as she could, with baby carrier in tow, of course. She remembered that her college offered online courses and searched the offerings for lectures about foreign places that she could watch on demand. I also encouraged her to write a short-term bucket list of day trips and even overnights that would be possible when her son got just a little bit older. And, of course, I encouraged Marla to put all of these activities on her daily schedule so that she was sure to make them happen. Clearly international travel was not in Marla's immediate future, but at least she could make exploring (albeit on a far smaller scale) a regular part of her life.

Spend some time studying the recreation/leisure/passions section of your values worksheet. Note those activities you truly value and think critically and creatively about how you can incorporate them into your week. Just a few minutes of values-based leisure activity can go a long way toward reducing stress and helping you feel like yourself again.

Ask for Help!

It seems completely logical: you're having difficulty coping with your anxiety/mood/fatigue/overwhelm, so you ask your partner/parents/sibling/in-laws/friends/neighbors to take your kid(s) for a little bit/listen to you vent/run some errands for you/bring over some emergency chocolate cake, after which you feel refreshed and ready to tackle the next parenting challenge. Makes sense, right?

I wish asking for help were that simple. I can't tell you how much time I spend encouraging moms to ask for help when they need it. But so many struggle with this, for a variety of reasons. Some, particularly those of the "sacrificial mother" variety, believe that it is their sole responsibility to care for their child, and that by asking for help they are lying down on the job. There are others who believe that asking for help signifies failure; that by requesting assistance, you're broadcasting that you really can't hack it as a mom. There are also those who desperately want help and are willing to accept it but don't directly ask for it, believing their loved ones should just know they need it and offer it to them. Other moms like the idea of help in theory but don't trust that their loved ones will do as good a job with kid-related tasks as they will.

Finally, there are moms who just don't feel comfortable asking for help. I've often heard things like "It's just not in my nature to ask people to help me." For some, it's a social anxiety or shyness issue. Asking for help makes them nervous, and they worry about inconveniencing other people. Others report that they've just never been the type of people who ask for assistance, having always adopted an "every woman for herself" mentality, regardless of the situation.

If you resist asking for help for any (or all!) of these reasons, I urge you to start challenging yourself to reach out when you need to. You want to be able to call in a relief pitcher before your anxiety, sadness, irritability, or other negative emotion(s) reach the point of no return and you end up in a mammoth maternal meltdown. Here are some strategies for effectively enlisting help from others:

1. **Actually ask!** You may know how stressed you are, but your friends and family may not, at least not until you explicitly tell them. I've worked with so many moms who assume that loved ones will always know when they're struggling and rush to their aid. When these loved ones don't rush to their aid, they often become angry and resentful. Which honestly isn't fair: how can your partner or mother or friend be expected to read your mind? Don't assume that anyone knows how much you're struggling.

2. **Be specific.** When you ask for help, don't just put out a general distress call. Be very specific about what you need and when you need it. Do you need a babysitter for a few hours on a Saturday? Do you need someone to pick up some diapers at the drugstore? Do you need someone to listen to you while you cry? Telling people that you're stressed and need help is certainly a good place to start, but to ensure that you actually get some assistance, think carefully about what you need and what specific action(s) someone will have to take to help you meet that need.

3. **Try to play to your helpers' strengths.** If you have a helpful neighbor who is weirded out by babies but is happy to take a Target run, ask her to pick up a few things for you rather than babysit. If you have relatives who keep telling you how much they want to see your kids, invite them over and ask if you can go out and take a little break while they're there. If you need emotional support or advice, call that friend who is thoughtful and sensitive and validating (much more on the importance of emotional support from friends in Chapter 11). You can even write out a list of potential helpers, noting what each person on the list is best at helping with.

4. **Don't look gift horses in the mouth.** You know the old proverb "Don't look a gift horse in the mouth?" I often talk to moms about what I call "the Gift Horse Problem." Moms often look in the (metaphorical) mouths of well-meaning relatives or friends who offer to watch their kids, decide that these hypothetical helpers' bathing/lullaby singing/meal selection skills are not up to snuff, and refuse the help.

If you are lucky enough to receive a babysitting offer, and you know that the potential babysitter will provide your child with TLC and keep your child safe and secure, by all means, say yes to that babysitter! And use your time off to get some much-needed rest, which will ultimately help you parent more effectively. I promise your kid will survive, even if he eats candy or goes to bed at 10:00 P.M. or watches 3 hours of TV.

5. **Recognize that asking for help is not a signal that you're failing at motherhood.** I'm aiming this at moms who worry that asking for help will betray them as frazzled messes. What I'm hoping you've gotten from everything you've read thus far (and especially from Chapter 2) is that all moms are frazzled messes sometimes. Anyone who's ever been a mom knows this to be true. Asking for help is not going to out you as some incompetent disaster. Instead, it will out you as a mother who looks out for her own mental health and takes active steps to cope when her mom brain is overloaded (lots more on moms' futile attempts to act and look perfect in Chapters 7 and 8).

6. **Start small.** If you feel uncomfortable asking for help, for whatever reason, start by making small requests of notoriously accommodating people. If you have a really friendly neighbor with older kids who has repeatedly offered assistance, for example, try asking her to perform a quick task like bringing in your packages when you're away. Keep asking for small things from generous people until you feel ready to make some larger requests. I'm certain you'll find that loved ones and friends are happy to help you and will not feel at all inconvenienced, as long as you are asking for things that are specific and reasonable. And if you find that a particular friend or family member appears to be inconvenienced, scratch that person off your list of potential helpers. As you've probably noticed, what I'm describing here is an exposure plan for asking for help.

I do recognize that for some moms, particularly those who are socially anxious or shy, asking for help remains a tall order, even if they follow all the suggestions I've given above. If you're one of those moms, stay tuned: later in the book, you'll learn additional strategies that will make it easier for you to ask for what you need.

The importance of Saying "No"

Volunteer for the bake sale committee at the preschool.

Take your toddler to visit your aunt who lives 2 hours away.

Join a Mommy and Me music class so your friend's kid will have a friend in his class.

These are just a random sample of the many requests faced by Martina, a patient of mine with a young daughter. Martina came to my office each week oozing with resentment, rattling off the most recent demands coming in from her kid's preschool, her relatives, her friends, and even her partner. After Martina finished venting, I'd always ask her the same question: "Did you say yes to everything that was asked of you?" Unfortunately, she'd usually say "yes" to me, too.

Martina, like many moms, felt compelled to say yes when a favor was asked of her. She told me that she just really wanted other people, particularly other moms, to like her. I completely got that, because I too am an inveterate people pleaser. Martina also felt that saying yes to things like bake sales and family visits was something that came with the job of mom—a version of the "sacrificial mother" idea we discussed before. Whatever the motivation behind her yesing, it was leaving Martina with no time for self-care or values-based activities.

I don't think many people think of occasionally saying no as a form of self-care. But if my work with moms is any indication, saying yes too much can become a huge issue and can get in the way of a mom's health and well-being. Moms have to be strategic about what they say yes and no to. Otherwise, their lives will be dictated by the needs of their kids or other mothers or relatives, which will invariably contribute to increased anxiety and stress, as well as low mood and mom brain burnout.

Based on my work with moms, here is a random sample of mom-related things that you can pretty easily say no to:

1. Volunteering for a school event that you technically can attend but really don't want to
2. Attending a kid event you don't want to go to (Really—you can skip a few peewee soccer games and send your partner or grandparents in your stead. I promise: your kid will not remember!)
3. Driving cranky kids to visit family
4. Signing your kid up for something at a time that will majorly inconvenience you
5. Taking your kid to a playdate that will rile her up and leave her overtired

Moms often have trouble deciding whether or not to agree to a given request. If that's the case for you, I recommend falling back on the tried-and-true CBT technique of considering the **benefits and drawbacks** of saying yes. Here is Martina's list of the benefits and drawbacks of saying yes to enrolling her daughter in a kiddie music class with her friend.

Benefits

- *It may be fun for Ada.*
- *It will be a change of pace for Ada.*
- *It will endear me to Joseph's mom, who I like and would like to become better friends with.*

Drawbacks

- *Cost.*
- *It will mess with Ada's nap schedule.*
- *If Ada naps less, I will have less time to myself.*
- *I can't stand those Mommy and Me classes.*
- *I won't actually have the opportunity to hang out with Joseph's mom during the class, and we will have to leave immediately after so that we can get home for nap time.*

Note that there are some clear benefits here, as well as some clear drawbacks. I encouraged Martina to consider them both and decide which side carried more weight. After going back and forth, she decided to skip the class, despite the fact that it could theoretically be good for Ada and would probably help her win points with Joseph's mom. Martina just really didn't want to attend the class, both because she loathed those classes (as did I, incidentally) and because it would mess with Ada's nap, which would then mess with her only time off during the day.

When you weigh the benefits and drawbacks of saying yes to something for your kid, you may find that it's *your kid* who will reap the benefits and *you* who will suffer the drawbacks. This was the case for Martina. Had she said yes to the class, Ada would have benefited (as the class would have been a new and maybe fun experience for her), but Martina would have suffered (loss of money, time, and nap— and, if my experience is any indication, public humiliation thanks to falling on your ass while trying to hold on to a chain of scarves during a song about fall leaves). Again, we all expect to sacrifice our own needs for those of our kids. But if you evaluate a request and find that the benefits for your kids are not super-compelling and the drawbacks for *you* are significant, consider saying no.

One more point about saying no: If you do decide to say no, do not apologize for doing so! An apology implies that you've done something wrong. It is *never* wrong to say no for the sake of your mental health. Simply state that you are not available to do what was asked of you and move on with your day. If you have difficulty doing this, stay tuned: we will be talking a lot more about how to effectively say no in the context of a variety of relationships, including those with your partner (Chapter 9), extended family (Chapter 10), and friends (Chapter 11).

Below, I discuss a type of mom request that can be particularly difficult to navigate: the pressure to volunteer at school.

How to Engineer Your Volunteering

I'm not going to lie: I've always felt I should say yes when asked to volunteer at my kids' schools, starting when they were in day care. I know, I know—as a CBT therapist, I am supposed to be questioning the *shoulding* I'm doing here. Who says I "should" volunteer? What are the benefits and drawbacks of my saying yes? Is leading a bunch of kindergartners through the maze of the school book fair really bringing me joy? Or is it just contributing to my overall mom brain stress?

I recognize that the pressure I feel to volunteer is largely self-imposed and that volunteering often comes with substantial drawbacks (it's time-consuming, it can be boring, it can stress me out). But I've honestly always seen myself as someone who would be involved in my kids' schools. School volunteering is values consistent for me; I very much value being involved in my kids' day-to-day lives.

When I first started volunteering for stuff, I really did not enjoy myself. At all. But then one year I volunteered to participate in Theme Day at Matty's school, where parents were asked to present on a topic that fit with an overall theme, "innovation." I decided to speak about *Hamilton* and Lin-Manuel Miranda, a topic about which I was extremely passionate.

Do I think that the kindergartners and first graders really understood how revolutionary a rap musical about Alexander Hamilton was? Probably not, but they did seem to like the clips I showed, and I loved being able to share my love of theater with them. Matty, a *Hamilton* fan himself, beamed from the audience. After that day, I realized that I need only say yes to volunteer experiences that interest me and play to my strengths.

If you, like me, value saying yes to school volunteering, choose your activities strategically. Draw on your talents and interests and make it fun for yourself. And as always, feel free to say no to volunteer opportunities that don't work for you because they're stressful or inconvenient or just uninteresting.

Don't Forget about Your Mental Health

By reading this book, you're showing a commitment to your mental health, as the book's main objective is to help you navigate the cognitive and emotional upheavals of new motherhood. Despite this fact, I felt I would be remiss if I didn't explicitly mention mental health in the chapter about self-care. We've already discussed a number of strategies aimed at helping you combat stress and anxiety, like using evidence, exposure, and mindfulness. If you're actively practicing these strategies, be sure to add them to your daily schedule to ensure that you're making them a regular part of your routine.

Further, throughout the book I urge you to seek help from a mental health professional if you find that your problems with anxiety, depression, body image, relationships, or any other issues are too difficult to manage on your own. I've reminded you of this before, and I will remind you again: **There is no shame in seeking mental health support if it will help you function more effectively as a person and as a mother.** In the Resources you'll find guidelines for connecting with a mental health professional.

"Why Can't My Life Be More Instagrammable?"
Coping with Comparison Making and Social Media

It was one of those mornings. Cassie had overslept and was racing to get dressed for work and get out the door while her son was having a melt-down, ranting about the kid in his kindergarten class who stole one of his Hot Wheels cars. When Cassie and her son finally made it to school, they had to pass the phalanx of "yoga moms," pristine in their skintight exercise clothes, flat-ironed hair, and full makeup. And leading the pack was their patron saint, Maddie Fields, with her bleached-blond hair and impeccable figure. Cassie, who was half-dressed and hadn't brushed her hair, tried not to make eye contact with anyone as she ushered her still-yelling son into school. Cassie didn't understand why she couldn't be like Maddie or any of the other yoga-pantsed moms she saw. She wondered how these women could have it all together while she was falling apart.

Rachel moved to the suburbs right before having her daughter and longed to connect with other mothers with babies. She decided to join the local moms' online group, where she hoped she'd find a community. But to her surprise, the posts on this page read like a diary of one-upmanship, with moms sharing details about the expensive music classes and exclusive preschools they frequented and organic foods they favored. Reading these posts, Rachel felt her anxiety mounting. Should she be enrolling Amelia in a music class? Was she doing Amelia a disservice by not putting her on the wait list for that (very costly) preschool? Should she toss all of her baby food and buy all-new organic stuff? Far from feeling comforted by other moms' posts, Rachel was consumed with doubt about her own parenting choices.

It was an exceedingly cold, dreary February day, and we in the Northeast were in the thick of what meteorologists termed a "polar vortex." Matty and I were both sick, and he had a fever, so I had to drop him at my parents' in the morning before I went to work. I finally made it to my desk, eyes watering and nose dripping, and opened up Facebook so I could get a quick mental break. A friend from college had posted a gorgeous picture of herself in a wide-brimmed sun hat, along with her uber-attractive husband and children, all frolicking on a sunlit beach. Her caption read, "Escaping the polar vortex!" Upon seeing this picture, I had several competing impulses: to anonymously troll my friend online; to stress-eat the entire bag of pretzels meant to last me several weeks; and to barricade myself in my office and never come out. I was sucked into my own vortex of all-consuming envy.

As our stories illustrate, Rachel, Cassie, and I all engaged in maternal comparison making and all felt a mix of negative emotions (anxiety, envy, guilt, self-doubt) as a result. Maternal comparison making is everywhere, as there is virtually no end to the moms to whom you can compare yourself (friends, family members, acquaintances, acquaintances of acquaintances, random women on the Internet), the topics available for comparison (how well you're balancing work and family, how put together you look, how involved you are in your kids' activities, where your kids are at developmentally), and the venues that inspire comparison making (preschool dropoff, birthday parties, soccer practices, and, most insidiously, the Internet).

Social media is perhaps the worst offender: it offers up a highly curated version of other people's lives, in which moms and their families engage in enviable activities while looking totally fabulous. It's virtually impossible not to compare yourself with the other moms you see on social media. Research has shown that moms who engage in this type of social comparison feel more overwhelmed and depressed and less competent as parents than moms who don't. Of course, if you're a mom who's ever compared herself with another mom, you don't need research to confirm what you already know— that comparison making, whether on social media or IRL, can leave you awash in bad feelings.

In this chapter, we'll take aim at comparison making in its many forms. In Chapter 8, we'll discuss a particularly problematic negative consequence of frequent comparison making, maternal perfectionism.

How We're Thinking When We're Comparing

Many of us go into immediate comparing mode the second we identify some-one (either in person or online) who bears even the slightest resemblance to us. We seem to do it almost unconsciously, as if there is a default setting in our brain causing us to quickly identify the target for comparison, evaluate ourselves against the target, and determine whether we are succeeding or failing relative to the target. Sometimes we feel good about where we land, but more often we feel like we don't measure up.

To override the default, we first need to understand what our compar-ing looks like. What situations and which people tend to inspire compari-sons? How are we thinking when we're comparing? The best way to answer these questions is to spend some time monitoring our comparison making, taking note of when it happens and what it looks like. Here's a review of some of the thinking traps most commonly associated with the trap of com-parison making:

• *Shoulds.* Often, when a mom compares herself to another mom, she only sees things that the other mom is doing and she is not. In the words of CBT pioneer Albert Ellis, she begins "*shoulding* all over herself" and winds up consumed with mom guilt. Just the other day I was talking to another mom who was extolling the benefits of music lessons for her son's cognitive development. I started to worry that we should have signed our sons up for music lessons and that by not doing so we had put them at a disadvantage. Needless to say, mom guilt ensued.

• *Discounting positives/negative filtering.* When comparing themselves to others, moms often focus exclusively on their flaws and shortcomings and ignore their positive qualities and strengths. For example, consider a mom who feels terrible about her messy home after seeing her friend's super-neat home, while conveniently forgetting that her home is messy because she's always doing awesome craft projects with her kids.

• *Overgeneralizing.* Moms sometimes hear one piece of information about another mom or kid and take it as evidence of a much larger truth about them. Social media often inspires this type of thinking: we see one fabulous-looking post and assume that the poster must have a much better life than we do.

• *Mind reading.* Mind reading happens when we assume that the moms to whom we are comparing ourselves (or the kids to whom we're comparing our own kids) are doing better than we are (or our kids are) without asking them how things are really going.

Once you've taken some time to monitor your comparison making and note your common thinking traps, you will be in a better position to critically evaluate your comparisons, using tools we'll discuss below.

Challenge Your Comparisons

So many of us compare ourselves to others without realizing that we lack sufficient information to draw any meaningful conclusions. This is especially true of Internet comparison making, when we tend to evaluate ourselves against a single post or picture coming from someone else. We need to consider whether we know enough about the person in question to make a fair comparison.

Let's look at my response to my friend's polar vortex post. I saw that picture and immediately assumed a number of things: that my friend was exceedingly happy, that she had a blissful family life, and that she had the means to escape the cold whenever she wanted to. But when I thought about it, I recognized that I was overgeneralizing and mind reading. I had not talked with or seen this friend for years and had no idea how well her life was actually going. The only information I had was a picture and a post—things that this friend purposely chose to show to everyone she knew.

Of course, it was possible that everything was going amazingly with my friend, and maybe she posted that picture to elicit envy. But it was equally possible that things weren't going well at all and she posted that picture in an effort to hide this fact from others (and perhaps from herself). Or maybe she'd had a tough year for some reason and wanted everyone to see that she and her family were doing better now.

I came to recognize that I knew virtually nothing about my friend's life or her intentions in posting that picture. Which meant that I was evaluating myself, the person I knew most intimately, against a single picture of someone I barely knew anymore. We have so much more information about ourselves and our own internal lives than we do about the lives of others. So *we* may know, as I did when I saw my friend's post, that we're cold and snotty and falling apart from stress. But would others recognize that we are, assuming that we did not tell them? And conversely, does a long-lost friend's carefully selected post tell us anything about her daily life? Of course not—which means that we simply don't have enough information about her to make a reliable, evidence-based comparison.

This is also true of celebrity mom social media posts. How many of you have followed celebrity moms, only to ooze with envy over the gorgeous photos of their amazing lives and (seemingly) super well-behaved, well-dressed children (frequently accompanied by #blessed or #grateful)? It is so important to ask yourself whether you have enough information about these women to make an informed comparison between your life and theirs—which, spoiler alert, you don't: you don't know a thing about celebrities, other than what they (and their massive PR teams) want you to see. Their pictures tell you nothing about their actual day-to-day lives and very well may not reflect reality. In the box below, I've included some tips for critically evaluating social media posters by doing a little bit of detective work.

I've been talking primarily about social media here, but moms also make ill-informed comparisons in "real life." Take Maeve, who took her 4-year-old son to the same local gym class every week. Before each class, another mom

---

Do Some Social Media Detective Work

Always envious of a friend or celebrity's social media posts? Some detective work can help you weed out the truly self-obsessed posters. Look for answers to the following questions:

1. What types of things do they typically post? Do they share news items or issues outside of their own lives, or are they mostly posting things about themselves?

2. Is every picture they post of themselves excessively flattering?

3. Do they seem to care about others? Do they respond to others' posts in a supportive manner?

4. Do they seem to be trying to sell or promote something?

If the answers to these questions indicate a truly self-obsessed poster, you'll know to take their posts with many grains of salt.

and her 4-year-old always sat on a bench, reading. The mom read a novel, and the 4-year-old read some kid book (and was clearly actually reading, not just flipping pages). In her head, Maeve named these people "Einstein Mom" and "Einstein Kid." As Maeve's son still used books primarily as launch pads for his Hess trucks, she worried that he was lagging behind developmentally. And she envied "Einstein Mom," who clearly knew some secret formula to get little ones interested in reading.

I challenged Maeve to consider how much she really knew about "Einstein Mom" and her son (starting with the fact that she called the woman "Einstein Mom" because she did not even know her name). Sure, "Einstein Kid" could read and seemed to be able to focus very well. But did Maeve know what it took to get "Einstein Kid" to read? Perhaps "Einstein Mom" spent lots of money on a tutor or on one of those child enrichment classes so that her kid could get ahead of the curve. Or maybe "Einstein Kid" was one of those off-the-charts gifted kids. If so, his excellent reading at age 4 indicated that it was he, not Maeve's son, who was on an unusual developmental trajectory.

In the absence of information about the Einstein family, Maeve simply could not make a fair comparison. Maeve and I decided to come up with a "backstory" for "Einstein Mom" in which "Einstein Mom" was an exacting reading teacher who withheld dinner from her son until he read several books and who rewarded him with a single grape every time he completed a paragraph. Thinking of this scenario made Maeve laugh, which helped to ease her anxiety when she saw "Einstein Kid" tackling his latest book. If, like Maeve, you have to create a ridiculous backstory to fill in the information gaps about another person, clearly you do not have enough information about that person on which to base a comparison.

Use *All* the Facts

Sometimes our comparisons are unfair because we do not have enough information to make an informed evaluation. There are also times when we conveniently choose to ignore information that could significantly impact our comparison. This can be viewed as an example of negative filtering, where we focus only on negative information about ourselves. We need to ask ourselves if we are considering *all* the information necessary to draw a reasonable conclusion.

Let's use Cassie as an example. She spends a lot of time thinking about hot mom Maddie Fields. She focuses on how beautiful Maddie looks and how frumpy she believes she looks in comparison. Not surprisingly, this leads to significant self-criticism. Cassie wonders why she can't get it together in the way Maddie can and feels pressure to work harder to look good in the morning.

But Cassie always conveniently forgets that Maddie has something that she does not: help. Maddie has a live-in au pair. So Maddie has another set of hands in the morning to help her get her kids ready for school. Which obviously leaves her with a lot more time to get *herself* ready for school. So yes, Maddie probably does look better than Cassie at dropoff. But this isn't due to any personal deficiency on Cassie's part and certainly isn't grounds for self-criticism. With only one set of hands, Cassie is doing the best she can to get herself and her kids out of the house.

As Cassie's story illustrates, we can challenge our comparisons and still conclude that we don't compare so favorably. After questioning her comparison, Cassie still acknowledges that Maddie Fields does in fact look way hotter than she does in the morning. But we can hopefully conclude, as Cassie does, that there are legitimate reasons for not stacking up that have nothing to do with personal shortcomings or screw-ups.

Expand Your Comparison

Jillian had recently become friends with a fellow preschool mom, Neena, on Facebook. Jillian was amazed to discover how much of a social life Neena and her son, Sunil, had. It appeared that every weekend Neena and her family were going to a different park, meeting up with a different group of toddlers and their parents. Jillian really hadn't put much effort into making mom friends and had never scheduled a playdate for her son. She had always been a homebody, even more so since having a child. She worried that her lack of interest and effort would hinder her son socially. She felt like she paled in comparison to Neena, who made sure that Sunil was always surrounded by kids his own age.

I challenged Jillian to expand her comparison by considering how she compared to Neena in other areas of parenting, not just in terms of social planning. While Jillian wasn't hosting epic playdates, she was very involved in her son's preschool, helping to make curriculum decisions that would impact her son's education. Neena, however, wasn't particularly connected with the school. Jillian also remembered that Neena and her husband were West Coast natives and didn't have any extended family out east. So presumably Neena needed to cultivate a support network of friends nearby. Jillian, on the other hand, lived close to her parents and in-laws and worked hard to ensure that they were a regular presence in her son's life.

The truth is that there are so many different areas in which moms can excel, due to their particular talents or interests or circumstances (or all of the above). Usually most moms will excel in a few different areas, but *no one* will excel in all of them. It's important to recognize that you can play to your strengths, and other moms can play to theirs, and it doesn't mean that any of you are better or worse mothers. If you're intimidated by another mother's strengths, please take the time to identify your own. And work toward incorporating those into your parenting. More on playing to your strengths as a mom in Chapter 8.

Revisit Some Old (Cognitive) Friends

In addition to the cognitive strategies discussed above, several of the tools we learned in previous chapters can be effective for managing comparison making. For example, you can always consider the evidence for and against a "thinking trap" thought. You'll likely find that this leads you to the strategies highlighted above: evaluating the information (or lack thereof) you have about the other person and expanding your comparison.

Another helpful approach we've already discussed involves asking yourself what you would tell a friend in your situation. In Chapter 4, I presented this as a strategy to help you cultivate self-compassion when you feel anxious. It can also be used to help you manage the guilt and self-blame that come with comparison making. Say, for example, you're having a conversation with a fellow mom who talks at length about her exercise regimen. While you listen politely, you privately *should* all over yourself, telling yourself that you *should* be exercising like this other mom does and *should* be able to make time for it, given that this mom works and seems to fit it in. You walk away from the conversation convinced that you are a "lazy ass" and feel awful as a result.

Now consider what you would say if a friend of yours (it helps to bring a real friend to mind) came to you and explained that she'd just had a conversation with an exercise enthusiast mom and felt like a "lazy ass" as a result. Would you say, "Yes, I totally agree with you, that mom is really keeping it tight and you need to start working out ASAP?" Or would you instead remind her that she is working incredibly hard as a mother, that exercise is difficult to fit in, and that she'll be able to work it in at some point? Might you even question the exercise enthusiast mom, wondering what she has to sacrifice to make her exercise dreams come true? Considering what you might tell a friend is a great way to get out of your own judgmental head and view a comparison-making situation more objectively and compassionately. It's essentially a way to trick yourself into considering all the reasons the comparison you're making is unfair and unhelpful.

When Comparing Is Helpful: Choosing the Right Targets

I've been talking thus far about the dangers of comparison making. There are times, however, when we can actually learn from the moms to whom we are comparing ourselves. Say you know of a mom who seems to be doing a better job than you are with prioritizing self-care or setting boundaries at work. It can be helpful to look at what this mom is doing and try to emulate her choices and actions.

The trick, of course, is to identify the right sort of mom to compare yourself to. To this end, consider the values you articulated in Chapter 3 and think of a mom or moms you know who seem to share these values. A mother who values the same things you do is a much more appropriate target for comparison than a mother who doesn't. After all, are you really interested in being like a mother who has a completely different set of values from your own? (Something to ponder when you're comparing yourself to certain celebrity moms!)

I'm sure all of you have at least one other mom in your life, maybe someone who has older children and has been doing this mom thing for a long time, whom you'd like to emulate. Miriam, mom of a 4-year-old, felt pressure to have another child, in large part because she was comparing herself to friends who were having their second or even third child. While these friends all extolled the virtues of having multiple children (making comments like "Now our family is complete!"), Miriam wasn't sure this was the right path for her.

Miriam decided to seek the advice of her older cousin, whose values she shared and who she trusted implicitly. She asked her cousin how she knew she was done having children. Her cousin shared that for her the decision came down to financial and emotional resources. She and her partner felt that a second child would stretch them too thin and decided that they had the money and energy for only one kid. Her cousin noted that she at times felt a twinge of longing when she saw someone else's new baby and always got annoyed whenever anyone asked her when she was having her second. But ultimately this did not shake her conviction that she had enough resources for only one child.

Her cousin's input enabled Miriam to make a decision that was right for her. Miriam continued to use her cousin as a point of comparison, even when she didn't actually go out and seek her cousin's advice. Whenever she found herself questioning any of her parenting decisions based on a comparison she made, she'd ask herself what sort of decisions her cousin would have made in the same situation. It helped her effectively work through her guilt and anxiety.

Don't Be Afraid to Unfollow!

If a particular friend's or celebrity's social media account is driving problematic comparison making for you, unfollow it. This goes for entire apps as well; if you find that Instagram or Facebook or any other app routinely inspires negative emotions, go ahead and delete it (or at least remove it from your phone, which limits the opportunities you'll have to check it).

I remember unfollowing a friend years ago, before I had Matty. I was ready to have a baby before my husband was, and I was consumed with envy every time I'd see another Facebook friend post pictures of herself and her newborn. I struggled with one particular friend, who was gorgeous and had a gorgeous husband and baby. For a while, I busted out all of my cognitive techniques every time she posted a new picture. But ultimately, I decided it would be easier for me not to follow her for a little while. I unfollowed her until I got pregnant and then followed her again. I've also periodically removed social media apps from my phone entirely, typically during those times when I noticed that I was feeling bad about myself every time I finished looking at them.

I encourage you to evaluate the benefits and drawbacks of following a particular celebrity or friend or engaging with a particular social media platform. If, for example, you identify the benefits of following a certain celebrity mom as "Has great ideas for vegetarian recipes" and "Has amazing thoughts about how to wear leggings" and the drawbacks as "Posts fill me with soul-crushing FOMO," it is absolutely time for you to stop following this person. This is true of personal friends on social media as well. There's no need to subject yourself to posts that will inspire upsetting comparison making.

Motherhood: Welcome to Judgment City

In the first half of the chapter we talked about comparison making that originates in our own mom brains; we identify a target to compare ourselves against and assess how we stack up relative to that target. Another possible (and extremely pernicious) source of comparison making is other people's judgments. When we're judged, we're compared against a (probably arbitrary) parenting standard and found to be lacking. We often respond with *shoulding*, guilt, and self-blame.

In one study, nearly two-thirds of American mothers surveyed reported being judged for their parenting decisions, most often by members of their own family. If my clinical experience is any indication, two-thirds is a gross underestimate. Many excellent books and articles have been written about our culture's excessively judgmental stance toward mothers; see the Resources for some of my favorites.

Let's take a moment to acknowledge the myriad ways in which American mothers are judged:

- **Overt in-person judgments.** This is where people will come right out and tell you that they don't approve of something you're doing as a parent. Sometimes it's very obvious, as when your mother lets you know in no uncertain terms that you should be feeding your kids differently/enforcing different bedtime rituals/exposing your little genius to more art and culture/[insert any other perceived maternal infractions here]. And sometimes these judgments can be of the more passive-aggressive variety. My favorite is the relative or friend who learns of a choice you've made as a parent and responds by saying, "Hmmm . . . that's interesting" or "I've never heard of doing that!"

- **Subtler in-person judgments.** I was once in the grocery store with Matty and very visibly pregnant with Sam. Matty was sitting in the cart, and I realized I'd forgotten to grab something a few aisles back. Instead of dragging my cart back there I left it at the end of the aisle, told Matty I'd be right back, and rushed to grab what I needed. When I was racing back to Matty, I ended up in the wrong aisle, and when I saw Matty was not there, I visibly panicked. Then an elderly woman cleared her throat and pointed at where my cart (and Matty) were, just an aisle away. This happened 6 years ago, and I can still bring to mind the withering stare that she gave me. She didn't even have to say anything—I knew exactly how she felt about my parenting.

   I know I'm not alone in this. How many of you have been on the receiving end of a dirty look when, say, your kid was tantruming, or you nursed your baby in public, or you let your kid watch the iPad at a restaurant so that you could eat your meal in peace?

- **Online judgments.** The Internet and social media have elevated judgmental mothering to an art form. I've found that moms who are friends on social media don't usually pass direct judgment on other friends' posts but tend to communicate their judgment in more subtle ways. I'm thinking of a mom I worked with once who posted a picture of her 5-year-old helping her make brownies. One of her so-called Facebook friends responded by asking if those brownies were made with "clean" ingredients, and if not, here was a dynamite recipe for "clean" brownies. If that's not a judgmental response, I don't know what is.

The more overt online judging seems to occur on those god-awful anonymous mom chat rooms/boards. Tina Fey (one of my personal heroes) was once quoted as saying that mom blogs "Have some of the worst human behavior I've ever seen in my life." I've worked with women who've logged many hours on these sites, and I never cease to be amazed by their stories— tales of venom spewed forth in support of organic diapers, child Mandarin-immersion programs, and gluten-free diets. These mom sites, originally created as communities where moms could build each other up, have instead become forums where moms can (anonymously, and therefore without consequence) tear each other down.

And even when other mothers aren't actually addressing you directly, it's possible to read judgment into their posts. Take Rachel, introduced above. She read other mothers' braggy posts about the expensive preschool and classes they sent their kids to as a commentary on her own choices not to do any of those things. This is true of friends' Facebook and Instagram posts as well. Seeing a friend's posted article about, say, the dangers of corn syrup while your son is wolfing down pancakes swimming in Mrs. Butterworth's can leave you feeling completely irresponsible.

• **"Expert" judgments.** Many parenting "experts" (I use that term loosely, as not all self-proclaimed experts actually live up to the title; more on this in the next section) write scores of articles and books about how you should be parenting. For example, consider the "cry it out" advocates/detractors, who either insist that crying it out is the only way to get your kid to sleep or maintain that it will cause a significant disruption in your attachment to your child. Whenever we aren't doing the thing the expert is advising us to do, we usually wind up feeling extremely guilty and beating ourselves up. While parenting "experts" aren't actually judging us personally, it can very much feel like they are (and it doesn't matter, because we're doing enough judging of ourselves without needing someone else to do it for us!)

I feel compelled to bring up nursing here, as it's a topic discussed on a near-constant basis by parenting experts. It's impossible not to judge yourself if experts are telling you that nursing is the best thing for infant and maternal health and you're formula feeding. I've worked with many moms who are so ashamed of formula feeding that they refuse to do it out in public, where they could be seen and judged.

Coping with Judging

Unfortunately, we moms don't have any control over the fact that we're judged by everyone. However, we *do* have control over how we respond to the judgment (or the perceived judgment), both cognitively and behaviorally.

Before we go on, I want you to take out your values sheet from Chapter 3. We'll be using it as a reference throughout this section. Thinking about how your values align (or don't align) with those of the people who are judging you can help you effectively respond to their judgments.

Consider the Messenger

Your first task in processing others' judgments involves thinking about *who* exactly is doing the judging. Oftentimes moms who are judged won't stop to consider whether the judger is a reputable source whose opinion they value.

Lillian was constantly judged by her sister, who had older children and fancied herself a parenting expert as a result. Nearly everything Lillian did was met with a disapproving stare or a judgmental comment ("Oh—you're letting Elissa skip her nap? That's really going to come back to bite you tonight!"). Lillian loved her sister but often emerged from their interactions feeling guilty for the things she was or wasn't doing.

I asked Lillian to consider the messenger here. Did she value her sister's opinion, and did she agree with her sister's parenting decisions? Lillian revisited the parenting section in her values worksheet and recognized that her parenting values were very different from her sister's. If she was being honest, Lillian felt that her teenage nephews could be "obnoxious" and didn't want her own children to turn out that way. If that was the case, then, why would she take any stock in her sister's parenting opinions?

Lillian agreed that whenever her sister openly judged her, she would remind herself that she had different parenting values than her sister did and that she didn't want her kids turning out like her sister's kids. While this didn't stop her sister from judging her, it did enable Lillian to cope effectively with these judgments and not get sucked into feeling guilty as a result.

What if the judgers are people you don't know or only vaguely know?

I'm always amazed at how much moms seem to value the opinions of anonymous moms posting in a chat room, random mothers on a community group page, or social media connections that they haven't spoken to since eighth grade. Rachel, for example, was extremely intimidated by the posts of random moms in her community moms group. She assumed that because these women recommended a certain preschool and music class and organic diet, these choices must be the right ones for her baby as well. But Rachel had no idea who these moms were, whether they were authorities on baby classes and baby food, or whether they had the same values she did. So she needed to learn to view these mothers' recommendations as what they were—simply a collection of opinions, rather than objective facts. She had to stop comparing herself to these random moms and learn to rely on her own values to guide her parenting decisions.

It's also very important to consider the messenger when he or she is a so-called parenting expert. There are plenty of excellent parenting specialists who are worth listening to (see the Resources section for a list of these), but there are also plenty of others who may not be. If you're reading an "expert" piece and find yourself mired in self-judgment as a result, take a minute to examine the "experts'" credentials. What is their background? Their training? If their training looks dubious (or if you can't seem to find any record of their training anywhere online), they're probably not worth your time.

You also need to determine how these "experts" approach parenting. You may be reading a piece written by card-carrying experts on, say, attachment parenting, but if you're not a fan of attachment parenting, their advice will not apply to you. It makes no sense to listen to "experts" who do not appear to share your values.

Remember That Even Reputable Messengers Don't Know Your Particular Story

But what, you might ask, if the "experts" are completely legit and you're still not doing what they recommend? Surely your *should*ing is justified in this situation, right?

You need to recognize that even advice from reputable experts may not apply to you. This is because **each mother is unique, and each child is unique,** and therefore generic recommendations often aren't relevant to a particular mother's individual circumstances.

Think about a mother who has a colicky infant. She may read all of the best infant sleep books and follow all of the expert recommendations and still not be able to get her kid to sleep, since her kid has colic and is super-uncomfortable. In desperation, she may do things that sleep books urge mothers not to do, like let her son sleep on top of her while she's lying on the couch, where he is most comfortable. This mom is clearly not following any "expert" recommendations. But she's doing what works best in her specific situation so that she and her kid can get some much-needed rest.

Nursing, of course, provides another relevant example. The professionals behind the American Academy of Pediatrics who recommend nursing do not know you personally. They do not know if your baby is refusing to latch on, or if your work situation renders pumping impossible, or if your nursing struggles are exacerbating your postpartum depression. You need to make a decision about breastfeeding that fits with **your particular life circumstances,** recognizing that the American Academy of Pediatrics' guidelines are generic.

Be Choosy about Your Environments and People

When Matty was a baby, I made friends with a woman whose son was Matty's age. I was lonely and didn't know many moms in the area, so we hung out a lot, even though I often felt bad about myself after I saw her. I remember one trip to the park where her son went racing up a particular climber and Matty hesitated, clearly afraid. I told him to go to another climber instead, and my friend told me she felt I should make Matty go on the frightening climber because he would benefit from being challenged. In hindsight I can see that my response was the right one for me (and for Matty), but at the time I worried that my friend might be right. Was I coddling Matty?

It honestly took me until Matty was 3 years old to realize that I felt bad after most playdates with this friend because she was constantly judging my parenting (and other aspects of my life). I decided to pull away from the friendship, which was ultimately a tremendous relief. If you have friends or even whole friend groups who tend toward the judgmental, you might want to consider breaking away from these women and focusing your energies on more supportive friends (much more on how to do this in Chapter 11). There is no reason for you to constantly subject yourself and your children to scrutiny.

You also need to be very choosy about the online environments you frequent. Moms often tell me about falling down the rabbit hole on mom chat boards or community Facebook pages and feeling miserable as a result.

But they keep visiting these sites again and again. Some consider these sites to be aspirational; they believe that by hearing what other moms are doing, they'll gain knowledge that will improve their parenting. Other moms tell me that they love witnessing the "drama" displayed on some of these sites. But it's often the case that the benefits of the more toxic sites (enjoying the drama, learning useful parenting information) are dwarfed by the significant drawbacks (feeling judged, experiencing mom guilt).

Here's an important rule of thumb: if you find yourself experiencing negative emotions after a deep dive into one of these sites, ask yourself whether visiting the site benefits you in any way, given the obvious drawbacks. If you can't identify any meaningful benefits, it's time to sign off.

I'll also remind you of something we discussed earlier: that it is OK to unfollow people. There is no reason for you to follow friends on social media who are judgy (or who inspire judgy responses from others). Again, think of the benefits and drawbacks of following these friends. If the drawbacks outweigh the benefits (as they often do), go ahead and unfollow.

Unplug Yourself!

As we've discussed, it makes sense to unfollow certain friends or celebrities or delete entire apps altogether if you find that they inspire problematic comparison making. Another way to ensure that you're minimizing the opportunities for comparison making and negative judgment is regularly unplugging yourself, putting all your devices aside for a set amount of time.

We all know that unplugging yourself is helpful for more than just curbing comparison making. It's also a great way to help us parent (and live!) more mindfully. Remember that pie chart I shared in Chapter 1, illustrating the many contents of my mom brain? I pretty much always have a large amount of stuff swirling around in there. And when I check my phone, even more stuff starts to swirl around, causing my brain to constantly ping with anxiety-provoking news headlines and comparisons and to-do list items. If I'm trying to play a game of *Clue* with my sons while all of this information is being downloaded into my mom brain, there's no way I'll be able to solve the murder.

There are lots of ways to effectively unplug yourself. It won't surprise you to hear that in CBT we tend to approach people's phone problems very behaviorally, by encouraging them to set limits and think critically about where they put their phones. Here are some tips for successfully unplugging yourself:

1. **Set a timer.** Before you start looking at your phone, set a timer to go off when you want yourself to stop.

2. **Check your phone at regular intervals.** As mentioned previously, I worked with a mom whose frequent phone use at work was interfering with her ability to get her work done. We agreed that she would check her phone for 5 minutes once per hour (always on the hour, at 1:00, 2:00, etc.). When the 5 minutes were up, she would resume working.

3. **Disable phone notifications.** If your phone pings every time there's activity on your Facebook account, you will never be able to resist the siren song of Facebook. Consider disabling the notifications on your phone.

4. **Take apps off your phone.** We discussed this earlier, but it bears repeating. Some apps can be accessed via your computer as well as your phone. You can remove these apps from your phone entirely and just keep them on your desktop (or get rid of them altogether).

5. **Physically move your phone.** So many moms check their phone before bed, charge their phone right on their bedside tables, and even engage with their phone if they can't sleep or wake in the middle of the night. If you think social media comparison making is stressful in the daytime, try doing it at night. Good luck falling asleep after reading about your friend's weeks-long trip to Bora Bora.

Try instead to leave your phone in another room overnight. My mom patients find this incredibly helpful. They tell me that it helps cut down on their comparison making and anxiety and makes it easier for them to sleep. Many feel considerable relief that their phone is nowhere near them at night.

You can also physically move your phone during the daytime. I do this quite often when I'm with my kids. If my phone is not physically next to me, I will not check it mindlessly. I will only put in the effort to get up and get it if I really need it.

One final thought on phones: If you have a partner, try to loop them into your phone plan. If they're constantly on their phone, it will make it hard for you to resist yours. See Chapter 9 for more on partner communication.

8

"Why Can't I Mom Perfectly?"
What to Do When You Expect Too Much of Yourself

"He's not usually like this! He's not usually like this!" This was Gia's refrain as she quickly ushered her 3-year-old son and 1-year-old daughter out of the library. Gia worked hard to cultivate an image of herself as a totally together mother with the "perfect family." Prior to the library trip, Gia had lectured her son about the importance of good behavior in public. Some good that did: in the middle of story time Gia's son got into some sort of dustup with another kid, ultimately resulting in a book-throwing match. Far from looking like the "perfect" family, Gia and her kids busted out of story time like fugitives running from justice. Gia was humiliated and frustrated by her inability to control her son's behavior.

Ellie's fourth birthday was fast approaching, and Tamara was stressed. Last year, she'd thrown Ellie a party in the backyard with a few outdoor games and a piñata. But then Ellie attended a slew of fancy birthday parties, complete with entertainers and swag bags worthy of the Oscars. While Ellie had no complaints, Tamara believed that she'd failed in the birthday department and felt guilty for not spending more time planning. She vowed to make up for it this year. She spent time at work doing research for the party, browsing YouTube to find the best local Queen Elsa impersonator and Etsy to find the perfect personalized party favor. As a result, she fell behind on her work and ended up having to finish work at home after Ellie went to bed. She also feared bringing any of this up with her wife, who would flip out if she knew how expensive this party was turning out to be.

When Matty was in kindergarten, I received an email requesting that parents create a Thanksgiving costume for a party at school. We were encouraged to consult Pinterest for ideas. I was intimidated by this assignment, as I am the least crafty person on the planet. But I decided that if other parents could do it, so could I. I signed on to Pinterest for the first time ever and saw a display of professional-grade Thanksgiving costumes and crafts. And I found myself thinking, "Hey, crafty Pinterest mom! Love your Thanksgiving cornucopia made out of your children's old rubber bottle nipples and receiving blankets! I'll be over here, trying to glue some glitter onto a piece of paper." I got so overwhelmed by my Pinterest searching that I ultimately gave up and threw something together at the last minute. At the Thanksgiving celebration, many of the kids looked like they belonged at the first Thanksgiving. Matty looked like a piece of seaweed that had washed ashore with the *Mayflower*. And I felt incredibly guilty for not putting more effort in.

As these stories attest, lots of moms expect themselves to mom perfectly, whatever the task before them. I don't need to tell you about the relentless pressure on American mothers (for some excellent writing on the subject, see the Resources). Messages abound, on social media and elsewhere, about all the things we can (and should) do to perfect our parenting. We're expected to put our kids first and provide them with every advantage, always with a smile on our faces. A slew of products are marketed to us that will supposedly help us achieve perfection: the workout that will give us the perfect post-baby physique; the scores of parenting books that will turn us into master parents; the "lifestyle website" that will teach us how to host seamless events. As we discussed in the last chapter, we often compare ourselves to other moms and believe we can (and should) strive to achieve their perfect-seeming lives.

But all this striving for perfection comes at a cost. When things don't work out perfectly, and they never do, many moms (like Gia, Tamara, and me) experience significant anxiety, frustration, guilt, and self-blame. I think a former patient, discussing her own tendency toward perfectionism, said it best: "In trying to do everything for everyone at 100% capacity, I end up with 0% left of myself."

The goal of this chapter is to help you recognize that you can't (and don't need to) do everything at 100% capacity all the time. I hope you'll learn to set your expectations more realistically and show yourself compassion when you can't achieve perfection. Being a mother is hard enough without expecting yourself to do it flawlessly.

"Does Wanting to Do the Best for My Child Really Make Me a Perfectionist?"

It can be difficult to identify perfectionism in the context of parenting. As parents we are committed to doing what's best for our kids. But there's a fine line between being a responsible parent and going overboard. Some moms have difficulty ascertaining where conscientiousness ends and perfectionism begins.

To determine whether you're falling into the perfectionism trap, conduct an "emotional check-in" with yourself. Are you feeling intense pressure to do something well or to behave in a certain way? Do you have difficulty letting go of some tasks, always believing you can do more or do better? Is "good enough" completely unacceptable to you? Do you experience anxiety, frustration, guilt (or all of the above!) as a result of your efforts? If you answered "yes" to any of these questions, you may be expecting too much of yourself and/or overdoing it. Consider taking a step back and assessing whether you can approach the task differently, using the strategies we'll discuss below.

Another way to spot perfectionism is to engage in helpful comparison making, noting how friends whose values you share handle a given situation. Angela, for example, expected perfect behavior from herself; she believed that she should only "lose it" with her children when they did something seriously wrong or dangerous. As a result, she pressured herself to "stay calm" and experienced significant guilt and frustration when she couldn't (which, if she was being honest, happened often). She decided to ask several close friends whose opinions she valued whether or not they expected themselves to stay calm with their kids (and whether or not they actually did). When they all responded to both questions with an emphatic "No!" she realized that she was being perfectionistic about her own behavior and needed to engage in some mindful self-compassion work (see Chapter 3 for relevant strategies).

"But Why Shouldn't I Try to Mom Perfectly?"

So maybe you can identify yourself as a perfectionist, but you don't really want to stop trying to be the best of the best. Here's the thing, though: I don't care what the ads say, or how celebrity moms look on Instagram—**none of us can mom perfectly,** even if we fervently wish to. Here are some reasons why:

1. We have limited resources. Time, energy, and money are finite resources for the large majority of us. We simply do not have enough of any of these things to ensure that everything we do as a mom (and partner, and employee, and friend) goes 100% according to plan without any complications.

To meet her goal of throwing the "perfect" birthday party, Tamara devotes daytime hours to research, which causes her to fall behind on work. And this party of her dreams (note that I said of *her* dreams, not her daughter's) is costing money that she maybe doesn't have. So she can throw the perfect party, perhaps, but it will result in decidedly imperfect work performance as well as a less-than-perfect financial picture for the month. Even if you, like Tamara, succeed in giving 100% to one particular project, other areas of your life will inevitably suffer.

2. We can't always control our environments. Let's say Tamara does manage to put together the perfect party but wakes up to a snowstorm the morning of the event. Tamara can't control her environment; she doesn't know whether it will keep snowing or the heat will go out in her house or the pizza place will forget to deliver the pizza (or deliver it 30 minutes late, leaving her to deal with 15 hangry 6-year-olds, my own personal nightmare come true). There is nothing Tamara can do about any of these issues, all of which could sink her event.

3. We can't always control our kids. Some parenting books would have us believe that if we only follow a certain method, we can get our kids to reliably sleep/eat/behave. But while we can certainly take steps to set the stage for good behavior in our kids, we cannot guarantee that said behavior will be on display, especially if our kid happens to be tired or cranky or sick.

Also, kids are changing all the time and can experience profound emotional and behavioral shifts that you may not be prepared for. You may think you've completely figured out your own kid and know just what to do to keep her happy, only to find that she's changed into a new person overnight. This is true of delightful babies who suddenly become "terrible twos" and also of older children whose transitions are more unexpected.

4. We can't always be our best selves. Even if our kids manage to act perfectly and everything in our environment lines up, we moms may not always be able to follow our own game plans. The same factors that influence our kids' behavior, like fatigue or hunger, may also affect our own behavior. In addition, we're contending with the confusing, mixed emotions that we discussed in Chapter 2, as well as the mental overload that is characteristic of mom brain. Given all of these factors, the likelihood that we can be our best selves most of the time is pretty low.

To illustrate, here's a random list of several things I did not do perfectly in the past week:

- Missing the deadline for purchasing baseball "spirit wear," so Matty won't have the baseball T-shirt he requested
- Going to the supermarket and forgetting the one item we desperately needed (laundry detergent)
- Getting frustrated and yelling at Sam for dragging his heels in the morning, only to learn later that he was coming down with a cold

Try as we might, we moms are bound to make mistakes. Lots of them. There will be many, many times when we ourselves get in the way of our own best-laid plans.

The bottom line here is that perfection is impossible. The more quickly you can accept this, the more quickly you can start using strategies to help you cope with your (and life's!) many imperfections.

Challenge Your Perfectionism by Changing Your Thinking

Moms who tend toward perfectionism often fall into predictable thinking patterns and hold themselves to unattainable standards. As a result, many of the cognitive strategies we've already discussed can be very useful for managing the anxiety, guilt, and other negative emotions that come with perfectionism. Let's take a look at how Carly, a self-admitted "control freak mom," uses these strategies to help her manage her perfectionism around her daughter's upcoming dance recital.

Carly enrolled her daughter in a local dance school with a reputation for being "low-key." One of the selling points of this school was that parents were allowed to make their kids' recital costumes instead of having to sink substantial amounts of money into professionally made outfits. Carly was relatively crafty and, when she signed Sabrina up for the class in January, figured this would be no problem for her.

Flash-forward to early June, when Carly was completely swamped at work and could barely find time to take a shower, never mind create a dance costume. Carly believed that she should be devoting time and care to the task, especially because she knew some of the other parents were "going all out." She worried that if Sabrina didn't have a super-bedazzled, fancy costume, she would "look like crap up there."

The first thing I asked Carly to do was to think about which thinking patterns she was using. She was able to identify a few: the *shoulds* (believing that she *should* be devoting time to making the costume); black-and-white thinking (assuming that if Sabrina's costume wasn't 100% fabulous, it would be "crap"); comparison making (comparing herself to the other parents); and catastrophizing (assuming that a subpar costume would be awful).

Once Carly recognized her problematic thinking patterns, I challenged her to examine the evidence for and against her thought that Sabrina's costume needed to be gorgeous to be acceptable. Here's what she came up with:

Evidence that Sabrina's costume has to be gorgeous to be acceptable

- *Some of the other parents are making what sound like elaborate costumes.*
- *Sabrina won't look as put-together as these other kids will.*

Evidence that Sabrina's costume does not have to be gorgeous to be acceptable

- *The dance school said that even a plain leotard would be fine.*
- *Sabrina does not seem to care at all about her costume.*
- *I chose this dance school because it has a reputation for not being concerned with things like costumes.*
- *Everyone always focuses on their own kids at these performances anyway; I will be the only one paying attention to Sabrina.*

I questioned Carly about the two pieces of supporting evidence she provided, as neither of them directly validated the idea that her daughter's costume had to be gorgeous to be acceptable. She ultimately had to admit that she couldn't come up with any facts that supported her thought.

I also asked Carly to think through the worst-case scenario and whether or not she felt she could manage it. She identified the following as the worst case: *Sabrina will be the only one in her dance class who does not have a superduper bedazzled costume.* Carly recognized that, should this scenario come to pass, she would be able to manage her guilt. After all, Sabrina was not one of those kids who really cared about clothes; she just wanted her parents to be in the audience. Carly acknowledged that her guilt would likely pass quickly once the recital was over and she moved on to "the next parenting drama."

I just described how Carly used cognitive strategies to manage perfectionism in the face of a stressful task. The same strategies can also be used *after* a task or event is completed if you perceive that things haven't gone perfectly and are criticizing yourself as a result. I've found myself in this situation many times. For example, one year I was a class parent (a role tailor-made for masochists) and along with the other class parent was responsible for planning and running the holiday party. The day of the party, I had trouble parking at the school and ended up getting to the party 5 minutes late. All the other parent volunteers were already there, and Matty was visibly distressed. Throughout the party, I was preoccupied with the fact that I was late and the other parents weren't and that the teacher and other parents and kids had probably seen that Matty was upset. Clearly, I thought, they all believed that I had totally botched this whole class parent thing.

Later that day, I tried doing some cognitive work on myself. I recognized that I was overgeneralizing (assuming that I was a terrible class parent based on one piece of data, my lateness) and catastrophizing, as well as engaging in black-and-white thinking (because I didn't make it to the party on time, I was the worst). I examined the evidence from the party and realized that there was little data to suggest that I had botched it. Yes, I did arrive late. But the kids (including Matty) all had a great time. I spent time talking to the teacher and other parents, none of whom seemed to be at all put off by my lateness. Plus, I brought Oreos with me. If you've got Oreos, do you really need anything else to guarantee a successful kid party?

Feeling Like the "Worst Mom Ever"?
Try Ranking Yourself on a Scale of Moms

I've found that perfectionistic moms often bestow the "Worst Mom Ever" title on themselves when they perceive that they've fallen short of perfection. Noriko gave herself this label when she forgot to put her daughter's lunch in her book bag for day care. "Only the 'worst mom ever,'" she thought, "would send her kid to school without lunch."

Moms like Noriko who call themselves "the worst" fall into two main thinking traps: overgeneralizing (Noriko assuming that one small mistake, forgetting her daughter's lunch, was evidence of a much larger truth about her parenting) and black-and-white thinking (Noriko assuming that because she wasn't 100% perfect, she was 100% the worst). I encouraged Noriko to challenge her thinking by using a classic CBT strategy, the continuum technique, to rank herself on a scale of moms. If you, like Noriko, think you're an abject failure as a mom, this technique will be helpful for you.

To make your own continuum, draw a line with 0 at one end and 100 at the other. The 0 represents the worst mom you can think of, someone who does everything wrong. This can be someone you know, a celebrity, or even a fictional character (I've heard everything from Joan Crawford in *Mommie Dearest* to Betty Draper from *Mad Men* to "my mother-in-law"). The 100 represents the ideal mom, a paragon of motherhood who never loses her temper or cool and whose children are always well behaved and gracious. When I do this exercise with patients, they usually tell me that they cannot think of a real person who fits the "100" description, so they end up choosing another fictional character (I often hear June Cleaver or another fictional 1950s-era housewife). Next, pick someone who's at a 50, halfway between ideal and horrible. Here's where moms are readily able to identify real people they know who fit this description.

Finally, ask yourself where you think you fall. Noriko thought back to the many mom tasks she had completed over the past week alone and was able to collect a significant amount of evidence that she had done a lot of things well (if not entirely perfectly). For example, she had prepared her daughter's school lunch every day but the one in question; she had successfully consoled her daughter when she had a nightmare and couldn't fall back asleep; and she had signed her daughter up for a summer camp that she'd researched thoroughly and thought would be a good fit.

Considering this evidence, Noriko was able to conclude that she would definitely fall above a 50 in the motherhood department. That is, she was better than average. Sure, she screwed up sometimes, but she did a lot of things well and clearly cared deeply for her daughter.

Nearly all of my patients who rank themselves come to the conclusion that, all things considered, they're better-than-average moms. And I always stress that there is no mom on the planet who's at 100; and in fact, you don't need to be at 100 (or even close to 100) to be doing a good job of mothering.

The continuum technique can be especially helpful if you're doing a lot of comparison making; you can use it to determine how you actually compare to your target mom and to other moms more generally. You can also focus your continuum on a specific parenting issue as opposed to a more general idea (like your being the "worst mom ever"). For example, Angela, the mom who believed that she should never "lose it" with her kids, would benefit from creating a continuum of moms, noting how much different moms yell and where she falls in relation to these moms.

Further, the continuum technique can help you cope with feelings of failure relating to all kinds of topics, not just motherhood. If you believe that you're a subpar friend, family member, or employee, you can rank yourself on a scale of friends or family members or employees. I think you'll find that you rank higher than you might have anticipated.

Bake a Perfectionism Pie and Then Take Your Slices

Remember the pie chart technique from Chapter 5? We used it to demon-strate the limited control we have in many anxiety-provoking situations. We can also use it to illustrate all of the out-of-control factors that can mess up our "perfect" plans.

Gia decided to make a pie chart depicting her library story-time disas-ter. She drew a "pie" including all of the factors that contributed to her son Will's behavior that morning. She then estimated the percentage of the pie accounted for by each of the factors. She assigned a greater percentage to those factors that she believed had had a greater impact on her son's behav-ior. Gia's pie is featured below.

How many slices of this pie could Gia reasonably be assumed to be responsible for? The lecture, of course. And perhaps she could have made sure Will had a good snack before they left the house. (Regarding the "sleep" slice of the pie, I do not think any mother of young children should claim responsibility for her kid's sleep. Even moms who employ the best sleep practices may have poor sleepers.) The lecture and hunger slices together account for 20% of the pie. This means that Gia had control over 20% of the factors that ultimately contributed to her son's meltdown.

Should Gia be brave enough to sign up for another library story time, she needs to change her expectations of herself. Rather than challenging herself to orchestrate the perfect story time, she needs to focus on doing the best she can with her two slices of the pie. She can own these slices and at the same time recognize that even if she does the 100% best job with her slices, many other forces may conspire to make the event a complete disaster.

If you're pressuring yourself to create the perfect event or host the perfect

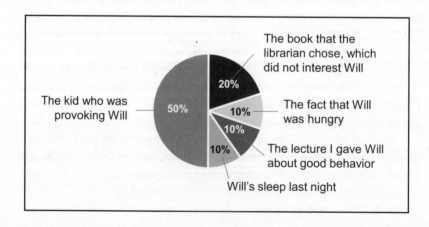

playdate or put together the perfect matched family costume for Halloween, consider making a pie chart and determining which slices of the pie you have some control over. Focus your efforts on those slices, but keep in mind that there are other slices that could very well thwart your grand plans. Here again you can see the acceptance and change concept from DBT playing out: you have to accept what you can't control and focus on what you can.

Ask Yourself, "What Is Perfectionism Costing Me?"

When I initially set out to make Matty's Thanksgiving costume, I really, really wanted to do a good job with it. This was his first year in a brand-new public school and one of the first opportunities I had to demonstrate what a thoughtful, engaged parent I was. I wanted Matty to fit in with the other kids, who I assumed would all be decked out in their Thanksgiving finery. I wanted to show everyone I was "on board" with the school's theme days and celebrations.

So as you know, I signed on to Pinterest, fully intending to make this costume. But when I looked up what other parents had done to make their kids' Thanksgiving costumes, my anxiety skyrocketed. For me to create an outfit that looked one-tenth as good as the ones on display would entail a significant amount of blood, sweat, and tears on my part. And given that most of my craft projects have historically ended in disaster (see: the great North Jersey pipe cleaner explosion of 1995), I couldn't even guarantee that putting in a ton of time and effort would yield anything remotely presentable. Plus I had a 2-year-old at home who was requiring my attention, not to mention my ongoing job commitments.

I wanted Matty to look perfect. I wanted to come off as the perfect kindergarten parent. I wanted to impress the class parents and teacher. But at what cost?

I decided to weigh the potential benefits of going all out against the potential drawbacks. Here's what I came up with:

Benefits of trying to make the "perfect" costume
- *Matty will look great.*
- *Matty will fit in with the other kids who have great costumes.*
- *Class parents and teachers will see that I'm a team player.*

Drawbacks of trying to make the "perfect" costume
- *Will take significant time, which I don't have right now.*
- *Will take significant energy, which I don't have right now.*

- *There is no guarantee that, despite my best efforts, this costume will turn out well.*
- *Crafting gives me anxiety.*

I weighed the benefits and drawbacks, and decided that I just didn't want to sacrifice my time, energy, and mental health for this cause. So I threw something together (which, as I mentioned, made Matty look like a piece of Massachusetts Bay seaweed) and sent Matty to school in it.

There were kids in his class who looked absolutely Pinterest-perfect at dropoff. Matty just wasn't one of them. I certainly didn't come across as the most perfect mom that day. And I'm not going to lie: I did feel like I'd failed at this particular parenting challenge, and I did feel self-conscious about my subpar effort. But I was able to recognize that these feelings were a small price to pay for avoiding a soul-crushing Pinterest deep dive.

One additional note on the topic of the benefits and drawbacks of perfectionism. Many of the more perfectionist moms with whom I work talk about the "icky" feeling they get when they perceive they are "half-assing" something. They truly feel uncomfortable when they don't think they're putting their best foot (or kid costumes or meals or parties) forward. I urge these moms to weigh this feeling of "ickiness" against the many things they have to sacrifice to get to perfection. Many end up deciding that they'd rather learn to endure the "ickiness" than continue to devote all of their time and energy to trying to meet unrealistic expectations. Below, I'll describe behavioral strategies aimed at helping moms tolerate the discomfort of acting imperfectly.

Challenge Your Perfectionism by Changing Your Behavior

As shifting your thinking can go a long way toward managing perfectionism, so too can changing the way you behave. Below, I share a number of helpful strategies for this purpose.

Cut Some Corners

Generally speaking, "cutting corners" is not seen as a positive thing; the phrase conjures images of lazy people shirking their responsibilities and doing a half-assed job. But if you're a perfectionist, committing ahead of time to letting go of some aspects of a project or experience can save you much-needed time and energy.

Kara, mom volunteer extraordinaire, decided to cut some corners with the annual preschool carnival she chaired. Kara had gone all out for last year's carnival. There were pony rides, bounce houses, and professional face painters. Kara herself designed T-shirts for the event and coordinated a number of different local food vendors to sell a diverse array of items. She brought in a karaoke machine and bins of craft supplies for art projects.

Everyone praised Kara on a job (exceedingly) well done. But Kara could barely take in the praise because she was completely depleted by the end of the event. When she agreed to chair the event again the following year, her family made her promise to do less this time around.

Here's what cutting corners looked like for Kara: She ordered generic T-shirts instead of designing them herself. She decided to serve only pizza instead of a variety of different foods from different vendors. She nixed the karaoke and provided art supplies for only one type of project. She kept the things that people really seemed to love: the pony rides, face painting, and bounce houses.

Kara had some difficulty cutting corners; she experienced that "icky" feeling of knowing she wasn't doing absolutely everything she could and worried that parents would find this year's carnival to be subpar. However, the parents and kids seemed happy, and most important, a significant amount of money was raised for the school, which was the whole point of the event.

Kara recognized that the only person who was truly affected by the "imperfect" carnival was her. She needed to lower her standards so she could survive future events with her sanity intact. Kara also came to understand that cutting corners was an exposure exercise for her. She knew that the more practice she got with lowering her standards, the more comfortable (and therefore the less "icky") she would feel.

Delegate, and Deal with It

In addition to doing away with some of the more labor-intensive aspects of the carnival, Kara reluctantly decided to delegate some tasks to her husband and willing friends. If you're a perfectionist, you know how difficult it can be to delegate. If you're not in charge of something, how can you possibly ensure that it's done according to your exceedingly high standards?

The answer, of course, is that you can't, which means that you have to live with the possibility (let's face it, probability) that things will not be done as well as they might have if you'd been in charge. Kara asked a friend to take care of the desserts, and when her friend ordered too few cake pops, some disappointed children revolted. This upset Kara, for whom running out of dessert was akin to serving cupcakes laced with E. coli. But Kara had to remind herself of the benefits and drawbacks of handing this task over to her friend. Yes, her friend had screwed up (a definite drawback), but Kara was spared yet another task that would have cost her additional time and energy (a definite benefit). And the truth was, there were plenty of alternative desserts for the kids to eat, so no one left the event hungry.

As Kara learned, the trick to delegating is coming to terms with the fact that others might not do the meticulous job that you would. Of course, you can try to avoid this by choosing only responsible people to delegate to. (Your neighbor who always backs his car into things? Probably not the best candidate to work the dunk tank.) But even then, you may find that the volunteer didn't quite do things to your standards. Hopefully, like Kara, you can remind yourself of the benefits and drawbacks of delegating, recognizing that the benefits (protecting your time, energy, and mental health) outweigh any drawbacks. We're going to talk a lot more about the importance of delegating, in the context of your relationship with your partner (Chapter 9) and extended family (Chapter 10).

Keep Yourself on Track with Schedules and Timers

If you're struggling to loosen your standards, try setting schedules and using timers, both of which will force you to set limits on yourself. Nicole was really into fashion and always wanted her 2- and 4-year-old sons to look red carpet ready. As a result, she routinely spent hours online shopping for her kids' latest duds. When she had only one kid, she truly loved finding him clothes. But she found shopping for two to be stressful, especially because she was "obsessed" with finding the best deals and scouring every available kid fashion site.

Nicole realized that her perfectionistic online shopping was overwhelming her and eating up some of the precious free time she had (not to mention costing her a fortune). She really liked being the one to buy kid clothes, however, and didn't want to delegate this particular task to her husband. So she decided to add clothes shopping to her schedule on a somewhat regular (but not too regular) basis. Before her scheduled shopping time, she made a list of the things she absolutely needed for each of her kids, along with two or three websites where she'd likely find these things. When she actually sat down to shop, she set a timer on her phone to alert her when her shopping time was over. And if she needed to shop for one specific item (say, for a new pair of sneakers to replace the pair that somehow got destroyed a mere two months after they were purchased), she set a timer for herself, ensuring that she only had time to buy the one item.

Scheduling and using timers enabled Nicole to stay in charge of the clothes shopping, which was important to her, while setting limits on how much of her time she devoted to it. Initially, she felt uncomfortable limiting her shopping time; she lamented that she might miss out on a really great deal or a really awesome outfit. But the longer she stuck with her schedule, the more comfortable she became and the happier she was to have more free time to devote to other things. As you've no doubt noticed, adhering to a shopping schedule was an exposure task for Nicole. And as with all exposure exercises, the anxiety/discomfort of the task decreased with continued practice.

You can use schedules and timers in a whole host of potentially perfectionistic situations. For example, if you worry that you're overpreparing for an event, like a birthday party, decide how much more time you actually wish to devote to preparing (or poll others if you're not sure how much time is reasonable). Then incorporate that prep time into your schedule and set a timer to alert yourself when that time is up. Schedules and timers can also prove helpful if you suspect you're becoming perfectionistic with routine kid stuff (e.g., spending too much time finding the "perfect" birthday gifts for friends or preparing for a school event). Once you've gotten used to following your schedule and timers, you'll find it easier to cope with the less-than-perfect outcomes.

Screw Up on Purpose

Daniella had been a perfectionist her entire life. Long before she had kids, she would take days to send a relatively mundane email to a coworker, reading and rereading it to make sure her grammar was "perfect." She spent hours getting herself ready for big events in the hopes of looking perfect and spent years (literally) planning what she deemed to be the "perfect" wedding (much to the dismay of her husband, parents, and in-laws).

Once Daniella had kids, her perfectionism hit a fever pitch, as there were suddenly so many more things she needed to do that theoretically could be done perfectly. This included everything from engineering perfect holidays to selecting perfectly matching outfits to finding the absolute perfect nursery school for her son to attend. I asked Daniella why she felt she needed to be perfect all the time. For example, what did she fear would happen if she sent an email with a grammatical mistake? Daniella didn't know, but suspected that it would probably "feel terrible" for her and that her coworker would think she was "stupid."

So I made her do it. Yep, therapist-sadist that I am, I actually made her send an email to a coworker that contained a misspelled word.

I should clarify that this assignment was an exposure exercise, one among many that I encouraged Daniella to carry out. The goal of each of these exercises was the same: to screw up on purpose. The consequences of messing up are never as terrible as perfectionists like Daniella fear they will be. And once they realize this, they become much less scared of messing up and much more willing to be less than perfect.

Of course I would never have encouraged Daniella to skip a crucial work meeting, send her son to school without his jacket in the winter, or try anything else that could be detrimental. But there were countless opportunities for her to practice small screwups. Daniella's exposure list included tasks like going to her son's day care with two different shoes on, walking around New York City with an umbrella when it was bright and sunny outside (my personal favorite because of the stares it inspired from confused New Yorkers), "forgetting" to RSVP to a birthday party, and not completing the book for her book club. Daniella worked her way up from the less stressful exposures at the bottom of her list to the more stressful ones at the top.

Over the course of her exposure practices, Daniella became increasingly more confident in her ability to tolerate the "icky" feeling that came with screwing up. She also learned that people did not react nearly as dramatically to her imperfect behaviors as she'd feared they would. Most important, she recognized that despite her planned mistakes, she was still successful as a mom and employee.

The Take-Home Message from Behavioral Strategies: You Don't Need to Be Perfect to Be Effective

Daniella's exposure work taught her that she didn't need to do everything perfectly to continue to function well as a mom and employee. If you practice lowering your standards, through exposures or cutting corners, I assure you that you'll come to the same conclusion.

Take some time to think back to your own parenting experiences that haven't turned out as you'd hoped they would. Were they unmitigated disasters? Or did things seem to work out all right in the end? I'm guessing that many of your parenting experiences have not gone smoothly but nonetheless have worked out fine, with your kids enjoying themselves in the end (or at least getting over their disappointments very quickly).

Much as we might want things like birthday parties and holidays (more on this in Chapter 12) to be perfect, our kids don't share our exacting standards and rarely if ever even notice when things have not gone according to plan. It's easy to lose sight of why we do things like throw birthday parties or volunteer at school. At the end of the day, we're doing this stuff for our kids, not for ourselves. And if they don't care about everything being perfect, why should we?

Focus on the Positive

Up to this point we've been discussing cognitive and behavioral strategies for lowering our expectations and standards. However, it's also important to focus on the positive—to recognize what we're good at and put these skills to use.

Keep a Diary of "Wins"

Most moms I know, even those who aren't preoccupied with being perfect, tend to focus on the things they perceive they're doing wrong or the strengths they lack. I can include myself in the mix here: I'm much more likely to use space in my mom brain to ruminate on my shortcomings than to acknowledge my talents and successes. You'll recognize this as an example of a thinking error we discussed in Chapter 4: discounting positives/negative filtering.

We need to challenge our tendency to discount positives by giving ourselves credit for what we're doing well. In Chapter 3 we talked about the lack of validation we get as mothers; few people tell us we're doing a good job. Actively acknowledging our wins can provide some of the validation we crave, which will help us soldier on each day, through family illnesses and toddler meltdowns and nauseating trips to trampoline parks.

There are a few ways we can provide ourselves with this validation. We can use the cognitive strategies we discussed above, examining the evidence and drawing a continuum, both of which demand that we collect data against self-critical thoughts. We can also keep a daily diary of our successes—parenting wins, work achievements, or any other situations in which our hard work or talents served us well.

I recently asked Aliyah, mother of a 4-year-old and an infant, to keep such a diary. Aliyah had hoped that her perfectionism would improve with her second child, since she now had some parenting experience under her belt. Instead, it seemed to have multiplied by a power of two. With both of her children, Aliyah always felt as if she was falling short of her (admittedly extremely high) standards.

Once she started keeping a daily diary of wins, however, Aliyah was surprised by the number of successes she was able to identify. Some were parenting wins (e.g., got Olivia to go down for her nap with minimal crying); some related to adult relationships (e.g., was able to be supportive via text to a stressed-out friend); and some were just random successes that brought her joy (e.g., was able to carry the recycling out to the curb without dropping any cans or bottles on the driveway).

Try keeping a daily diary of wins for yourself. Remember that no victory is too small, no talent too insignificant. Be sure to keep this diary on hand for those moments when you're berating yourself for falling far short of perfect. It will serve as a helpful reminder of all you've accomplished!

Play to Your Strengths

Once you've used a diary to acknowledge your strengths, start thinking strategically about how you can apply those strengths as a parent (and as a partner, friend, employee, etc.). When I was reflecting on the incident with the Pinterest Thanksgiving costume (the Pin-cident?), I came to the conclusion that I wouldn't get very far if I kept pressuring myself to do things I knew I was no good at. It would leave me feeling demoralized and "less than." Instead, I decided, I would try to play to my strengths. OK, so I couldn't make my son look good on Thanksgiving. But I *could* sit down with him and write a story about the First Thanksgiving. I *could* take him to the library and read Thanksgiving books with him. I *could* sing him that silly Thanksgiving song I learned in second grade.

I mentioned this in the last chapter, and I think it bears elaboration here: all of us moms should aim to play to our strengths. We need to stop focusing on the things we *can't* do and start focusing on the things we *can* do. It's important to figure out what we're good at and incorporate it into our parenting, whether it's crafting or singing, cooking or coaching.

Using her diary of wins, Aliyah made a list of things she was good at and a list of things she didn't do so well, which she titled "Aliyah's wins and fails." Aliyah considered her fails first. She was not much of a cook, which meant that she should probably stick to basic recipes rather than trying and failing to make gourmet meals like her foodie friends did. She didn't know the first thing about dance (nor did she care much about it), so she was clearly not the best candidate to be one of the backstage "dance moms" at her daughter's dance school. She was hopeless with Legos (an affliction she and I share) and had to concede that, instructions be damned, she was not going to be much help when her daughter needed an assist with the Lego Friends beach cabana.

Aliyah was, however, a good athlete, a good listener, and very organized. This meant that she was ideally suited to coach her daughter's peewee soccer team, comfort her daughter when she had issues with a mean kid at nursery school, and make/keep track of her infant son's doctor's appointments. Aliyah found that engaging in these tasks was so much more satisfying and validating than trying in vain to puree organic squash or corral a group of ballerinas backstage.

All moms are good at something (and usually, many things!) and benefit when they focus on the things they *can* do. What's more, many moms discover that they possess fairly obscure but surprisingly helpful talents that they can use to their advantage. I'm thinking of some of my own mom friends here—like my friend who is expert at making the sides of gingerbread houses stick together using the not-very-adhesive packaged icing; or my friend who specializes in the fine art of wrangling groups of kids at birthday parties; or my friend who is a ticket savant, able to secure seats to even the most popular kid shows and events.

What I've learned, and I think you'll learn too, is that playing to your strengths feels so much better than obsessing over your weaknesses.

9

"How Can I Nurture My Relationship When I'm Busy Nurturing This Kid?"
Navigating Changes and Challenges with Your Partner

Taylor and her husband both worked demanding full-time jobs. Before having their son, they agreed that they would share the parenting load 50/50. But by the time their son was a toddler and their daughter came along, Taylor's load had grown far heavier than her husband's. She was the one who spent her lunch hour at work managing doctor's appointments and buying kid stuff online and rushing to the grocery store. Her husband, meanwhile, spent his lunch hour exercising. Taylor kept the entire family's schedule in her mom brain and signed her son up for all of his activities. Plus Taylor was the only one waking up in the middle of the night when either kid cried out. Taylor felt significant anger and resentment toward her husband. Where was the "50/50 partner" she'd been promised?

Alice knew that being a parent would be incredibly stressful, but she and her wife had always approached every stressor as a team and didn't expect that parenthood would be any different. She was surprised, then, when parenting took a toll on her marriage. She didn't realize that she would barely see her wife—it felt like one of them was always off with one kid while the other was always off with the other one. Whenever they managed to have an actual conversation, it typically centered around the kids and often ended in frustration, especially when they discussed discipline issues. Alice thought her wife yelled too much, while her wife thought Alice was too lenient. Alice routinely referred to her kids as "the bombs that dropped on our marriage."

My husband travels a fair amount for work, especially during the summer months. Since both of my sons were born in April, this meant that there were weeks during the summer when I was on my own with a newborn, and later, a newborn and a 3-year-old. When my husband FaceTimed me, often from some hotel on the West Coast, I burned with resentment. Here he was, free to eat and sleep and move about as he pleased, while I was saddled with all the responsibility. By the time he returned home, I was angry at him and practically threw the children in his face. But he was always exhausted, having taken a flight at an inconvenient time to get home as soon as possible. He told me that he hated these trips and felt incredibly guilty for not being home. Which then made me feel guilty for feeling angry at him. Travel was an unavoidable fact of his job. Why was I taking it out on him? Why was I so mad when he was doing the best he could?

Numerous studies confirm what anyone who's ever had a child knows: babies put a significant strain on romantic relationships. Post-baby, marital satisfaction and frequency of sex decline. Clearly, Alice is not being over-dramatic when she describes children as bombs that drop on a relationship.

Couples with babies and small kids operate on little sleep and have wildly fluctuating emotions. They have virtually no time alone together to talk about the bomb that just dropped on them and how they can effectively manage it. Many couples, like Taylor and her husband, struggle to achieve a more fair division of labor. Further, each member of a couple comes to parenthood with his or her own set of values around parenting, which can become a source of conflict if their values differ significantly.

Marriages and partnerships are incredibly complex, and no two couples are the same. Covering all of the potential minefields for couples with little children would take an entire book (or more likely, a whole bunch of books; see the Resources for some suggestions). My goal in this chapter is not to provide comprehensive couples therapy, nor to suggest solutions for the many societal inequities that force moms into traditional gender roles (if only I could!). Instead, I want to share a number of clear-cut strategies from CBT and DBT that have helped my mom patients cope with the fallout from the kid bomb.

A few notes before we dive into the chapter. First, I use the term "partner," not "husband," throughout the chapter, and I do not assume that the partner in question is male; in fact, I've found that these couples strategies work well for individuals of all gender identities and sexual orientations. I also don't assume that the partner in question is necessarily the biological parent of your kid(s). I do assume, however, that the partner spends a significant amount of time with you and with your kid(s) and lives in your household (or at least stays with you very often).

Second, I recommend that you take some time to revisit the relationships section of your values questionnaire, and complete it if you have not yet done so (see Chapter 3). As you're reading about strategies for approaching your partner, it's important to remember what you value about being in a committed relationship and co-parenting. As always, let your values guide your decisions about whether and how you choose to address certain issues in your relationship.

Finally, my hope is that partners will get on board with these strategies, as some of them (e.g., dividing up family tasks) require their participation. However, if your partner can't get on board and your relationship is suffering, consider seeking couples therapy, where you can work on your differences together. See the Resources for more information about accessing couples therapy.

Schedule "Face Time" with Your Partner

If there is one message I want you to take away from this chapter, it's that **you need to talk to your partner.** I don't care how little space you have in your mom brain, or how little alone time you have with your partner; you need to make time for communication. I can't tell you how many times I've talked to moms about problems they have had with their partners that could have been avoided if they'd talked openly about their feelings and communicated their needs.

Perhaps the most significant barrier to getting new parents talking is purely logistical—they barely ever see each other, and when they do, they're usually covered in poop or staring dead-eyed at a show on Netflix. I'm always amazed by how abruptly communication patterns change when kids enter the picture. Moms who previously talked to their partners for hours over dinner every night will go days without talking to their partners about anything substantive.

Remember in Chapter 6 when we talked about adding basic things like showering and exercising to your regular schedule? I think it's also important to schedule in face time with your partner, when you and your partner take time out for actual face-to-face conversations. How frequently you do this is up to you, but I would suggest at least once a week. Decide on a time and place that works for both of you. Be sure to select a time when you're not typically wiped out, and commit to putting your phones away so you can really focus on each other.

I know that for some couples, finding time when both parents are available (and reasonably coherent) is a tall order. Mira and her husband both worked crazy hours and purposely worked late on alternate nights so that one of them was always home for bedtime with the baby. Mira recognized that they'd have to do their face time on the weekends. And because she went to bed far earlier than her husband did, she decided that talking during her daughter's Saturday naptime was the best option. Mira honestly wasn't thrilled about devoting time that she typically used for TV catch-up to sitting and chatting with her husband. But she recognized that this might be her only opportunity to talk to him, something she valued and recognized as important to the health of their relationship.

What Should I Do during Face Time?

So now you've scheduled face time with your partner. What should be on your agenda? You can of course use the time to catch up on your day or discuss the previous night's episode of *The Bachelor*. You can review your and your kids' schedules for the week and remind each other about commitments and responsibilities (much more on this later when we discuss the "List of Lists").

You can also use the time to have more difficult conversations—about your roller-coaster emotions, for example, or about something your partner did that upset you or something you need from your partner. Needless to say, it's much harder to talk about negative emotions than to gossip about why Jenn F. didn't get a rose last night despite her successful date. Below, we'll discuss a number of strategies for effectively venting, arguing, and asking for what you need.

What to Do When You Just Need to Hear "That Sucks"

Throughout the book we've talked about the emotional roller-coaster ride that is motherhood. You need to have sounding boards you can turn to—people who can listen to how you're feeling and offer validation or advice. Your partner is a prime candidate. Your partner likely knows you more intimately than anyone else. And your partner, like you, is experiencing firsthand what it's like to have really small kids. (Of course, there are plenty of times when you might want to vent *about* your partner or when you feel like your partner is too closely involved with situations with your kids to be an effective sounding board. That's when you turn to friends. More on that in Chapter 11.)

Scheduled face times with your partner are prime opportunities for venting, when you can let your mom brain emotions loose (think of it as a more public version of an "emotional check-in"). Before you start venting, however, I recommend that you clarify exactly what you need from your partner. Do you just want an audience while you yell and scream at the universe, or do you need help solving a problem (or both)?

So many moms I've worked with have complained that their partners respond to their venting by trying to problem-solve. In fact, this scenario was featured in one of my very favorite shows, *Parks and Recreation*. In the episode, a very pregnant Ann gets upset when her baby daddy Chris keeps trying to cure her pregnancy ills with foot rubs and health-food remedies. At the end of the episode, Chris realizes what Ann really wants from him: simply for him to listen to her and respond, "That sucks."

If all you need to hear is "That sucks," tell your partner that, before you even start venting. For example, "I want to talk about my nursing issues, but I don't want to try to solve them. I've spent 6 months trying to solve them. I just want to dump out my feelings and use some expletives and then get some ice cream. Sound good?" If, on the other hand, you want to problem-solve, tell your partner this, too. Maybe you need feedback on a situation at work or want to brainstorm how to sleep-train more effectively. Whatever you need, let your partner know (much more on how to ask for what you need below).

What to Do When You Want to Lock Your Partner Out of the House

New parents often disagree on things. Unfortunately, differences of opinion are an inevitable part of new parenthood—we all love our kids a lot, we want what we believe is best for them, and we will fight to the death to get it. In some cases, these disagreements culminate in screaming matches, where unkind words are hurled back and forth. This is especially likely to happen when both partners are sleep and energy deprived and lack the mental resources to filter what they're saying to each other.

So many new parent conflicts go something like this: Tired, irritable

Jeff makes a decision or has an opinion that tired, irritable Carissa is not on board with. Carissa, fully in emotion mind due to the aforementioned sleep deprivation and irritability, lashes out at Jeff, accusing him of being wrong. Jeff lashes out in return, defensively arguing his case. Screaming ensues. Anger persists. Ultimately, no changes are made.

As an alternative to that scenario, consider this one: Tired, irritable Amy notices that she's getting really angry with Greg. Instead of choosing this moment, when she's fully steeped in emotion mind, to tell Greg what she really thinks of him, she decides to take an "adult time-out." She tells Greg that she's upset and can't deal and needs to take some space and cool off a bit. She lets Greg know that she'll be coming back to him (perhaps during their next scheduled face time?) to discuss her feelings.

It won't surprise you to hear that I favor the second scenario over the first. Emotion-mind moments like these are the very worst moments to talk with anyone—partners, friends, kids—about negative feelings and grievances. We simply will not be able to approach these topics in a measured way that inspires understanding and problem solving; instead, we will yell and be on the defensive.

I urge you to consider taking an "adult time-out" when you're very angry or frustrated with your partner. Once you've had a chance to cool down, plan out how and when you are going to approach your partner about your feelings. Rehearse what you are going to say ahead of time so you can make your case in a calm, confident manner.

Scheduled face times present an ideal opportunity to discuss bad feelings and perceived slights. In fact, I think the "face" aspect of face time is particularly important here. I am constantly urging moms not to engage in disagreements over texts and email. It is impossible to read tone or body language over texts/emails, and texts in particular are often sent off quickly and impulsively, resulting in both partners saying things they instantly regret.

Below, we'll talk about how to engage in a face-to-face conversation about a conflict or difference of opinion using "I" statements, validation, open-ended questions, and summary statements.

Start Off with "I" Statements

To effectively communicate your anger, hurt, frustration, or any other negative emotion, try using "I" statements. With "I" statements, you discuss conflicts in terms of how they made you feel, rather than in terms of all of the things you perceived your partner did wrong. I know that many people view "I" statements as somewhat of a couples therapy cliché. However, I find them to be extremely effective for communicating negative feelings in a measured, nonjudgmental way.

A mom I once worked with, Gloria, recounted how she yelled at her husband for allowing their daughter to go on an age-inappropriate slide at a birthday party. Her comment to her husband went something like this: "Seriously? Do you not see the sign that says that that slide is for children over 5? SHE IS 3!!! She could have broken her neck!!!" As you can see, Gloria attacked her husband here and implied that he was an irresponsible parent. Her husband responded that she was being "overprotective" and stormed off.

Here's an "I" statement version of the same comment: "I worry when you let Ella play on equipment made for older kids. She is a risk taker, as you know, and doesn't know her limitations. I fear she'll hurt herself. Can we talk about how to keep her safe?"

"I" statements are effective because they do not inspire defensiveness in the other person (unless they are just insults masked as "I" statements, as in "I really feel upset when you're acting like a complete asshole"). In her comment to her husband, Gloria basically accused him of being negligent, which caused him to defend his own behavior. In the revised comment, Gloria just expressed her feelings—and how can her husband possibly argue with her feelings? The revised comment would be far more likely to lead to an apology and problem solving (especially if it's followed by validation—see below) than a blowout fight.

Validate, Validate, Validate (and Then Validate Some More)

Validation is a core concept in DBT. According to DBT, validating another person does not mean agreeing with the person. It involves communicating that another's thoughts, feelings, and behaviors are understandable, given the circumstances. Validation also involves acknowledging any aspects of another's perspective that may actually ring true.

According to Marsha Linehan, creator of DBT, validating another person's perspective has several important benefits. It lets the person know that you're listening and value the person's opinion. By indicating that you understand where the person is coming from, you're shifting focus away from trying to determine which one of you is "right." This reduces anger and defensiveness and makes effective problem solving and emotional support far more likely.

Remember my story about my husband's traveling? I was so, so angry at him for not having to be home with the kids that I truly didn't consider his perspective. Here was my assumption: that he was sleeping as late as he wanted; that he was eating delicious food and getting to schmooze with actual adults who didn't want to talk about anything related to babies; and that he was enjoying the (typically far superior) West Coast weather.

But here was my husband's reality: he was waking every morning at 5:00 A.M. East Coast time (our daily wake-up time at home), which was 2:00 A.M. West Coast time; his day was so packed with meetings that he had to grab gross lunches from the hotel lobby; and he had to attend work dinners every night during which he had to be "on," even though he'd been up since 2:00 A.M. He usually took a red-eye to get home as soon as possible after his meetings were over, which meant he was walking through the door of our house on 4 hours of sleep, max. And he was wracked with guilt for missing the whole week and not being there for me and the kids. Sounds just as glamorous as I'd pictured, right?

I wish I'd approached my husband with the aim of validating his experience. If I had, I would have recognized that he had had it pretty bad, too. Instead of yelling at him, throwing the kids in his face, and storming off, I could have said something like this: "It sounds like your trip was incredibly stressful and that you barely got any sleep. It was really stressful here, too, which is why I'm at the end of my rope. So we're both exhausted and stressed, which sucks. What can we do about it?"

Acknowledging that the week sucked for both of us would have made it feel like we were a team (misery loves company, right?) instead of adversaries. Perhaps we could have put our heads together and figured out a way to relieve our stress—maybe by calling a grandparent or friend or sitter over to give us both a break (since we clearly both needed relief). And validating each other would have spared hard feelings on both sides.

To validate successfully, you have to truly listen to what your partner is telling you about his or her experience. If you're having trouble listening, consider asking your partner open-ended questions, which demand an actual explanation instead of a "yes" or "no." This would mean the difference between "Were you pissed at me when I invited our neighbors to stay for dinner?" and "You seemed pissed off after I invited our neighbors to stay for dinner. Can you tell me why?" Asking open-ended questions like this will encourage your partner to share more and demonstrate that you're interested in the response.

I also encourage you to periodically summarize what your partner is saying. For example, "So you felt like I went ahead and invited them to stay without asking you if it was OK, when you were hoping for a nice quiet evening at home." By making summary statements, you're demonstrating that you're listening and ensuring that you're understanding what your partner is expressing.

Once you and your partner have validated each other, consider moving on to problem solving. If, however, one or both of you is too steeped in emotion mind to problem-solve effectively, make a plan to problem-solve at a later time, perhaps during your next scheduled face time.

There is a particular type of validation that I think is especially important for new parents: validation of your partner's parenting values. See the box on the facing page for details.

How to Ask Your Partner for What You Need

So many moms complain that their partner is not meeting their needs. These needs are sometimes of the practical variety (e.g., partners not pulling their weight with household chores—more on that in the next section) or the emotional variety (e.g., partners not being available as an emotional sounding board), or both. When I ask these moms if they've ever asked for what they need, many of them confess that they haven't. Some believe that their partners should be able to intuit what they need and don't believe they should have to explicitly ask them. Others just don't feel comfortable asserting themselves.

I said this in Chapter 6 regarding asking for help, and I'll say it again here: you cannot expect your partner or anyone else to be able to know what's happening in your mom brain or intuit what you need in any given moment. If your needs aren't being met, whether they're trivial or significant, it's imperative that you communicate this to your partner. Fortunately, there is a strategy from DBT, DEAR MAN, that makes asking for what you need relatively easy.

DEAR MAN is an acronym that stands for Describe, Express, Assert, Reinforce, stay Mindful, Appear confident, and Negotiate. In the box on page 172, I define each of the components of DEAR MAN.

To clarify what a DEAR MAN approach looks like, let's talk through the example of Donya, who used DEAR MAN to get her husband to change his behavior around her parents.

Donya's husband, Brian, was never particularly patient with her parents, who Donya acknowledged could be "overbearing" and "opinionated."

Validating Our Partner's Parenting Values

We all come to parenting with very different ideas of how children should be raised. These ideas are often a product of our own upbringing. Sometimes we model ourselves after our parents, making similar choices to the ones they made for us. Other times, we consciously try to do things very differently from the way our parents did them.

At the start of the chapter I mentioned Alice, who was frustrated by how much her wife Shannon yelled at their children. Alice came from a home where emotions—good or bad—were not usually expressed. Shannon, on the other hand, came from a self-described "loud" family, where everyone expressed emotions very dramatically. While Alice was uncomfortable with yelling, Shannon didn't see anything wrong with it; in fact, she believed that Alice was too lenient and "let the kids get away with everything."

In treatment, Alice worked to develop her validation skills. With time, Alice was able to see that neither she nor Shannon was "wrong" in the way they approached discipline; they were both just influenced by the very different ways they were disciplined as children. Once Alice was able to validate Shannon's perspective, she was in a much better place to have a series of thoughtful conversations with Shannon about how they could implement time-outs when the kids misbehaved, a better alternative than yelling or failing to respond.

But after Donya and Brian had children and Donya's parents started coming by all the time, Brian reached a breaking point. He grew tired of hearing their opinions about how he should parent and was annoyed that they continually brought over (huge, impossible-to-assemble) new toys for the kids.

As a result, Brian started leaving the room whenever Donya's parents arrived at their house, which created an awkward situation for Donya. She felt compelled to explain where Brian was ("He's working on a project in the garage"; "He had a really long week at work and he needs to rest"). This was starting to upset Donya, especially after her mother asked her if Brian "hated" them. Donya decided to use DEAR MAN to discuss this issue with Brian.

DEAR MAN Defined

- **Describe.** Describe the situation in question in very clear terms, using facts only.
- **Express.** Express your feelings and opinions about the situation. This is a great place to use "I" statements.
- **Assert.** Clearly ask for what you want, or say no if you do not want to do something that's been asked of you.
- **Reinforce.** Reinforce the other person by describing the positive consequences of her doing what you've asked her to do (and/or the negative consequences if she doesn't do what you've asked her to do).
- **stay Mindful.** Remain focused on what you need. Don't get distracted, and stay on topic. Be a "broken record" and continue to ask for what you need. If the other person attacks you, ignore his attacks and continue to ask for what you need.
- **Appear confident.** Maintain eye contact. Adopt a confident physical posture. Speak loudly and clearly. Don't weaken your argument with phrases like "I'm not sure."
- **Negotiate.** Be open to reducing what you're asking for or exploring alternative solutions to the problem. If the situation involves you saying no to something, think about things you are comfortable saying yes to that might solve the problem.

During their next scheduled face time, Donya presented a DEAR MAN appeal:

- **Describe.** "Every time my parents come over, you leave the room. Last week my mother asked me if you 'hate' them and asked what they'd done to make you avoid them."

- **Express.** "When my parents come over and you disappear, I really struggle. I feel pressure to make excuses for you and awkward when I'm making those excuses. I feel sad that you don't have a better relationship with my parents, and I feel bad for my parents, who know that you don't like them. I also feel angry with you for not making more of an effort, even though I recognize that my parents can be really difficult sometimes."

• **Assert.** "I would really like it if you would make a conscious effort to actually talk with my parents when they come over."

• **Reinforce.** "If you made more of an effort, I would be in a far better mood at the end of those visits. As a result, we'd be far less likely to fight after they leave. I worry that if things keep going as they are, I will start to feel very angry and resentful, which will drive a significant wedge into our marriage."

• **stay Mindful.** When Brian emphasized how "annoying" her parents could be, Donya validated his perspective and continued to emphasize that she wanted Brian to stay in the room and talk with her parents when they came over.

• **Appear confident.** Donya decided to practice her appeal to Brian ahead of time, looking at herself in the mirror while making her request. She focused on making good eye contact, speaking loudly and clearly, and adopting a confident posture. By the time she actually made her appeal to Brian, she was firm and direct.

• **Negotiate.** Donya and Brian talked through a number of different ideas to "sweeten the deal" for Brian. Donya agreed that she would talk to her parents about stopping the constant flow of toys. Donya and Brian also discussed the possibility of coming up with a few conversation topics in advance of her parents' visits. There were certain things, like home renovation/repair ideas and traveling, that Brian actually enjoyed discussing with her parents; it made sense, then, for him to plan to bring up these topics. Finally, Brian and Donya agreed on a "signal" that Brian would give Donya if at any point her parents were really bothering him. At that point, Brian would take his own adult time-out for a few minutes, while Donya would try to change topics and involve her parents in something different (e.g., taking them outside to look at the garden, asking her son to sing them a song from school).

After their DEAR MAN discussion, Donya found that Brian was far more willing to be present and patient with her parents. His behavior was by no means perfect, and there were certainly times when his adult time-outs lasted longer than she would have liked. But generally speaking, the situation improved significantly.

Don't Forget the Positive Feelings, Too!

To this point, we've been talking about discussing negative feelings with your partner. But it's also important to let your partner know when you're feeling happy or doing well. Consider sharing those moments when you're feeling great about parenthood—when your kid has done something amazing, perhaps, or when you feel you've crushed it as a mom. I've found that parenting wins are even more gratifying when you're able to share them with a partner.

You should also make sure to express gratitude when your partner has done something you've appreciated, whether it's something minor or something labor-intensive. Some examples of things your partner might do that are worthy of a "thank-you" include accompanying your kid to a preschool gym party you're desperate to skip; taking charge of the nursery school pickups so you can spend more time at work; making kid lunches; or giving you an unsolicited back rub.

Yes, you need to let your partner know when you've been disappointed or when you feel you need more. But you need to balance that with positive feedback so that your partner knows you're recognizing the efforts made and feels encouraged to keep making them. Positive feedback also helps cushion the blow of any negative feedback you do give. One mom I worked with started every face-time conversation with a positive comment before moving on to negative emotions or grievances.

While we're on the topic of gratitude, remember that you deserve to feel appreciated, too! Even if you and your partner have an agreement (based on practical needs and availability) that you'll handle certain tasks with the kids, you have a right to expect regular expressions of gratitude. Go ahead and ask for them, using your DEAR MAN skills.

Date nights are great opportunities for you and your partner to express appreciation to each other. See the box on the facing page about how to do date nights right.

While we're talking about focusing on the positive, one more point: try to remember that you and your partner are in this together. I mentioned this idea before, when discussing my husband's business trips. Had we approached the situation as team players (both of whom desperately needed to get benched for a while so that we could recharge), we would have focused our efforts on recharging as opposed to bickering. If you can view yourselves not as adversaries but as teammates who have each other's back, you'll be so much more likely to respond to stressful situations with collaborative problem solving.

How to Do Date Nights

Regular date nights can be very helpful for maintaining intimacy and remembering who you were before you had kids. But it can be tough to make them a priority.

If you find date night impossible, for either financial or logistical reasons (or both), you may need to get creative. In Jancee Dunn's terrific book *How Not to Hate Your Husband after Kids,* she discusses sharing babysitting duties with another family so that you regularly leave your children with them for date nights and they regularly leave their children with you. When your kids are older, you can look into community-wide parent nights out, which are often available at churches, synagogues, YMCAs, or kid play/gym spaces. As Dunn points out, these places are often considerably less costly than individual babysitters.

I also tell my mom patients to try to engineer regular date nights at home. For example, you can commit to one weekend night a week or every other week when you and your partner wait to eat dinner until after the kids are in bed and do something fun after dinner, like watch a movie or have sex (more on that in a bit). This of course becomes more possible as your kids get a little older and are more reliable nighttime sleepers.

If you can, try to steer your date night conversation toward positive, non-kid-related topics (or at least try to avoid the boring, logistical kid stuff, which is better saved for your face times). You might even want to think up some good nonkid topics ahead of time or plan to use the opportunity to express appreciation to your partner. Whatever form it takes, aim to make your "date night" an opportunity for positive partner interactions.

Let's Talk about Sex

Here's some news I doubt any of you will find shocking: according to research, couples report having less sex after a baby arrives. This is especially true during the first months after a baby is born. For a number of reasons, sex after baby may not be super-appealing: we have less time and energy for sex, we're always exhausted, our mom brains are overtaxed and often consumed with complicated feelings, we may be undergoing hormonal changes (especially if we're nursing), and we may be recovering from birth injuries. Many moms report that nursing in particular serves as an anti-aphrodisiac. As a mom once told me, "I used to look forward to taking my boobs out for sex. Now that I spend all day with my leaky boobs hanging out, I look forward to putting them away."

Sex doesn't always improve after babies become toddlers. If you've spent all day with kids hanging all over your body, you may not be excited about an activity that involves an adult person hanging all over your body. And of course, toddlers seem to intuit when you and your partner are about to get it on, choosing that exact moment to wake up and scream for you.

Many of the moms I treat are reluctant to talk to their partners about sex. Which I get: it's an awkward topic. But maintaining an open dialogue is so important. You need to let your partner know where you're at, even if you're revealing that you don't want to touch him or her with a ten-foot pole. At the very least, it will give you the opportunity to explain your lack of desire so that your partner can validate your experience.

Openly discussing sex will also give you both the opportunity to consider different methods of maintaining intimacy. There are many ways you can express affection without actually having to have sex, by doing things like setting aside time to snuggle in front of the TV (or even just choosing to sit next to each other while you're checking your phones). Further, any sort of positive interaction with your partner, be it helping each other out, expressing gratitude, or saying something flattering about the other's appearance, can set the stage for intimacy.

There may be specific circumstances (times of day, certain environments) in which you feel more interested in sex, or there may be certain things you can put into place that will make sex more likely. Isla, for example, found that she was much more likely to want to have sex at night if she got a break to do her own thing after dinner. She told her husband this, and he agreed to completely take over the kids' nighttime routine at least one day a week so that Isla could have her downtime.

In fact, Isla and her husband went so far as to designate Friday night as "sex night." I know making a plan for getting it on doesn't sound romantic, but it can ensure that it actually happens. And if you know sex is coming, you can think about it ahead of time, which can make it easier to get into the mood when the time comes.

The most important thing you and your partner can do is keep talking about sex, even if (or especially if!) it's the last thing on your mind. Like Isla and her husband, you should devote time to figuring out what you can both do to maintain intimacy.

One last note: Some couples find that they continue to struggle with intimacy issues even after making a concerted effort to talk openly about them and problem-solve. If this is the case for you and your partner, consider seeking out sex therapy (for you, your partner, or both of you together). For more on sex after baby, including information about sex therapy, see the Resources section.

Divide and Conquer: How to Share the Household Load

Remember Taylor, from the start of the chapter? Before her son was born, she and her husband agreed to split the child care 50/50. But once her kids entered the picture, she found herself doing the majority of the child care, including the nighttime comforting. Taylor felt extremely resentful toward her husband and didn't understand how they'd strayed so far from their original plan of joint parenting.

For his part, Taylor's husband, John, wasn't actively shirking responsibilities; he had just fallen into the habit of letting Taylor take the reins. Taylor admitted that while he always did what was asked of him, she rarely asked him to do things. This was because she often found it easier just to go ahead and do things herself.

I've heard some version of Taylor's story many, many times, from mom patients as well as friends. It always goes something like this: well-meaning couple vows to co-parent, only to have Mom end up with the largest share of the parenting burden. This is consistent with what's been found in numerous research studies, which indicate that mothers spend more time with children and more time on household tasks than do fathers.

The gender gap in parenting is a complicated problem, born of long-held cultural expectations for what maternal and paternal roles should be. Most child care tasks are still thought to be "women's work," and women are socialized from a young age to be the ones to do it. Moms often shoulder what is commonly referred to as the "mental load" or "invisible labor": they are tasked with nearly everything that needs to be done to run a household, like scheduling appointments, purchasing clothes and gifts, communicating with doctors and teachers, and providing emotional support. You may also have heard of the concept of "the second shift," describing how working mothers are expected to work two jobs (their day job and their job managing kids and household responsibilities).

Clearly, this inequity is a huge issue that will be remedied only by a large-scale shift in norms, attitudes, and expectations (for some interesting writing on what needs to happen for this to occur, see the Resources). We can, however, strive to make changes at a more micro level by using CBT strategies to create a more fair division of labor within individual partnerships.

Two notes before we move on. First, I'm aware that not all of you want to mess with the division of labor in your house. You may be OK with things as they are and even value being the one "in charge" of everything (this should be reflected in the values worksheet you completed in Chapter 3). If so, no need to upend things.

Also, same-sex couples are known to divide household work more evenly than their heterosexual counterparts. However, this does not mean that same-sex couples are immune to difficulties with equitable parenting. For example, one of my patients and her wife were committed to splitting tasks 50/50. But because her wife earned more, her wife's work was deemed more important. This meant that my patient was often left to pick up the household slack when her wife was swamped at work.

Divide Up Your "List of Lists"

Earlier in the book I mentioned a *New York Times* editorial entitled "Mom, the Designated Worrier." In it, Judith Shulevitz argues that moms tend to be the ones who worry and this worry inspires them to take charge of child care and household responsibilities. Moms keep track of these responsibilities in what Shulevitz calls the "List of Lists," which details everything that needs to be done for the kids and all the steps that each of these tasks entails.

The problem with moms being the keeper of the List of Lists is that their partners are sometimes not privy to what's on the list. Like Taylor's husband, partners often don't even know what needs to be done. It just gets done, so they assume all is well.

If you're looking to parent more fairly, you need to sit down with your partner and write out your "List of Lists." You need to include all kid- and household-related tasks. No task is too insignificant (in fact, it's often the case that insignificant tasks, taken together, end up being very time-consuming).

Once you've got the List of Lists in front of you, you need to decide who will be responsible for each of the tasks. One important factor to consider is logistics. Don't assign yourself or your partner any tasks that you cannot actually carry out due to, say, your work schedules or other commitments. Find tasks that work for each of you, given your respective schedules. Even moms or dads who have busy, inflexible work schedules can find things to do that don't have to be completed on a certain schedule or at a certain time, like online shopping for next season's clothes, vacation planning, or compiling and boxing old baby stuff.

Another important factor to consider is each partner's strengths. Remember in Chapter 8 when we discussed the importance of playing to your strengths as a parent? You and your partner need to be realistic about your talents and choose tasks from the list that you are best suited for.

Take me and my husband, for example. When it comes to picking out little boys' clothes, I am far better suited to the task. However, when it comes to pitching a tent, my husband clearly has me beat. This means that I buy the clothes and my husband is in charge of the Cub Scouts stuff. (And I mean *all* the stuff—attaching patches to my son's uniform, keeping track of den meetings, volunteering at den and pack meetings, etc. If all he did was take Sam on the twice-yearly camping trips, I'd end up being stuck with the bulk of the Scouts burden.) We've divvied up our List of Lists according to what each of us does well.

It's important to note that tasks on the list don't need to be divided exactly 50/50. If one parent works far more hours than the other, or is responsible for something significant (like helping aging parents, for instance), it might make sense for the parent who has more time to take on more tasks. What's most critical is that you and your partner spend time going through the list together and mutually agree upon which of you will take on which tasks, based on your schedules and strengths.

On the next page, you'll see an excerpt from Taylor and John's List of Lists. Notice that they're each assigned specific tasks so that both of them know exactly what they're responsible for. And notice too that, as with my husband and Cub Scouts, each of them has taken on different tasks in their entirety, not just one small aspect of a task.

Finally, their list refers to their shared calendar, something I urge all families to adopt. This should be a calendar that includes all relevant kid, work, and family commitments and that each partner can see and contribute to. Personally, I've found an online shared calendar to be most effective, although some of my patients still like using large whiteboards.

Remember that the List of Lists has to be updated often as the kids get older and more activities get added into the mix. Be sure to keep it current, or else it will cease to be helpful.

Writing out the List of Lists and assigning tasks sounds straightforward in theory, but can actually be quite challenging. The following are a few difficulties that my mom patients commonly face, along with ideas for navigating them.

An Excerpt from Taylor and John's List of Lists

John

Prep Brendan's lunch for nursery school daily
Dishes (including bottles): Mon, Weds, Fri
Take out garbage (Thursday)/recycling (Friday)
Brendan's pee wee soccer: Sign up (deadline in August); Purchase
*   uniform, cleats, shin guards; Note games on shared calendar; Prep*
*   Brendan for games*
Yard work: mowing, planting
Laundry on weekends
Nighttime: if either kid cries out second half of night (1–6)

Taylor

Schedule doctor and dentist appointments (and put on shared
*   calendar)*
Buy birthday gifts for family and friends
Dishes (including bottles): Tues, Thurs, Sat, Sun
Buy kids' clothing
Laundry on weekdays
Nighttime: if either kid cries out first half of night (8–1)

Taylor and John

Attend doctor and dentist appointments
Attend events at Brendan's school
Grocery shopping (switch off weeks)
Stay "in the loop" with nursery school (ensure that school sends emails
*   to both of us)*
Weekend plans with friends or family (note on shared calendar, check
*   with other person)*

Unwillingness to Change Due to Resentment

A lot of moms have difficulty moving past their anger and resentment and are closed off to the possibility of change. They feel they shouldn't have to spend time coaching their partners on what needs to be done with their kids and believe their partner should just know how to do these things. If you're a mom like this, I urge you to take a step back and try some validating.

Before she tackled her List of Lists, I encouraged Taylor to work on her resentment toward John by trying to validate his experience. Taylor recognized that John did in fact want to share the child-care responsibilities but felt clueless about what to do. He had confidence in her parenting abilities, so he leaned on her. Once Taylor was able to validate John's perspective, she was in a far better headspace to sit down with John and discuss their lists.

I also think acceptance is key here. Your partner, whether due to upbringing or societal expectations or anything else, may not be able to tackle parenting tasks without some coaching. Maybe your partner truly does not know that scheduling regular doctors' appointments and dentists' appointments for the kids is necessary, that signup for preschool occurs 6 months before school actually starts, and that Grandma's birthday is on March 25.

So you may just have to be the teacher. You may have to devote one or five or ten face-time conversations to letting your partner know what needs to be done and how to do it. You may have to start with smaller requests and build to bigger ones, or you may have to break a more complex task down into smaller pieces that your partner can tackle one at a time. Yes, this might be time-consuming on the front end. You may feel like banging your head against the wall when your partner is honestly baffled by how to make pancakes or how to set up a carpool. But it will ultimately save you a ton of time over many, many years when your partner can take ownership of certain aspects of household labor so that you don't have to. Consider it an investment in your future.

Waiting Too Long

Divide up your List of Lists *as soon as possible* after your first kid is born—whenever you've gotten the lay of the parenting land and know what needs to get done. I can't tell you how many moms complain to me that patterns they established when the kids were babies persist through toddlerhood and beyond. Establishing themselves as the "person who gets up with the kids" is a prime example; many mothers filled this role early on (partly by necessity if they were nursing) and continue to do so until their kids absolutely won't accept anyone else at night. Deciding early on that the nonnursing parent will be on wakeup duty for any non-nursing-related issues can solve this problem. (By the way, I am living proof that this works. To this day, when Matty calls out during the night, he says, "Mommy or Daddy! Mommy or Daddy!")

Failing to Collaborate

Marta returned from her List of Lists discussion feeling very frustrated. Apparently, she and her husband ended up fighting: "It was me telling him what to do, and him feeling bullied and telling me I was 'nagging.'" I told Marta that I understood her frustration, as well as her husband's. I stressed that their List of Lists conversation, and all of the parenting conversations thereafter, needed to be collaborative. Marta and her husband had to work together to make decisions, so that they both felt involved and invested. Only then would they each feel empowered to take the lead on some aspects of parenting.

When you're discussing your List of Lists, make sure that you and your partner are DEAR MAN-ing each other, stating your needs and preferences and opinions in an open, validating manner.

Unwillingness to Relinquish Control

In my work with moms, I've found that a significant barrier to fair parenting can be the mom herself, who wants things to be more equal in theory but has no desire to relinquish control. As a result, she chooses whether and how her partner will be involved in parenting tasks. There's actually a name for this phenomenon: maternal gatekeeping.

Rebecca, for example, was a laundry gatekeeper. She wanted laundry done her way, and when her husband couldn't meet her exacting laundry standards, she just took over, closing the gate on her husband's laundry opportunities. I've had moms tell me this about routine tasks like dishwashing and meal prep, as well as more kid-focused things like making and attending doctors' appointments and birthday party planning. They don't like the way their partner does these things, so they just go ahead and do them and shut their partners out, even though it's time-consuming for them and leaves them feeling angry and resentful.

Remember when we talked about delegating in Chapter 8? I mentioned that sometimes the people to whom you delegate will not perform according to your standards. This is true of partners as well. They may not make lunches or beds as well as you do, nor match socks and shirts as successfully (not that I have any personal experience with that one). But as long as your partner is doing things in a satisfactory manner (e.g., the kid is actually wearing socks) and you feel that you could benefit from his or her assistance, please challenge yourself to accept what's offered. You might even want to talk with your partner ahead of time and agree on acceptable minimum standards for various List of Lists tasks (e.g., the minimum number of times per week laundry needs to get done; the minimum amount of vegetables that needs to be force-fed to your kid during lunch).

Think of it as an exposure exercise. Letting your partner take over certain things might make you anxious and uncomfortable at first, but over time you'll grow accustomed to the way he or she does things. And again, remember to play to your strengths. If there's a task that your partner is hopeless at, go ahead and save that task for yourself. But be sure that your partner is taking on a commensurate load in areas in which he or she excels (or at least performs adequately!). Once you've gotten used to delegating, you will feel incredibly relieved to have a lightened load.

10

"Who's the Mother Here?"
Coping with Extended Family

Peggy lamented to friends that she was living the "mother-in-law cliché." Her mother-in-law was everything you saw in the movies: she showed up at Peggy's house unannounced, dramatically stated her opinion about everything from baby carriers ("Why are you walking around all day with that baby strapped to you???") to day care ("Would it be possible for you to pick Gavin up a little earlier? It's really a long day for him"). Peggy's husband recognized that his mother could be a handful but did not want to say anything to her for fear of hurting her feelings. Peggy, for her part, tried to be patient but truly didn't know how much more of it she could take.

Lorelei knew that local family members could be intrusive, but when she learned she was having twins, she was grateful to have parents and siblings nearby who could help her. But after her twins were born, she was shocked by how little her family actually showed up. She assumed her parents would be the type of grandparents her best friend's parents seemed to be—totally involved and in love with the kids. Instead, her parents, newly retired, spent most of their time playing bridge and traveling, stopping at her house only when it was on their way to someplace else. And her brother and sister were far less interested in the twins than Lorelei expected they'd be. Lorelei complained that she might as well be living far away from her family, for all the help and support they gave her.

Before she had her son, Imani didn't realize how sad she would feel when she saw grandparents at the park or in the library. Her father, who raised her, had died several years before. She missed him terribly, often thinking about how enthusiastically he would have embraced the grandpa role. Imani sometimes resented her friends whose parents and in-laws lived nearby and were a huge part of their kids' lives. They seemed to have this enormous supportive network of family members, and she was all on her own.

I come from a family of huggers. My husband comes from a family of huggers. Imagine my surprise, then, when Matty did not want to hug his relatives. When he was small, Matty simply was not interested in cuddling with anyone other than me and my husband and Sam. Contrast this with Sam, who to this day would happily hug the FedEx delivery person who periodically shows up at our doorstep. When Matty was little, I felt compelled to apologize to relatives for his apparent lack of warmth—giving them the "it's not you, it's him" speech—and was truly embarrassed by Matty's behavior. I found myself forcing him to say warm hellos and goodbyes to his relatives, which didn't feel right to me but seemed like the appropriate thing to do.

Relationships with extended family are always complicated and become infinitely more so when children are thrown into the mix. I included one extra vignette above but could have shared many more, encompassing the varied experiences that new parents can have with their relatives.

Whatever your particular family stressors may be, there are excellent strategies from DBT and CBT that can help you cope with them. Of course, family issues involve other people, and you can't directly change others. So you've got to focus on changing your own thoughts and behaviors, in the hope that doing so will inspire your relatives to change, too.

Two things before we move on. First, I recommend you take a minute now to look at the extended family section of your values worksheet. These values will help guide your decisions about how to interact effectively with your relatives.

Second, the CBT and DBT strategies in this chapter are meant to address common problems that arise in extended families when children enter the picture. However, they probably won't help you end your family's decades-old blood feud with Aunt Jean. If you are looking to work on long-standing family issues, consider seeking out family therapy or an individual therapist who can help you work through family problems. You may also benefit from family-focused therapy if you find that your current difficulties with your extended family are significantly impacting your day-to-day life. See the Resources for more information about accessing support.

Don't They Have Their Own Lives?

Like Peggy, many of us experience some version of the cliché of the overin-volved relative. "Overinvolved" can mean many things—an aunt who con-stantly pops by unannounced, a grandpa who questions every single pedia-trician recommendation, or a great-grandma who insists on viewing every one of your infant's poops (that's a personal example, sadly). Further, moms vary widely in terms of what they consider to be "overinvolved"; behaviors that feel intrusive to one mom might feel helpful to another. However you define "overinvolved," if you feel like a relative is invading your space (physi-cal, emotional, or both!), it's important to engage your best validating and DEAR MAN skills.

Find Something—Anything!—to Validate

Remember in the last chapter, when we discussed the importance of vali-dating your partner during a conflict? I noted that trying to understand where your partner is coming from can help you better see things from his/her perspective, hopefully setting the stage for less anger and more effective problem solving. Validation is similarly helpful when approaching conflicts with relatives.

When I worked with Peggy, who had the clichéd "mother-in-law from hell," I encouraged her to try viewing the situation from her mother-in-law Ruth's perspective. Peggy noted that her husband Tom's two siblings lived far away, which broke Ruth's heart, because she could not see her grandchil-dren on a regular basis. She was thrilled when Peggy and Tom, who lived close by, had a baby; she could finally be the doting grandma she couldn't be for her other grandchildren (and she took the role of "doting grandma" to new and spectacular heights).

Also, Peggy recognized that many of Ruth's opinions were dated; they reflected the prevailing wisdom about child rearing from Ruth's days as a young mother. When Ruth constantly barraged Peggy with advice, she did in fact think she was giving Peggy some useful information, not realizing that it was hopelessly out of date.

So when Peggy found herself aggravated during Ruth's latest rant about swaddles, she tried to remember just how much Ruth cared about Gavin (and was able to acknowledge that yes, a swaddle blanket might strike a loosey-goosey 1980s-era mom as a "torture device"). Validating Ruth in this way didn't drastically change Peggy's opinion of her; Peggy was still extremely frustrated by her constant intrusions and judgmental comments. It did, however, put Peggy into a somewhat different mom brain space; she went from feeling only anger and resentment toward Ruth to also feeling something like empathy for her. As a result Peggy felt more open to working on the relationship.

While validating, it can also be useful to remind yourself about the positive aspects of the relative in question. In Chapter 3, we discussed the thinking trap of discounting positives/negative filtering. When we fall into this trap, we focus only on negative feedback or negative aspects of ourselves and ignore the positive. I've found that this can happen with our relatives, too—we are often so annoyed by their negative qualities that we ignore their strengths. When asked to consider Ruth's strengths, Peggy acknowledged that Gavin was "obsessed" with Ruth and that Ruth was always available to help out and give her and her husband a break, no questions asked. Peggy acknowledged that she truly appreciated this.

Recognize What You Can and Cannot Change

After she spent some time validating Ruth, I asked Peggy to consider what she felt she could change about her situation with Ruth and what she felt she couldn't change. Unfortunately, there are always some aspects of your relationships with overinvolved relatives that cannot easily be fixed, like their locations or long-standing aspects of their personalities (sorry, but Uncle Russ is always going to live down the street from you and will never stop believing that all your problems could be solved if you could just "learn to chill"). But there are other aspects that are indeed amenable to change, and should therefore be the focus of your efforts and energy.

Peggy's list looked like this:

What I cannot change

1. *Where I live and where my in-laws live*
2. *The fact that Ruth is exceedingly opinionated*
3. *The fact that Ruth has no filter*
4. *The fact that Ruth wants to see Gavin so often*
5. *The fact that Tom loves his mother and wants to accommodate her*

What I can change

1. *When the frequent visits from Ruth occur*
2. *Whether I am around when Ruth comes to visit*

3. *What we do when Ruth comes to visit*
4. *How often I take Gavin to my in-laws'*
5. *How I respond to Ruth's critical comments*
6. *How I talk to Tom about his mother*

What I like about a list like this is that it shifts your attention away from the things you can't possibly fix and forces you to think about the things that are in fact in your control. This will hopefully lead directly to the next step in dealing with overinvolved relatives: boundary setting.

Boundary Setting 101

Once you have a list of things you can and cannot change about your relationship with an overinvolved relative, use it to start thinking through whether and how you wish to set boundaries with this person. I know the notion of "setting boundaries" has become somewhat of a pop psychology cliché. However, I believe boundary setting is a critical exercise, in that it forces moms to think very carefully about what they will and will not accept from family members (and then convey this to them—more on that in the next section).

The boundaries you set can be general ("I don't want Mom popping by unannounced") or specific ("If my sister accompanies me to Lucy's dance recital, she needs to not scream so loud in the audience that everyone turns around to look at us"), physical ("I will not provide my dad with a key to our house") or emotional ("I will not stay in the room if my brother is pummeling me with criticism"). Each mom's desired boundaries are going to depend on her own particular circumstances and values. Make sure to consult your values worksheet as you're thinking through your boundaries.

Boundaries can be set in a number of different areas. They can relate to how family members are treating you or your kids or how they act at certain events or in certain places. For example:

1. How often visits occur
2. When visits occur
3. What happens during visits
4. How often/what types of things are purchased for your kid
5. Appropriate times for phone calls/FaceTime calls
6. How many family members are allowed to visit at one time
7. Which groups of family members can visit at one time
8. The type of behavior you will or will not accept from family members

When setting boundaries, be sure to consider not only the things you can change, but also the things you can't. For example, if, like Peggy, you have a family member who lives very close to you and wants to see the children all the time, it is probably not reasonable for you to set a boundary limiting those visits to once every three months.

Here are the boundaries Peggy came up with, as well as those of Carmen, a mom who lives far away from the rest of her extended family.

Peggy's boundaries

1. *Ruth can come over frequently, but we will ask her to come over at regularly scheduled times each week. That way she has guaranteed time with Gavin and we know when she'll be coming.*

2. *Ruth's regular babysitting times will occur on the two days I'm at work. She'll pick Gavin up early from day care and spend the whole afternoon/evening with him.*

3. *If Ruth wants to come on the weekends, we will ask that she tell us ahead of time when she's coming. I will try to take those opportunities to run errands and meet self-care goals I've set for myself. If Tom and I need to be in the house, we'll ask her to take Gavin out to the park or library or other places.*

4. *When possible, we will protect Sunday afternoons/evenings as time for only the three of us to spend together.*

5. *If Ruth starts loudly asserting an opinion I don't agree with, I will not sit and take it. I will make up some excuse to leave the room and take an adult time-out. If I return and the rant persists, I will do what I do with Gavin when he can't break out of a crying fit— suggest a change of scenery or venue.*

6. *If Ruth's opinions become too much for me to bear, I will talk with her about them, using DEAR MAN strategies.* [More on this in the next section.]

Unlike Peggy, Carmen lived halfway across the country from her family—both she and her husband were from the Midwest, where their families continued to reside, and Carmen and her family lived in New Jersey. Carmen had to set boundaries relating to how family visits would go and how they'd communicate and how much stuff family members would send her kids.

Carmen's boundaries

1. *When it's time for visits, we can have a maximum of four people staying with us. If more than that number wish to visit, they'll have*

    to stay in hotels. We can alternate which family members get to stay with us and which have to stay in hotels.

2. *When we visit our families, we will alternate which families we stay with.*

3. *We will establish a regular time for FaceTime calls so that family members are not FaceTiming during tough times of day (like during dinner or the nighttime routine).*

4. *I'll ask my sister not to text me at all hours of the day demanding pictures of the kids. I'll try to upload pictures of the kids to a shared album on Sunday nights so that everyone can see them.*

5. *We'll ask parents and siblings to send gifts only when there's an occasion to do so.*

6. *When our families are visiting, we'll ask that they babysit at least one night so that we can go out and get some space from them and from our kids.*

Note that both Carmen's and Peggy's boundaries are highly specific. As is always the case with behavioral work, change will happen only if you articulate exactly what you will be doing differently. In Carmen's case, it's the difference between stating, for example, "When it's time for visits, we can't have too many people staying with us" and "When it's time for visits, we can't have more than four people staying with us." Only a highly specific request like the latter is likely to be honored.

Once you're done drafting your boundaries list, I highly recommend sharing it in a DEAR MAN discussion with your partner. Many of these boundaries require the cooperation of your partner, so it's important to get feedback. If Peggy, for example, wishes to block off Sunday nights for family time, her husband needs to agree to commit to this to ensure that it happens.

In addition, your partner should have the opportunity to weigh in on how these boundaries will affect members of his or her family of origin. Remember, when setting boundaries it's important to consider those aspects of family members' personalities and circumstances that most likely can't be changed. Your partner is in a better position than you to identify which boundaries will be a total "deal-breaker" for his or her parents, siblings, and other relatives. Also, as we'll discuss below, if you want your partner to join you when you're communicating your boundaries to family, he or she will have to be on board with everything you're asking for in order to have an effective exchange. Regular face times are a great opportunity for discussing family boundary setting.

Communicate Your Boundaries

I know what you're thinking: "These boundaries look great and all, but good luck explaining any of these things to my mother."

I don't doubt that your mother is a formidable opponent. I'm not so naïve as to think that all of your requests will be honored; it's entirely possible that your mother will never stop showing up at your house unannounced. But assertively expressing boundaries is a far better option than suffering in silence. In my experience with moms, it almost always leads to at least some changes in relatives' behavior and helps moms feel more empowered.

Remember the DEAR MAN skills we learned in the last chapter? You'll want to use the exact same skills when you're making boundary-related requests to your relatives. In fact, whenever you're asking anyone for something you need, DEAR MAN skills will help you get what you're looking for.

Here is an example of Peggy's DEAR MAN appeal for having her mother-in-law watch her son on regularly scheduled days each week:

- **Describe.** "Now that Gavin is getting older and I'm settling back in at work, I'm trying to work on a weekly family schedule."

- **Express.** "I get so stressed out trying to make it home on time on the days that I work. I'm also feeling a push to get all of us—me, Gavin, and Tom—into a regular routine, which I think will reduce stress and overwhelm for all of us."

- **Assert.** "I think it would be great if you could come and see Gavin on the same days each week, Monday and Wednesday. Those are the days I work late and could really use the help. You can pick Gavin up as early as you'd like from day care and spend the rest of the day with him."

- **Reinforce.** "It will be so wonderful for Gavin to have 'grandma days,' when he knows he'll be able to spend time alone with you. Which I think will be great for you, too, since he definitely acts differently when Mommy and Daddy aren't around. I have to confess that I have difficulty when I don't know who's coming by, and as you've probably noticed I can get a little bit prickly when I have an unannounced houseguest. If I know when you're coming, I can make sure we have extra food for dinner and will be far less likely to get stressed out."

- **stay Mindful.** Peggy continued to ask for what she needed in spite of Ruth voicing concerns that she wouldn't be allowed to see Gavin on days other than her assigned days.

- **Appear confident.** Peggy maintained eye contact and a firm, level tone of voice.

- **Negotiate.** Ruth ultimately stated that she was fine with coming those two days, but really wanted more opportunities for Gavin to come to her apartment so she could "show him off to everyone in my building." They agreed that they'd bring Gavin to her apartment every other Saturday morning. Peggy realized that this was a win for her and her husband too, since it afforded them the chance to run errands or exercise or just spend some time together. Peggy and Ruth also came up with a plan for any times Ruth wanted to visit Gavin outside of her assigned days. She would text Peggy to see if that time worked, and if not, the two of them would find a time that worked better.

Note that Peggy uses lots of "I" statements and frames the entire scenario in terms of herself. She does not make it about how Ruth's frequent, unplanned pop-ins drive her crazy; instead, she makes it about how stressful it is for her to maintain a schedule and balance work and life.

Peggy's plan didn't go perfectly. Despite coming on her regularly scheduled days, Ruth did "pop in" at other times, often claiming she had something she needed to give them or Gavin. But the pop-ins were far less frequent than they had been, and Peggy felt far more in control of the situation.

Some Tips for Effective Boundary Discussions

Despite how neatly I've laid it out here, DEAR MAN conversations with (loving, well-intentioned) relatives can be difficult. Here are some pointers for making them easier:

1. **Rehearse ahead of time.** Remember in the last chapter, when we discussed the importance of rehearsing stressful conversations ahead of time? It helps ensure that you get your points across with confidence and without lapsing into emotion mind. I'd recommend having a friend pretend to be the relative in question so you can practice responding to any reservations he or she might raise.

If you and your partner are presenting your boundaries together, you both need to rehearse. I've heard moms complain that when they try to state their case to a relative, their partner inadvertently undercuts their message by using noncommittal language or watering down the request. It's difficult to set boundaries with relatives if it's clear that you and your partner are not in total agreement.

2. **Don't work on all of your boundaries at once.** Hitting your relatives with everything you want at one time ("So, by the way, if you could visit only on Saturdays, stop buying Jaden Lego sets with 800 pieces, not throw shade at Jaden's preschool teacher in front of him, and not bring 50 bags of food every time you come over, that would great!") will overwhelm them, causing them to forget the individual requests you made. You've got to ease them into your boundaries, one at a time. And you may have to work on a boundary for a while, periodically reminding them about it, until they truly get it. If you think your boundaries will be a particularly tough sell, you might even want to adopt a "foot in the door" strategy, where you ask the relative for something small at first and then gradually ask for more.

3. **Be mindful of the difference between assertive, passive, and aggressive.** In my experience, relatives' opinions and critical comments are often delivered in one of two ways: an aggressive way, where relatives state what they believe in a loud and hostile manner; or a passive–aggressive way, where they communicate their thoughts without directly saying how they feel (I've mentioned my favorite version of this, when a relative tells you that a certain child-rearing strategy of yours is "interesting" or that she or he has "never heard of that before"). Some moms come to believe that they have to fight fire with fire and respond with passive aggression or all-out aggression, depending on what was dished at them.

I urge you to resist the impulse to respond in kind and to consider an assertive approach instead, where you calmly, firmly, and clearly ask for what you need. (Here's the good news: if you're using DEAR MAN skills, you're automatically being assertive.) Regardless of how your relatives approach you, I guarantee you will be more successful with your boundaries if you respond to them with assertiveness.

4. **Do it in person.** I talked in the last chapter about fighting over text and email, stressing that important conversations should be had in person (or at least over the phone or FaceTime if the person in question lives far away). I feel similarly about boundary discussions. I don't think communicating boundaries via text or email is effective. As I mentioned, it is hard to read a person's tone in texts and emails. What you perceive to be assertive may read to a relative as aggressive. Also, face-to-face conversations give relatives the opportunity to respond to you in real time, so you can negotiate with them.

5. **Don't forget to acknowledge successful changes.** Be sure to give your relatives credit for any boundary-related changes they've made. Peggy,

for example, reached out to Ruth to thank her for watching Gavin during her workdays, noting how much Gavin loved getting picked up early from day care and spending time alone with Grandma. As with partners, praise will keep your relatives doing what you'd like them to do and make them more receptive to making additional changes.

Think Critically about Responding to Criticism

Ali lived in the same town as her brother and his wife, and each family had two young kids. She was thrilled to have the opportunity to experience parenthood alongside her brother. She was not prepared, however, for how different their parenting styles would be. Her brother and his wife had an opinion on everything: screen time (they forbade it; Ali and her husband embraced it); sleep training (they thought it was cruel; Ali thought it was necessary); and nursing (they thought it was essential; Ali chose to formula feed).

Ali understood that all moms and dads parented differently and were entitled to their opinions. However, her brother and his wife couldn't seem to stop criticizing Ali's choices. An example was Ali's brother's statement on screen time: "Al, just so you know, our pediatrician told us that little kids shouldn't be spending more than an hour per day on screens. Your little guys are watching way more than that. It could be bad for their development. You really should consider limiting their screen use." Comments like this played on repeat in Ali's mom brain and made her feel less inclined to spend time with her brother.

I totally understood where Ali was coming from. It can be really difficult to endure criticism and can make you want to avoid the critical family member(s). But as a CBT therapist, I am never in favor of avoidance as a coping strategy. Here are some ideas I gave Ali for how to manage her feelings toward her brother and his wife:

1. **Don't take the bait.** Initially, Ali found herself defending her parenting choices. After her brother's comment about screen time, for example, she reminded him about their cousin's daughter, who had been addicted to Candy Crush since before she could talk and, at age 9, seemed to be doing just fine. But Ali realized that she was never able to change her brother's mind; and in fact, every time she tried to defend herself he doubled down on his initial opinion.

So Ali committed to not taking the bait when her brother and sister-in-law made a critical comment. Instead, she and I chose a stock phrase

("OK—I'll think about that") and decided that she would deploy that phrase after a critical comment was made. She would then attempt to change the conversation as quickly as possible. If she couldn't, she would consider taking a quick adult time-out, in the hope that she would return to the room more composed (and that her brother and sister-in-law would have moved on to another topic).

2. **Validate, and consider the messenger.** As we discussed, it can be helpful to try to understand where your relative is coming from. Validation and considering the messenger can help you respond to critical comments with compassion instead of irritation.

Ali recognized that her sister-in-law came from a large family with an "every person for him/herself" mentality. Her sister-in-law described her childhood as "chaotic" and noted that she wanted things to be different for her own children. So she decided to embrace structure and follow recommendations to the letter. Ali completely understood her sister-in-law's desire for structure, given how she'd been raised.

In fact, many of Ali's sister-in-law's parenting values were informed by her chaotic childhood. As a result, her values (and those of Ali's brother) were quite different from those of Ali and her husband. Knowing this, Ali made a concerted effort to "consider the messenger" as she listened to her brother and sister-in-law's latest comment about the "right" way to feed babies or the optimal time to start nursery school.

3. **Speak up and use DEAR MAN if you have to.** If committing to not taking the bait and validating is not helping you manage your negative feelings about your critical relatives, might I suggest telling them how you feel?

Full disclosure: Moms hate when I suggest this. They don't want to have a confrontation. They've got their hands full dealing with their little kids and their partners—why force their mom brains to focus on something else? But if the alternative is avoiding their relatives, I strongly urge them to consider it.

You won't be surprised to hear that I recommend engaging in a DEAR MAN conversation with your critical relative. Make sure you go heavy on the "I" statements; this will make the conversation about you, not about the other person and minimize the chances that you will offend your relative or put him or her on the defensive.

Here are some highlights from a DEAR MAN appeal that Ali shared with her brother:

"I get upset when you and Lisa state your opinions about my parenting. I understand that you're well intentioned and want to be helpful, but it makes me feel like I'm being criticized and puts me on the defensive. Can you trust that if I'm looking for guidance or your opinion, I will ask for it? And I will extend the same courtesy to you—I will wait for you to ask before I offer any opinions."

If you're going to have a conversation like this with a critical loved one, all of the rules we've discussed thus far about difficult conversations apply: think of what you want to say and rehearse ahead of time; find a time to talk when neither of you will be distracted; and try to have this conversation in person or over the phone or FaceTime and not over email or text.

4. **Consider the positive evidence.** When processing criticism from a relative, it can be helpful to consider his or her positive attributes. Ali, for example, acknowledged that her brother and sister-in-law were very "fun"; they enthusiastically interacted with her children, paid them lots of attention, and invited them to join on fun outings with their own children. Ali truly valued having them in her children's lives.

Considering the positive evidence won't inure you to criticism. However, it will remind you of all of the good things about your relationship (and/or your kids' relationship) with the relative in question, which can make loudly stated opinions somewhat easier to swallow.

Do They Just Not Like My Kid?

At the beginning of the chapter we met Lorelei, who was surprised by how little her parents and siblings wanted to see her twins once they were born. For all the moms I meet who complain of overly intrusive relatives, there are an equal number who complain that their relatives are not nearly as involved in their kids' lives (nor as helpful) as they hoped they'd be. I've heard two versions of this story: either that relatives don't come around or that relatives come around but don't interact with the kids at all. The latter situation can be particularly galling, because moms find themselves in the position of having to feed and entertain their relatives at the same time as they're trying to feed and entertain their kids.

Unfortunately, you can't force an underinvolved family member to become that classic doting relative, dispensing love and fresh-baked brownies with reckless abandon. But you can take steps to improve his or her relationship with your kid (and with you). As with overinvolved family members, you can start by validating and considering what you can and cannot change. You can then focus on communicating your feelings and directly asking for what you need.

Find Something to Validate and Recognize What You Can Change

Understandably, moms like Lorelei feel incredibly hurt and disappointed when their relatives don't seem to take much of an interest in their children. While acknowledging that these feelings absolutely make sense, I urge moms to try validating their relatives' perspectives. It helps them empathize with their relatives, which, as with overinvolved relatives, can make them more amenable to working on the relationships.

Lorelei, for example, recognized that her parents had been talking about retirement since she was a teenager. Both had worked demanding jobs, and both were dying to travel and pursue long-ignored hobbies. It made sense, then, that spending time at home with a small baby wasn't necessarily at the top of their priority list. Lorelei's brother and sister were both younger than she was and both single. Lorelei recognized that when she was their age, she was like them—focused on friends and dating.

Further, when validating underinvolved relatives, there are often generational issues to consider. Some relatives may be "out of the loop" of child care, either because it's been so long since they've done it themselves or because they have never been parents and therefore have no experience. It may be a lack of confidence, not a lack of caring, that accounts for certain family members' disengagement.

Once you've tried to view the situation from your relative's perspective, consider all of the things you can and cannot change about the situation. Lorelei acknowledged that because of their stages in life (retirement and swinging singles, respectively), neither her parents nor her siblings prioritized babysitting. And there was nothing Lorelei could do to manufacture enthusiasm for the baby that was not there. She could, however, change how she communicated to her parents and siblings. To this point all she'd done was stew about their lack of enthusiasm and complain to her husband about it.

How to Ask for a Little More from Your Relatives

I've worked with so many moms who privately seethe with disappointment and hurt over their relatives' underinvolvement, yet don't want to approach their relatives about it. Yes, I get that the idea of calling up your parents and saying "What's up with you not liking my kid?" is not super-appealing. But there are more measured ways of communicating your disappointment and asking for change. As when you're hurt by your partners, you can use "I" statements and engage in a DEAR MAN appeal.

Examples of effective "I" statements for underinvolved relatives include "I feel hurt when I hear you've been in my neighborhood and haven't stopped to visit us"; "I feel disappointed when you turn down invitations to events at Lily's preschool"; and "I feel confused when you text and tell me how much you miss Nicky but then don't respond to my texts offering dates to come and hang out with him."

You'll recall that "I" statements are effective because they don't involve blaming the other person for anything, which typically inspires defensiveness. Instead, they simply communicate how you feel, which paves the way for effective DEAR MAN-ing.

Use Your DEAR MAN Skills

You may resist the idea of DEAR MAN-ing your relatives, believing that doing so will "force" them into spending time with your kids when they don't really want to. But have you considered that certain relatives may be happy to help with your kids but don't think to offer, perhaps because they don't realize how important their presence is to you? Or maybe they're waiting for *you* to reach out to *them*. One mom I worked with, Kala, thought her mother-in-law had no interest in helping with her son, only to learn that her mother-in-law was hanging back in an effort to avoid coming off as intrusive. She was waiting for Kala or her wife to directly ask for help.

If you want a certain relative(s) to be more present, go ahead and use DEAR MAN to ask. It's essential that you be specific in your requests for help or support. An appeal to "be more involved in the kids' lives" is far less effective than an appeal to "come over on Saturday nights for dinner with us" or "come and watch Sarah while we go to Ian's doctor appointment." Try to be strategic about when you ask for help, choosing a day when, say, you know your mom doesn't have mahjong or your sister has off from work. You should also be prepared to continually make specific requests for help as the need arises.

Lorelei strategically used DEAR MAN with her parents and siblings whenever she needed help or wanted to see them at a specific time. Here's her DEAR MAN appeal to her parents concerning her daughters' first dance recital:

- **Describe.** "Elena and Emme's dance recital is in two weeks, and I'd love you both to come."

- **Express.** "It means a lot to me when you're present for the kids' milestone events. I know you guys are busy and loving all of the new activities you've been engaging in since your retirement. But I feel sad, and sometimes hurt, when you turn down invitations to these events, because I want you to be a strong presence in the kids' lives."

- **Assert.** "I would love you to be our guests at the recital on Saturday and then join us for lunch at the diner afterward."

- **Reinforce.** "It will be so wonderful for the girls to see you both out in the audience; they are so proud of their dancing and will feel so good that their grandparents are cheering them on. It will also be a joy for me to get to experience their first dance recital with you."

- **stay Mindful.** Lorelei continued to ask for what she needed in spite of her mother expressing some reservations about missing her book club.

- **Appear confident.** Lorelei maintained eye contact and a firm, level tone of voice.

- **Negotiate.** Lorelei's parents agreed to come to the recital but asked if they could skip the lunch afterward so that her mom could catch the tail end of her book club. This was not ideal for Lorelei, as she wanted her parents to join her for lunch, but she recognized that actually having her parents at the recital was the most important part of her request.

Lorelei found that DEAR MAN worked sometimes, but not always. Ultimately, she had to come to terms with the fact that her family members simply didn't show the enthusiasm toward her kids that she'd hoped they would. She and I talked about how she could cultivate a community of close friends who could provide the support and enthusiasm that her parents and siblings couldn't. We'll talk much more about finding a community of friends in the next chapter.

Be a Coach

As discussed above, some relatives may keep their distance from your kid because of a lack of confidence in their ability to interact with little ones. This may be due to their age or personality or any number of other things. If you suspect that this is the case, I recommend you plan activities for this relative and your kid and aim to tag along. It helps to pick activities with which the relative in question is comfortable. Once there, use the opportunity to engage in some subtle coaching.

For example, say Aunt Steph loves to shop, and you know your daughter would love it if Steph took her to the mall. But Steph is hesitant to do this, as she "has no idea what 5-year-olds like" (surprisingly, she doesn't know which jeweled tiaras are on trend). Why not accompany Steph and your daughter on a shopping trip, encouraging your daughter to tell Steph what she likes and encouraging Steph to tell your daughter funny stories about how she dressed as a kid (in an outrageous manner similar to your daughter's, if memory serves)?

Over repeated activities like this, your relative will grow more comfortable with your kid (and your kid with him or her). Hopefully, you'll eventually be able to remove yourself altogether from their interactions.

How to Cope When a Loved One Is Absent

Remember Imani, who was struggling to cope with the absence of her father? Many moms who've lost beloved family members find that their grief is reignited on a regular basis whenever they see kids in person (or even on TV) who have loving extended family relationships that their children will never have.

Initially, much of my work with these moms involves encouraging self-compassion, stressing that their grief as well as their resentment makes sense given the loss they've suffered. If you are struggling, I encourage you to mindfully acknowledge your feelings of loss and grief and resentment rather than trying to ignore or dismiss them (for pointers on how to do this, see Chapter 2).

Needless to say, working through grief is often a lengthy, difficult process and requires far more time and attention than I can give it here. Below, I share some relatively simple coping strategies. For more on managing grief, see the Resources.

1. **Take out those photos and videos.** Show your kids pictures of your lost loved one and prominently display them around your home. As your kids get older, tell them stories of the person in the picture. Also consider showing them videos of your loved one, if you have them. I can't tell you how happy I am that both of my kids can identify my maternal grandmother, the inimitable Grandma Hearts, in pictures.

2. **Celebrate on birthdays and holidays.** On what would have been the 100th birthday of my paternal grandmother (a.k.a. Grandma Teeth—don't ask), all of her kids, grandkids, and great-grandkids ate chocolate chip cookies, her favorite treat. It provided me with the perfect opportunity to tell my kids about her. I also recommend continuing holiday rituals favored by your lost loved ones and letting your kids know where the rituals originated.

3. **Share their "greatest hits."** Did your relatives have any characteristic phrases that you can use too? (I use a favorite line of my Grandma Hearts', "I need my medicine," which meant that she wanted a hug or kiss from us.) Perhaps there are songs your loved ones favored or activities they enjoyed? If so, share these with your kids and let them know what it was like when you sang these songs or participated in these activities with your loved one.

4. **Use your loved one as a model.** You can look to your lost loved one as a model for how to interact with your children. Imani, for example, wanted to model her own parenting after her father's. I asked her to make a list of examples that typified her father's parenting style, including how her father responded when she was targeted by a kindergarten bully and how her father structured her bedtime routine. Imani felt that by consciously choosing to parent as her dad did, she was ensuring that he played a role in the upbringing of her son.

5. **Seek out "friends who are family."** If you don't have much family support, either because loved ones have died or because they live very far away, try to cultivate a network of supportive "friends who are family." For details on how to do this, see Chapter 11.

What to Do When Your Kid Doesn't Play Along

You'll recall that I struggled when Matty was little and refused to hug relatives (and barely even said "hello" and "goodbye" to them). After a year of overapologizing about Matty's subpar greetings, I started to notice articles in the mom blog-iverse about the perils of forcing kids to hug their relatives. Many parenting experts argue that forcing a kid to hug someone else undermines a fundamental principle that we want all children to learn: that they are in control of their own bodies and should never have to be affectionate if they don't want to.

So I decided to stop forcing Matty to hug his relatives. And then I had to ask myself why I cared so much whether or not he greeted his relatives warmly.

I think for me, part of the forced affection issue had to do with my unfortunate drive to please people. I wanted to make sure that relatives who took the time to schlep to my house felt they were getting their money's worth. I also wanted these relatives to see me as a good parent who was encouraging good social skills in my kid. And of course, I loved Matty and loved my relatives and so naturally wanted them to love each other.

As you know, I preach acceptance all the time, and I ultimately had to come to my own place of acceptance about this issue. Matty's relatives wouldn't get the enthusiastic kid greeting that Sam nearly always gave them, and my apologizing for it would only draw more attention to it. As we discussed in Chapter 8, we cannot expect ourselves to be able to control our kids' behavior all the time. I ultimately realized that it wasn't my job to make my kid act a certain way to impress our relatives. It was my job to encourage my kid to be who he was, even if it meant he wasn't the huggiest person on the planet.

I also challenged myself to consider the evidence and think about the moments in between Matty's lackluster hellos and goodbyes when he enthusiastically showed relatives his president coins or cajoled them into doing stomp rockets with him. I realized that those moments were rewarding for relatives and showed them the type of kid Matty was, even if his greetings did not.

If you're struggling with the way your kid acts around your relatives, I recommend that you consider the evidence, as I did. Are there ways in which your kid does successfully connect with your relative(s)? Is there an activity they both enjoy, or something they both love? I imagine you'll identify at least something on which your child and the relative in question can connect. And once you find this thing, encourage those continued connections, as I now encourage Matty to share his baseball cards and play backyard wiffle ball with our family members.

Finally, acknowledge that you might be doing a bit of mind reading with your relatives. I certainly was: I assumed that relatives would see a scowl on Matty's face and automatically judge my parenting and even judge him. But I had no evidence that any relatives were judging us. And even if they were, I still had ample evidence to suggest that we were doing a good job with Matty. He was clearly a happy kid, even if he was sometimes cranky during family visits.

11

"Where Has My Social Life Gone?"

Fitting Friendships into Your New Life

Shortly before having their daughter, Renee and her husband moved from New York City to a New Jersey suburb. Renee had tons of friends in New York, mostly childless college friends and coworkers. But she knew virtually no one in New Jersey. Her husband resumed work almost immediately after their daughter was born, which enabled him to quickly reengage with other adults. Renee, on the other hand, was on maternity leave and completely on her own. While she wanted to connect with her old friends through texts and phone calls, the hours she was available (and awake enough) to text and call her friends tended to be the hours her friends were at work. And if she was in fact able to reach old friends, she sometimes found it hard to relate to them. She had no energy to seek out new friends and didn't even know how she would go about doing that.

After Daisy had her son, she was thrilled to discover a local new moms' group on Facebook which met regularly to socialize, both with and without kids. Daisy attended all of the group's playdates and meetups. She was grateful for the company and initially loved being a part of a community. But over time she began to feel pressured by some of these moms. One of them sold high-end cosmetics on Facebook and continually urged her to buy products. Several others tried to rope her into volunteering for their town's newcomers' club, which was not something she really wanted to do. At a certain point, the pressure started getting to her, and Daisy began to question whether the friendships were worth it.

A few months after I had Matty, I decided to attend a support group at a local lactation center, hoping to meet some other new moms. When I arrived at the group, I immediately felt awkward, as a number of women were nursing their babies out in the open and I, modest to a fault, didn't feel comfortable nursing mine. Shortly after the group started, a woman shared her nursing story: her son had bitten off part of her nipple (yes, you heard that right), but she was so pleased to announce that she had decided to continue nursing anyway. I immediately felt alienated from this woman, as I was 100% confident that for me, a ripped nipple (a ripple?) would have been an instant deal breaker. I was generally intimidated by the nursing fervor of these women. I decided that because I wasn't similarly enthusiastic, I didn't belong with them. I left the group and never went back.

In 2018, one of my favorite contemporary authors, J. Courtney Sullivan, wrote a piece for the *New York Times* titled "The Absolute Necessity of the New-Mom Friend." In it, Sullivan, a new mom, discusses how critical it is for her to have friends who are also new moms with kids the same age as hers. She describes her mom friends in this way: "I trust these women more than anyone. We take advice from each other before doctors or parenting books. We often make different decisions for our children, and yet there is never a hint of judgment. As we've found our footing, our conversations have moved to topics beyond babies."

I love this piece, because having mom friends was a lifesaver for me and has been for many women with whom I work. Those early days and years with young children can be extremely isolating and lonely. Mom friends, who are in the trenches with you, can be an invaluable source of companionship, advice, validation, and commiseration. Unlike your partners or extended family members, they are in the unique position of knowing exactly what you're going through and can chat openly with you about the mundane personal experiences that consume your mom brain: nursing, sleep training, tantrum managing, and so on. They can also serve as sounding boards if you're having issues with your partner or extended family. If your extended family lives far away or isn't very involved with your kids, your mom friends can serve as "friends who are family," providing you with much-needed support. I've found that as kids get older, mom friends become even more important, as you need a village to help you navigate carpools and sports team sign-ups and the school system.

Yet finding a community of mom friends can be challenging. Like Renee, you may feel like your old friends are difficult to access. Like Daisy and me, you may find that the moms you meet don't seem to be good matches for you, either because they pressure you into doing things you're not comfortable doing or because, well, you can't seem to get past their ripples. As we discussed in Chapter 7, you may also feel judged by the moms you meet.

This chapter is devoted to helping you meet the challenges of finding supportive friends. We'll discuss strategies for reconsidering your friends list, seeking out new friends, engaging with new friends, and coping with pressure from friends. My hope is that you'll be able to find mom friends like Sullivan's, comrades-in-arms who can help you navigate the many parenting battles ahead.

Before we continue, be sure to revisit the friends section of your values worksheet. As was the case for partner and extended family relationships, your values will inform the decisions you make about how you'll want to set boundaries with friends. It's also helpful to compare your stated values to those of your potential friends, as moms with values similar to yours are likely to be good matches for you.

Ask Yourself, "Is This Friendship Still Working for Me?"

We've discussed how having a baby can change partner and family relationships. Friendships, too, can be altered significantly by the arrival of little ones, in a number of different ways. For starters, some moms, like Renee, find it hard to connect with old friends once they have children, for reasons both logistical (hard to find mutually available times to talk/visit with each other) and emotional (hard to find mutually satisfying conversation topics). Other moms find that they want different things from their friendships after they have a kid and recognize that their old friends no longer meet their needs. I've also heard new moms confess that they don't have the energy for certain high-effort friendships and feel like a "bad friend" as a result.

Becoming a mom fundamentally changes you, so you need to accept that your friendships will fundamentally change, too. However, this does not mean that these friendships are over. Instead, it means that you need to think critically about these friendships and decide whether (and how) you can change them to better fit with your current life.

Take a minute to think about all of the friends you were in regular contact with before you had your kid (and I don't mean following on social media; I mean actual text/email/phone exchanges or in-person visits). Once you do this, consider each friend and ask yourself, "Is this friendship still working for me?" Make a list of every friend who inspires a "no" answer.

There are a number of reasons a friendship might no longer be working:

1. *Logistical issues.* It's simply too difficult to see/communicate with this friend due to schedules/mutual busyness.

2. *Too little in common.* You find that you no longer have much to say to a friend from your past. If your lives have taken very different paths, you may not be able to relate to each other.

3. *Emotional effort.* I'm speaking here of the "high-effort" friend, who wants to communicate a lot, often seeks out your advice or reassurance about things, and/or spends a lot of time venting to you. This friendship might entail more emotional effort on your part than you're willing to put in.

4. *Too judgmental.* We talked about judgmental friends in Chapter 7; these are the "friends" who make you question your choices (parenting or otherwise) and cause you to feel "less than."

5. *Too stressful.* These are the friends who are always informing you about the latest dire kid illness or threat to national security. You may have much less tolerance for these friends now that you have a kid who could theoretically contract said illness and be impacted by said national turmoil.

6. *Too uninterested.* These are the friends who seem to lose interest once you have a baby, perhaps because they can't identify with your new life and priorities.

Once you've compiled a list of friendships that aren't currently working, think through the pros and cons of each of these friendships. On the facing page, you'll see a pros/cons list completed by Renee. You can see that each of her friendships has clear benefits and drawbacks. In situations where the benefits of the friendship outweighed the drawbacks (which initially appeared to be all of them), I recommended she try to change her expectations and/or set new boundaries. When her boundary setting with one friend ultimately proved unsuccessful, I recommended she consider a "breakup." We'll be discussing changing expectations, boundary setting, and friend "breakups" in much more detail below.

Adjust Your Friendship Expectations

When it comes to making old friendships work again, changing your expectations is easier than the alternative, changing a friendship's boundaries, in that it's all in your control. You just have to rethink what you can reasonably expect to get out of the friendship in question.

Renee's friend Caroline freely admitted to "not being a kid person." She visited Renee and the baby in New Jersey shortly after the baby was born, then went radio silent. Renee periodically reached out to Caroline via text,

Renee's Pros/Cons Friendship List

Friendships That Are No Longer Working

1. *Caroline: Not interested in my kid, hasn't been reaching out to me.*
   - *Pros of the friendship: Long history of being very supportive of me. I love hanging out with her. I want to know what's going on in her life.*
   - *Cons of the friendship: She's not super-interested in kids and I think feels disconnected from me as a result.*
   - *Decision: Maintain friendship but change my expectations of her.*

2. *Lorrie: Lives across the country. Due to time zone differences haven't been able to get her on the phone or FaceTime. Feel guilty texting her during the day when she's at work; when she's home from work, it's late for me, and I don't want to be texting.*
   - *Pros of the friendship: My best friend from childhood, knows me better than anyone, loves hearing about Rose, gives me a break from talking about babies all the time.*
   - *Cons of the friendship: We're never able to connect.*
   - *Decision: Maintain friendship but discuss boundaries with her. Maybe we can find a regular time on the weekend that works for both of us to FaceTime, or we can start a regular email correspondence?*

3. *Tanya: Constantly texting me about kid-related dangers; judging me for not taking adequate precautions with Rose.*
   - *Pros of the friendship: Old friend who knows me very well, nice to have a friend who has a baby.*
   - *Cons of the friendship: I often feel judged and anxious after talking to her.*
   - *Decision: Maintain friendship if we can agree on boundaries regarding whether and how Tanya talks to me about anxiety-provoking topics.*

4. *Doria: Constantly texting me about work drama, tends to be emotionally needy*
   - *Pros of the friendship: She is hilarious; I love hearing her stories.*
   - *Cons of the friendship: She demands instant responses, which I don't feel able to provide right now.*
   - *Decision: Maintain friendship if we can set boundaries on texting.*

and Caroline always got back to her right away. But Caroline rarely reached out herself. This was a big change; when Renee lived in New York City, Caroline had been a constant source of emotional support.

Renee still wanted Caroline in her life but recognized that she could no longer count on her as a consistent emotionally supportive presence. Renee resigned herself to the fact that she would have to find other friends to fill the supportive role Caroline once played. However, she recognized that Caroline could provide her with a much-needed break whenever she didn't feel like talking about babies. So Renee made a point of going into the city by herself once every few months to have a kid-free dinner with Caroline. This served to maintain the friendship and kept the door open for more outings like this in the future, when Renee was no longer nursing and had more flexibility.

Like Renee, you may find that certain friendships on your "not working for me" list can be resuscitated if you consciously change your expectations. Take some time and think through each of these friendships. What can you reasonably expect from each of these friends, at this stage in your lives?

And on the flip side, what kind of friend should you expect yourself to be to them? This is an important question, which may inspire you to set parameters for the friendship that you can follow. One mom I worked with recently had a friend who was always texting her with anxiety-provoking information, and she decided to ignore this friend's texts when they came in, choosing instead to read them at times when she felt equipped to respond. Actually, the "don't respond to texts right away" rule has served many of my mom patients well; it enables them to respond in their own time, when they feel they have the patience and mom brain space to do so. It also sends the message to the friend in question that you aren't likely to respond right away, which often discourages them from continuing to send time-sensitive texts.

Once you shift your expectations, you'll be far less likely to feel angry or resentful of friends who aren't playing the role they once did. You'll also hopefully be more inclined to give yourself a break when you can't be the friend to them that you once were.

Set New Boundaries with Old Friends

If you can salvage old friendships by shifting your expectations, do so. But if changes on your end won't suffice, you may have to actively engage your friends(s) in a discussion about boundaries. I've found that friendship boundary discussions are fairly painless when you have young kids, as children provide the ideal "It's not you, it's me" excuse. You can totally blame the friendship changes on your time- and energy-consuming kid, not on anything specific to the friend in question. You won't be surprised to hear that, like boundary conversations with extended family members, boundary conversations with friends are best conducted with DEAR MAN principles in mind.

Renee decided to have a boundary discussion with her friend Doria, whom she described as "emotionally needy." Renee loved Doria; Doria was "a hoot," and Renee loved hearing all about the Kardashian-style drama in her life. But Doria also demanded a lot of Renee; it was Renee she texted when she was in the midst of this drama, venting and soliciting Renee's advice. When Renee's daughter was born, Doria at first laid off the texting. But with time, Doria started texting again, to the point where she was texting multiple times per day and would send texts like "Helllloooo? Are you there???" if Renee didn't respond in a timely fashion. It was driving Renee insane.

Renee wasn't thrilled to have a DEAR MAN conversation with Doria; she didn't feel like she had space in her mom brain to deal with this and worried that she would offend her friend. We spent time crafting the conversation, and Renee rehearsed it ahead of time, with me playing the role of Doria. Renee deliberately made her appeal about trying to reduce her stress and her screen time, rather than about Doria. Here's a snippet of Renee's DEAR MAN conversation, which she delivered over the phone since she didn't often see Doria in person.

- **Describe.** "I've decided to work on limiting my phone time during the day."

- **Express.** "I've been really overwhelmed of late, and I think it's because I'm spending far too much time on my phone, texting as well as looking at social media. My brain feels overstuffed, and I'm having difficulty being mindful when I'm working and parenting."

- **Assert.** "I'm trying to carve out specific times when I am on my phone and chatting with friends and family. I'd like to find a regular time that you and I can text."

- **Reinforce.** "If we have a regular time to text, I'll be far less distracted than I am now, and I can really focus on our conversation."

- **stay Mindful.** Renee stayed on the topic, even when Doria clearly wanted to talk about that new guy who just moved next door to her.

    • **Appear confident.** Renee did her best to speak in a confident tone of voice.

    • **Negotiate.** Renee asked Doria for her help in finding a regular catch-up time.

At one point, Doria commented, "What, are you trying to get rid of me?" and Renee responded with validation; she explained that she understood Doria's concern and reassured Doria that she absolutely was not trying to get rid of her. If she were, would she be asking her to set up a regular check-in time? She also reminded Doria that she was working on her phone time with others as well.

This seemed to satisfy Doria, and she and Renee found a mutually agreed-upon time to text. Renee was pleased to discover an unanticipated benefit of setting a regular texting time: by the time Doria reached that time, she had already moved past many of the issues that she would have texted Renee about earlier in the day.

How to Break Up with a Friend

Breaking up with friends is extremely awkward and hard to do. Fortunately, I've found that most of my patients can manage even the most difficult friendships with boundary setting. There are, however, circumstances in which breaking up with friends may be warranted. This includes:

1. When you consistently feel negative emotions (sadness, anxiety, anger, negative self-judgment, guilt) during or after your interactions with this friend
2. When you perceive that this friend is constantly judging you
3. When you dread hearing from this friend or spending time with her or him
4. When this friend is continually demanding more of your time and energy than you feel able to provide
5. When this friend doesn't respond to boundary appeals
6. When the friendship is one-sided; this friend asks much but gives little in return
7. When you don't like how you behave when you're with this friend

Some toxic friendships can be ended by attrition. Remember in Chapter 7, when I shared the story about the mom who was always judging me for not challenging Matty enough on the playground, among other things? I was able to end that friendship fairly easily. I simply stopped reaching out to her, and when she reached out to me, I always said I wasn't available for a playdate. Eventually I stopped hearing from her entirely.

If you're not lucky enough to lose toxic friends by attrition, you may have to have a breakup discussion. I strongly recommend such a discussion over "ghosting," which I believe is a very unfair way to respond to someone who at one point was a part of your life. (I'd add that moms who ghost are often forced to answer for their actions, by, say, mutual friends to whom the ghosted friend has complained.)

In a breakup discussion, I recommend letting honesty and genuineness rule the day. Consider starting out by discussing how much this friendship meant to you at one time. Then, using your best "I" statements, explain why the friendship is no longer working for you. Try to emphasize why the friendship isn't a good fit for you, rather than what you perceive to be your friend's flaws. You're basically having a DEAR MAN conversation, but without the negotiation piece. There's no compromise here; there's just you communicating a decision you've made.

Renee had one childhood friend, Tanya, who also had a baby. Renee really struggled with Tanya, who was constantly passing on scary news about the latest threat to babies and often judging her for not taking extreme measures to keep her baby safe. Renee tried to set boundaries with Tanya but was ultimately unsuccessful. So she eventually decided to end the friendship. She spent time preparing what she was going to say and practicing with her husband. Her appeal looked something like this:

"I know we've been friends since we were little, and I've so appreciated our friendship over the years. You helped me get over my breakup with Andrew, and I was happy to be there for you during your horrible semester abroad. But since we became parents together, I've struggled to respond to your texts and phone calls. When you tell me scary news about threats to babies and then imply that I'm not taking appropriate precautions to protect Rose, it makes me feel anxious and judged. I'm having trouble managing these emotions, along with all of the other negative feelings that come with motherhood. For that reason, I need to take a break from our friendship."

Note that Renee was resolute in her request; she didn't imply that a negotiation was possible. She deliberately chose to ask Tanya for a "break" as opposed to an absolute ending, in the hopes that maybe one day their friendship could be rekindled.

I'm not going to lie: Tanya did not take too kindly to this. She spoke of this being a "betrayal," saying that Renee, because she was at the same stage of parenting, had been the friend on whom she'd relied for support, and now she was yanking that support away. Renee stressed how sorry she was and how she truly wished for the best for Tanya and her son. Renee also acknowledged her own role in this: that she didn't have the mom brain space to be a strong support to Tanya and felt that Tanya deserved to find someone else who did. Like Renee, if you feel you have played a role in the demise of a friendship, it's important to acknowledge it.

Once you've decided that you need to break up with a friend, know ahead of time that it may not end well. I recommend having a discussion like this face to face if at all possible and rehearsing it ahead of time. I also recommend that you have your own support person at the ready, to whom you can "download" after the conversation is over.

Find Friends That Fit the New You

Hopefully, you emerged from your friendship reevaluation with several important friendships still intact. Even if that's the case, however, you'll probably have to find some additional new-mom friends. Your BFF who lives across the country might be your favorite person on the planet, but you still need someone who lives 5 minutes away and can loan you baby sunscreen when you unexpectedly run out. It also helps to have friends in your time zone who you can text at 5:00 A.M. because you know they're up with their kids too.

As Daisy and my experiences attest, finding new-mom friends is not easy, and false starts are inevitable. I've found that the experience is similar to the experience of finding friends when you arrive at college. In the beginning, as you're struggling to adapt to new circumstances, you cling to which-ever friend candidates happen to be the most readily available (this was how I found myself attending a frat party with my freshman roommates when all I wanted to do was go out for ice cream and watch The Simpsons). But as you start adapting, you begin homing in on the types of friends you really need. The tricky part isn't meeting new friends; it's meeting new friends who are a good fit for you.

Sometime during my third or fourth week of college, I complained to my mom that the girls I was living with seemed to have totally different interests from mine. She asked if I'd met anyone who appeared to be more on my wavelength, and I told her that two girls who lived across the hall seemed like possible friend candidates. My mom encouraged me to march across the hall and ask these girls if they wanted to hang out with me. At first this sounded ridiculous to me; I didn't want to put myself out there like that, and I worried about being rejected. But ultimately, faced with the prospect of nursing Diet Cokes at yet another kegger, I relented and knocked on the door. This led me to Becky and Abby, two women who are among my very best friends to this day.

Like branching out from your first roommates in college, making like-minded new friends requires effort. Many of the moms I work with bristle at this idea. They're already working hard enough at parenting; do they really need to work hard at something else? But I always assure them that the benefits (see J. Courtney Sullivan's quote above) outweigh the drawbacks (time, letting your guard down, running the risk that the person in question isn't looking for a new friend). By the way, regarding that last issue: I've found that most new moms are desperate to meet other new moms. I can't recall a time when a patient reached out to a potential new friend and was rejected. Many new moms feel completely alone and are overjoyed when a friend candidate sends them a lifeline.

In instructing moms on how to approach and connect with new friends, I rely on my own and patients' experiences as well as on DBT, which offers a number of interpersonal effectiveness skills focused on how to find friends and get them to like you. Below, I list a number of places where you can look for new friends, and discuss a number of different conversation entry points.

A Road Map for Finding New Friends

In no particular order, here are a number of places where my patients, my friends, and I have successfully found new friends. (Keep in mind that, although I'm talking about mom friends in a general sense, there are lots of male couples with babies out there who also might welcome some new friends who are navigating the same parenting territory.)

1. **The neighborhood.** When you're out walking with your kid in the stroller, make a note of other moms with strollers. If you see the same moms repeatedly, consider approaching them. Also be sure to attend neighborhood events, like block parties.

2. **The park.** You've all been in this situation: You're pushing your kid in the swing, some other mom comes up next to you and starts pushing her kid in the swing, and you start talking nonsense to your kid, in an effort to avoid having to talk to this mom. Might I suggest you actually try talking to this mom? (See below for information about starting conversations.)

3. **New-mom groups.** Many communities have new-mom groups, which are often publicized on community Facebook pages or local magazines or websites (like the Patch). If you search these places and can't find anything, consider posting on your community's social media and inquiring about other moms who might be interested in establishing a group.

4. **Lactation support groups.** No, my personal example didn't portray these support groups in the best light. But I think my experience was unusual. I do wish I'd given my local group another chance, especially because I now know of several women who've made close friends at groups like these.

5. **Kid classes.** Another great place to meet mom friends is at kid classes—gym classes, music classes, or even library story time. In my opinion, these classes benefit moms more than they benefit kids. They give moms a reason to get out of the house and expose them to potential new friends.

6. **Groups with common interests.** People tend to like other people with similar values, interests, lifestyle choices, religious proclivities, and political views. Consider joining a group of like-minded others, either in person or online (on a site like *meetup.com*), where you'll be exposed to a number of potential friends. There are also groups for moms who are experiencing particular physical or mental health challenges and/or who have children experiencing challenges.

7. **Exercise classes/training groups.** In addition to helping you meet fitness goals, exercise classes/training groups (like running clubs) can be great places to meet new mom friends. So you can honor multiple values at once! Added bonus: many gyms and YMCAs provide child care.

8. **Playdates outside your house.** Instead of just hosting one mom and her kid at your house, why not suggest meeting at a park or play space for a playdate? That will give you and your mom friend the opportunity to connect with other moms. (Plus you won't be stuck frantically cleaning up your house before the playdate starts.)

9. **Fix-ups.** In her *Times* piece Sullivan mentions being introduced to other new moms by mutual friends. This sort of friend fix-up can work really well. Do you have a friend who mentioned a friend of hers who has a kid your kid's age? Consider asking your mutual friend to fix you up. Interestingly, you need not even meet this new friend in person; Sullivan talks about being fixed up with a new mom with whom she had an exclusively text-based relationship for many months.

10. **Online chat rooms.** And speaking of friendships taking many forms, I know of moms who met friends in online mom chat rooms or forums or social media groups and communicate with these friends solely via email and text. With that said, I want to remind you of what we discussed in Chapter 7: some of these rooms/forums can be toxic, so be sure to visit only sites that make you feel good. If you can't find a group that speaks to you, consider starting one of your own. The *New York Times* published an excellent guide about how to do this, which I've listed in the Resources.

11. **Apps.** There are apps devoted to helping moms connect with each other. See the Resources for more details.

How to Make Your Approach

If you're the outgoing type, and already comfortable in your new-mom skin, you might not need any tips about how to start talking to a prospective new friend. For everyone else, here are some tried-and-true new-mom conversation starters:

1. **Ask questions.** Start out a conversation with a simple question. I think "How old is s/he?" (referencing that mom's kid) is a great opener when you see a mom at the park or while walking your kids in their strollers. Honestly, any generic question about a mom's kid is likely to lead to a positive response. You can also ask generic questions about the mom, like "Do you live nearby?"

2. **Note similarities between the other mom's kid and yours.** If you happen to notice something—anything—in someone else's kid that reminds you of your kid, it can serve as a great conversation starter and point of connection. For example, "I see your daughter has a binkie. My son has one, too, and I have to physically force it out of his mouth!" Commiseration often follows, which can lead to a deeper conversation.

3. **Use brutal honesty.** This was the path I chose with Becky and Abby. I basically said to them, "I am not connecting with my roommates, and I need some friends. Will you be my friends?" I'm not suggesting you say anything quite that desperate/awkward, but you can certainly make a genuine appeal, something like "I've been looking for other new moms to connect with. Would you be interested in doing a playdate or grabbing coffee sometime?" I wouldn't necessarily lead with this line, but if you've been successfully small-talking with a mom and get the sense that she's a good friend candidate, you might want to bite the bullet and ask her out.

4. **Share something you like/admire about the other mom.** DBT recommends telling someone you like her or like something about her (without being excessively flattering). In mom terms, this might mean starting a conversation by telling a mom how much you covet her chic diaper bag or tricked-out stroller or admiring her kid's cute outfit. As you know, flattery can really get you places.

5. **Ask about a mutually interesting topic.** Do you see a mom carrying a tote bag from the local preschool? Take the opportunity to ask about her experiences with that school. Moms love to "pay it forward" by sharing what they've learned about schools or camps or kid activities. You can also approach a mom about non-kid-related topics. Remember my story about seeing a mom at a party in a *Hamilton* T-shirt and engaging her in a discussion about it? I'm still friends with that mom.

I've found that new moms usually benefit from a few types of friends who serve different purposes. Based on my totally unscientific study of myself, my friends and family, and my mom patients, I've compiled a list of a bunch of different types of mom friends you might want to seek out, featured in the box on the facing page. You may be lucky enough to find one or two friends who fit several of these descriptions, or you might need multiple friends to fill these roles.

Use Exposure If You're Having Trouble

Love the idea of approaching new mom friends but finding it hard to do? Maybe you're worried about what these moms will think of you. Maybe the idea of walking into a large gathering of moms, as you'd find in a mom support group, is too overwhelming. Or maybe you don't feel like you have any space in your mom brain to devote to socializing.

If you're struggling for any (or all) of these reasons, I'd suggest taking a behavioral approach and applying the exposure skills we discussed in Chapter 5. Remember that exposure involves systematically approaching situations/people that you've been avoiding. Make a list of several possible situations in which you could meet new moms and plan to seek out these situations, one by one. It might be easiest for you to start with the least daunting situation and then move on to the more daunting ones.

Jamila wanted to find new friends but avoided socializing for fear that she would be judged and ultimately rejected. Her experiences with high

A Field Guide to Mom Friends

- **The Lifer:** Your true BFF. You've been close forever. She knows you better than anyone else. She's always there to provide emotional support and validation. If you're lucky enough to live close to her, she can provide support whenever you need it.
- **The Commiserator:** The friend to whom you can commiserate and vent, via text or in person. Ideally, this is a fellow mom with kids around your kids' ages, who can uniquely relate to your situation.
- **The Adviser:** The friend whose parenting values match yours and whom you therefore trust to give you advice on all things parenting. If this friend has slightly older kids, all the better; she can tell you what worked for her kids when they were at your kids' stages.
- **The Carpooler:** The friend who lives near you and can help you out— she can watch your kid for a few minutes if you need to run to the store, or swap carpooling duties with you, or loan you her snowblower on a blizzardy afternoon.
- **The Insider:** The friend with the inside scoop on everything. This friend knows all about the best kids' products and activities and has the lowdown on the local preschools.
- **The Social Butterfly:** The friend who gets you out of the house when you desperately need an airing. If you're a party girl, perhaps you select a fellow party girl for this task; if you're a "see a movie and drink coffee" girl, look for someone who enjoys those things, too.
- **The Connection to the Outside World:** The friend who, either because she does not have children or because her children are older, serves as an emissary from the world outside of young children. She can talk to you about books and movies and travel and many other non-kid-related topics.

school "mean girls" were still fresh in her memory, and she didn't want history to repeat itself. However, faced with the prospect of spending the winter months with only a 1-year-old for company, she decided to make an exposure list and work through it. She was far more intimidated by joining a large group of moms (say, in a local mom's group) than she was by approaching individual moms, so she decided to start with individual approaches and work her way up to groups. Here's what her exposure list looked like:

1. *Text Jen's friend, a local mom, and ask about meeting up.*
2. *Approach fellow mom at park.*
3. *Approach fellow mom(s) at music class.*
4. *Post on Facebook about seeking out other moms for a social group.*
5. *Attend local lactation center group.*
6. *Attend local moms' social group.*

Before Jamila tackled any of these tasks, we brainstormed relevant small-talk topics she could raise. We also rehearsed together—she pretended I was a mom at the park, or her friend Jen's friend, and we role-played what she would say. This preparation helped her feel more confident when she made her approaches.

Jamila and I also set realistic goals for each of these exposure practices. For example, for her first music class exposure, she decided to try to target just one mom and make just one comment to this mom. Had she tasked herself with going to music class and making a best friend for life, or engaging the whole room in a fascinating discussion, she would have caved under the pressure. Setting smaller goals, particularly during the first attempts at exposure, made it much more likely that she'd be successful.

Hopefully, approaching social situations with an exposure mentality will help you meet your social goals. If you've tried an exposure approach and continue to struggle, you may benefit from doing more focused work on social anxiety. In the Resources I provide the name of an excellent social anxiety workbook.

Set Boundaries with New Friends

OK, so you've made some new mom friends. Great! I wish I could say your work is done . . . but it's possible that, as with your old friends, you'll have to set some boundaries with these new ones.

We talked earlier about the guilt that many moms feel when they contemplate ending or making changes to a friendship that isn't working. I find that this guilt is particularly pronounced when a new mom friend is involved. Typically, new-mom friendships start out full of enthusiasm; both moms are sleep deprived and stressed and thrilled to have someone to relate to. But when the dust settles, moms may find that some of these first new friends are not a good fit. They may, however, feel obligated to continue these friendships, as they had expressed such enthusiasm early on and don't want to risk hurting someone they know is already riding the emotional roller coaster of motherhood.

If you find yourself in this position, try to work through the guilt. Consider the benefits and the drawbacks of the friendship in its current form and whether the benefits outweigh the drawbacks, or vice versa. Also, while you're thinking about sparing your new friend's feelings, consider your own feelings as well. If the friendship is compounding your own already considerable stress, it's important that you make a change.

You may be able to set friendship parameters for yourself without having to say anything to your friend. Tessa, mom of a 9-month-old and a 3-year-old, met Audrey at a hospital birthing class when she was pregnant with her first kid. At the time, she was thrilled to have a local pregnant friend. But as time passed, and Tessa met more new moms with whom she connected, she stopped wanting to hang out with Audrey, who was constantly venting about her own situation and not giving Tessa the opportunity to vent.

Tessa couldn't end the friendship, however, as Audrey lived in her neighborhood and they had several mutual friends who often socialized as families. So Tessa decided that she would no longer agree to hang out with Audrey one-on-one; she would only socialize with her when their kids or other moms were present. She also stopped responding to Audrey's texts immediately, waiting until she felt she had the time and mom brain space to do so. By setting these boundaries, Tessa was able to minimize her time alone with Audrey as well as Audrey's texting without completely alienating or offending her.

If setting your own parameters doesn't work, you may have to have boundary discussions with your new friends. For guidelines on how to do this, check out Renee's boundary discussion with Doria, described above. Once again, I think the "it's not you, it's me" appeal can work here, especially because a new-mom friend is experiencing the same stress as you are and at the very least should be able to empathize with you.

Also, remember to really focus on the "negotiate" aspect of DEAR MAN; hopefully, you and your friend can mutually make a plan for navigating the friendship (e.g., setting regular times to hang out, text, or talk) that works for both of you. Angel, for example, was overwhelmed by how often her neighbor popped in unannounced. She had a DEAR MAN conversation with her neighbor, noting that she enjoyed her company but became overwhelmed when she came over without warning. They agreed to take a twice-weekly morning walk around the neighborhood together, which seemed to work for both women.

Finally, as with old friendships, if boundary discussions with new friends prove unsuccessful, you might have to have a "breakup" discussion. Use Renee's discussion with Tanya as a model for how to do this effectively.

It's OK to Say No to Friends' Requests

Daisy, whom you met at the beginning of the chapter, struggled when her new-mom friends started making requests of her. Eventually, the pressure to honor these requests became too overwhelming for her, and the friendships no longer seemed worth it.

Remember in Chapter 6, when we talked about saying no as a form of self-care? I want to remind you of that here, because you'll likely find yourself fielding lots of requests from new-mom friends. Sadly, peer pressure isn't just for middle schoolers; moms can feel pressure from other moms to do and buy a whole host of things. I've worked with some moms who start to feel taken advantage of, as they repeatedly say yes to things they don't actually want to do.

I get it: it's hard to say no to your friends. You've finally made some new pals, and you don't want to risk losing them. But you've got to prioritize your own mental health over, say, being in the good graces of the nursery school PTO president. As I've underscored many times in the book, you can't possibly be all things to all people, and your mental health needs to be a top priority.

In Chapter 6, I recommended that you respond to requests by making a pros/cons list. What are the benefits of saying yes to a given request, and what are the drawbacks? Here is a list that Daisy made when she was deciding whether or not to attend a "cosmetics party" that one of her new mom friends, Alanna, was hosting in her home:

Benefits
- *It will endear me to Alanna.*

Drawbacks
- *Cost—the cosmetics are expensive.*
- *I'm not actually in the market for new cosmetics.*

- *I'll have to devote some of my precious free time to doing something I don't want to do.*
- *I don't want to sit around listening to Alanna talk about beauty products.*

In this case, the drawbacks far outweighed the benefits, so Daisy decided to RSVP "no" to her friend's event. Alanna's approval simply wasn't worth the cost. Daisy had to accept that Alanna might be annoyed with her . . . which, by the way, she was. Ultimately, after Daisy said no to several such events and failed to buy any products, Alanna stopped reaching out to her. Daisy felt bad about this but was ultimately relieved; she no longer had to cope with guilt every time she got an email invite about Alanna's latest party.

If you're a mom like Daisy who defaults to "yes" every time a mom friend asks you for something, I urge you to think through the pros and cons of each request and say yes only when the pros outweigh the cons (or when you perceive a real need, as might be the case with a friend who is sick or very overwhelmed). And of course, keep in mind that the friends who get annoyed with you whenever you say "no" might not be the types of friends you truly want!

Do You Have to Be the "Wine Mom"?

Before we wrap up, I wanted to mention one particular type of mom request I've been hearing about a lot recently: to attend boozy "moms' night out" gatherings. I can't count the number of memes I've seen about moms needing wine and moms drinking to cope, not to mention all of the Real Housewives on TV and the Bad Moms in the movies and countless other media examples of boozing mamas. Not only do these movies and memes suggest that turning to alcohol is the best way for moms to manage stress; they also indicate that boozing is the social experience all new moms should covet. (They also trivialize alcoholism, which is a very real problem for some moms. For an excellent piece of writing about this, see the Resources.)

If you're someone like me, who is not and never has been a party girl, know that there are many other ways to socialize that do not involve drunken "girls' nights." It's totally fine if that's what you're looking for, but it's also fine to say no to these gatherings in favor of more low-key outings with fewer people. (You can also choose to attend but only drink soda. I've done this. No one cares.) I personally spent a lot of time feeling guilty about saying no to "girls' nights" before I started showing myself some compassion and realizing that these nights were stressful for me. If I was going to get a night away from my kids, I sure as hell didn't want to waste it doing something that stressed me out further. If you also aren't a fan of boozy "girls' nights," I encourage you to find the people and social environments that engage and relax you and devote your time and energy to them.

12

"Why Isn't Anyone Having Fun?"

Surviving Vacations, Holidays, and Special Events with Young Kids

Vanessa couldn't wait for her family's end-of-summer beach trip. At 3 and 5, her kids were both finally potty trained and no longer fearful of the water. For the first time since becoming a mother, she had high hopes for a fun and (relatively) relaxing getaway. Sadly, her hopes were dashed about 10 minutes into the trip, when her younger son reported that the sand was "itchy" and that he only wanted to play in the pool. What followed was a series of complaint-filled days: in addition to the aforementioned itchy sand, there was too much sun, too little sun, it was too hot, it was too cold, the sunscreen burned, the ice cream was better at the last beach they went to, and generally speaking everything was vastly superior at home. Vanessa and her husband spent the majority of their vacation walking to and from the beach (arms laden with towels, beach umbrellas, sand toys, snacks, etc.) rather than sitting on it. Vanessa returned home far more stressed than when she'd left.

Patti was excited when her 3-year-old daughter, Isabelle, was chosen to be the flower girl in her cousin's destination wedding. The day of the wedding, Isabelle woke at 5:00 A.M., ready to go, even though the wedding didn't start until 7:00 P.M. Patti expected that Isabelle would nap that afternoon, but she was too excited to be in a hotel room and adamantly refused to lie down. By 5:00 P.M., Isabelle was a complete meltdowny mess, and Patti had to struggle to get her dressed and to the venue. While they waited for the wedding to begin, a well-meaning member of the catering staff offered Isabelle strawberries. Minutes before Isabelle's big debut, Patti was in the bathroom, frantically wiping a huge strawberry stain from her dress. When it was finally Isabelle's time to make it down the aisle, Isabelle froze. Completely. Patti, who was totally disheveled (having spent the past 10 minutes on her knees cleaning strawberry stains in the bathroom), had to pick Isabelle up and walk down the aisle with her, in front of everyone. When Patti finally sat down, exhausted and stressed, she burst into tears.

I am a big-time fan of Halloween. I couldn't wait to have a kid, if only because it would provide me with a socially acceptable rationale for trick-or-treating as an adult. Two days before what was to be Matty's first Halloween, there was a freak snowstorm in the New York metro area, and Halloween in our town was canceled. I was so disappointed, I cried. As it turns out, virtually every holiday those first few years was a bust. For example, Matty's first Passover seder (my husband and I cleaning up matzoh detritus all night), first Hanukkah and Christmas (toys ignored, dreidel nearly swallowed), and first birthday (very intelligent brother-in-law somehow cannot operate camera, precious memories never recorded). We celebrate all the major Jewish and Christian holidays in my family, so we were constantly presented with fresh opportunities for massive disappointment.

You may have noticed a theme running through all the stories I just shared: Mom has high expectations for a holiday/vacation/occasion, expectations are not met, Mom's fragile spirit is crushed. In my first years of parenting, my mom brain was often consumed with high expectations/massive disappointment scenarios, most of them involving special occasions. Honestly, I found the majority of my vacations, holidays, and special events to be excessively complicated but kind of fun at best, and abjectly miserable at worst.

We moms often have such high hopes for our kids' first holidays and vacations and other special events. Some moms have fond childhood memories of these types of occasions and want to do whatever they can to ensure that their children have similar memories. Other moms, whose childhoods were not as happy, are driven to provide their children with the experiences they never had. Either way, the stakes are high: moms feel compelled to make their kids' events as magical as humanly possible.

As much as we might want to make things magical for our kids, however, we moms are not magical, and as a result we can't always engineer the holidays and vacations of our dreams. So we're left with a choice: we can keep shooting for the moon and experiencing the dreaded high expectations/massive disappointment combination, or we can decide to lower the stakes.

You won't be surprised to hear that I recommend lowering the stakes. This can be accomplished through cognitive work, which can help you manage expectations and cultivate acceptance. At the same time, you can employ a number of behavioral strategies, like scheduling, goal setting, and focusing on self-care, that can help you manage your stress (and increase the chances that you might actually enjoy yourself a little bit).

I can't promise that these strategies will erase the angst of holidays and parties and family trips. But if my experience is any indication, they will certainly help make these occasions more bearable, both for you and for your kids.

Don't Expect to Be Santa (a.k.a. Think Differently about Vacations, Holidays, and Special Events)

Remember when we talked in Chapter 8 about needing to accept that you can't mom perfectly? I noted four reasons that perfection always eludes us: we have limited resources; we can't always control our environments; we can't always control our kids; and we can't always be our best selves. These reasons apply especially well to holidays, vacations, and other special events.

1. **Limited resources.** Special occasions would be amazing if we had unlimited money to spend. We could vacation anywhere we wanted, at a place with a huge staff to indulge our every whim and 24-hour babysitting services. We could hire a company to cater all of our holidays and parties and clean up when the guests leave. Having unlimited time and energy would also help, enabling us to think through every possible detail of an event and consider every contingency. But of course, our resources are finite, and as a result things like vacations and holidays usually end up stretching us pretty thin, financially as well as emotionally.

2. **Unfamiliar environments.** Special occasions also typically occur in unfamiliar environments, like a relative's home over the holidays or a cramped hotel room in an unfamiliar vacation spot. When you're at home, on your own turf, you can easily find a spare sippy cup and throw a load of laundry in and whip up a quick batch of mac and cheese. But when you're on unfamiliar terrain, it takes a lot of effort just to do basic things like get yourself and your kids dressed and fed, not to mention all of the other atypical things you have to do when you're away or celebrating an occasion.

And if you're staying with relatives, you're always subject to their "house rules," which may be very different from yours. This can be particularly problematic when these relatives don't share your parenting values. I've worked with several moms who dread staying with their siblings, whose sleep and screen time rules are completely different from their own.

3. **Kids are monsters.** It goes without saying that we can't always (ever?) control our kids. This is especially true during special occasions, when kids are exposed to lots of unfamiliar things that prime them for bad behavior. They're off their regular schedule and routine. They're often given loads of sugary snacks and, in the case of the holidays, lots of toys. They may skip naps and have difficulty sleeping if they're staying in hotels or relatives' homes. They may be surrounded by lots of unfamiliar family members who freak them out and/or spoil them relentlessly. (If my experience is any indication, kids tend to act differently when large groups of relatives are around. When Sam sees his cousins, he morphs into a combination of John Cena and that diabolical scientist guy from PJ Masks.)

4. **We can't always be our best selves.** Holidays, trips, and special events are often stressful situations for adults; we're off our routines and subject to other people's whims and preferences. When you add cranky, out-of-sorts little kids to the mix, we're primed for adult-size meltdowns.

Clearly, we need to expect and accept that any sort of special event with little kids will be challenging, for all the reasons mentioned above. There are also challenges specific to certain types of special events. Take vacations, for example. Some mom writers have suggested that the term "trip" be used when describing family getaways, since the term "vacation" implies relaxation and restfulness. Vanessa's experience illustrates this perfectly— her vacation was extremely effortful, her kids complained constantly, and she spent far more time traveling to and from the beach than actually sitting on the beach. Sadly, unless you leave your kids with a babysitter, your days of sipping mai tais and reading novels by the pool are over, at least until your kids get significantly older. And even if you have the luxury of taking a vacation away from your kids, you may have difficulty truly relaxing, since part of your mom brain will probably be occupied with what your kids are up to and how they're doing.

Holidays, too, can be tough. Many of us have beloved holiday traditions that become impossible to uphold once we have a needy, unpredictable little person in our care. For example, one of my mom friends lamented that since having kids, she could no longer continue her years-long Thanksgiving tradition of lounging for several hours while watching the Macy's parade on

TV. This truly felt like a loss to her. Others feel sad that they cannot spend time cooking or shopping or having catch-up conversations with rarely seen relatives. And as I mentioned above, many of us are wedded to certain ideas about how holidays with kids should go and feel super-disappointed when things don't turn out as we hoped they would.

And of course, there are special events, which, as Patti's story attests, become decidedly less special with kids. Ever take a nursing infant to an 8-hour-long bat mitzvah? I have! My experience at my niece's bat mitzvah epitomized what it's like to attend a celebration—be it a bar or bat mitzvah or christening or wedding—with a really small kid. When not frantically wiping the spit-up off my dress, I was obsessing over how I could strategically time my nursing so that I didn't miss any important moments (I should note that my sister-in-law, also nursing at the time, had to be interrupted mid-feed to run out onto the dance floor for my niece's candle-lighting ceremony). My nephew's bar mitzvah, 3 years later, was on a boat, which meant that I had to spend the entire time making sure that Sam, hopped up on sugar, didn't, you know, jump overboard. Bottom line: it's nearly impossible to fully participate in and enjoy special events when you're trying to keep a kid afloat (literally and figuratively).

I honestly wish someone had sat me down and shared everything I just shared with you, urging me to accept that vacations and holidays and events would be really different and extremely challenging once I had a kid. Of the Top Ten Most Stressful early parenthood moments I can call to mind, at least half occurred in the context of holidays or vacations or other special events. (Have I mentioned the 3:00 A.M. drive with Sam from my mother-in-law's house back to my house on Christmas Eve? How about the Jersey shore trip when 4-year-old Matty decided that a daily 4:00 A.M. wake-up call and 4:00 P.M. meltdown was a good plan for the week?)

If I'd accepted ahead of time that things like Halloween and Christmas and family bar mitzvahs and beach trips were going to be different and complicated, I would have been far less devastated when they didn't go according to plan. I also think I would have been less focused on trying to control every aspect of my experience and instead could have availed myself of some helpful cognitive strategies, like considering the worst-case scenario, approaching things with a "screw it" attitude, and setting the bar low.

How Bad Can It Really Get?

In Chapters 4 and 8, we talked about managing worries and perfectionism by considering the worst-case scenario and what you would do to manage it. This can also be an effective strategy to use in advance of vacations, holidays, and other special events. Catastrophizing seems to go hand in hand with overblown expectations; along with expecting that events will go perfectly, we tend to assume that if they don't, they'll be unmitigated disasters. Considering the worst-case scenario can help you manage your catastrophizing and therefore your anxiety about upcoming occasions.

Anita literally spent weeks preparing for her daughter's first holiday card photo shoot. She'd always envied her friends' adorable cards and was so excited to finally have the chance to send one featuring her own child. She ordered five different dresses online and three different pairs of shoes. She sprung for the expensive photographer and changed the photo shoot time twice, hoping for the ideal time slot that would catch her daughter at her most well rested. She spent time on an online photo site picking out different borders and backdrops.

As the photo shoot day approached, Anita's mom brain became consumed with worries about it. What if her daughter didn't sleep well the night before? What if she got sick? What if she was freaked out by the photographer and screamed for her parents the whole time?

In hopes of quieting her mom brain, Anita talked herself through these three questions:

1. "What is the worst-case scenario?"
2. "What is a more realistic (based on the evidence) scenario?"
3. "If the worst-case scenario does come to pass, could I manage it? What would I do to manage it?"

Here's what Anita came up with:

Worst-case scenario

Charlotte doesn't sleep at all the night before. She cries inconsolably through the whole photo shoot, and we can't get a single shot of her not crying. She gets snot all over her face and dress.

More realistic scenario

Charlotte is wigged out by the photographer. Glen and I have to make silly faces behind the camera and take out her stuffed animals and make them dance around. We need to give her Doggy to hold in the pictures. We get lots of bad shots and one or two decent ones.

How I'd manage the worst-case scenario

If every professional picture was truly awful, I would suck up the loss of money, scrap the photos, and take my own pictures. Or I could deliberately use one of the terrible photos in the card and add a funny title to go with it, like "Guess not all of us are in the holiday spirit!" That would certainly make my card stand out among the other ones featuring chilled-out, smiling kids (whose parents clearly served them cookies laced with Benadryl).

Anita comforted herself with the knowledge that even if the worst-case scenario came to pass, she'd be able to make do. Like Anita, we moms are generally pretty resourceful and are nearly always able to manage effectively, however far off course things go. By thinking through how we'd manage the worst-case scenario, we can problem-solve ahead of time and have several contingency plans in place even before an event or experience begins.

In addition to asking yourself to think through the worst-case scenario, you can question how "catastrophic" it would truly be if, say, your holiday card turns out crappy one year, or any other special event does not go according to plan. Consider whether the event or experience in question will mean anything to you in, say, one month, or 6 months, or a year from now. Will you even be thinking about your holiday card from this year after the holidays are over? What about a less-than-optimal vacation or party? While I was super-upset about Matty's first Halloween, we've since had many, many fun Halloween celebrations, and that first crappy Halloween no longer even registers for me. As important as any specific special occasions might seem now, they are merely drops in the huge bucket of holidays, events, and vacations you'll spend with your children.

Just Say "Screw It"

For me, and for many moms I work with, accepting that things like holidays and vacations will never be the same post-kids can be difficult. I personally felt like I had to mourn twice—once for the types of vacations, holidays, and special events I used to enjoy before I had kids, and once for the idealized experiences I thought I'd be able to have with my kids but clearly couldn't.

That said, while I mourned the loss of holidays and vacations I'd never have, I also learned to embrace an unexpectedly positive aspect of acceptance. Knowing that these occasions would be complicated and basically out of my control now that I had little kids, I could choose to say "screw it" and relieve myself of the responsibility for making the entire experience perfect for my kids.

In case you haven't figured this out already, I am not the type of person who usually says "screw it." Like any good CBT therapist, I am extremely planful and goal oriented and focused. But somewhere between my niece's bat mitzvah and my nephew's bar mitzvah it occurred to me: on certain occasions, I could just decide not to care. At my nephew's bar mitzvah, for example, I didn't have to care about my kids' eating or how well behaved they were. I didn't have to care if they stained their khaki pants 30 minutes after they put them on. All I had to care about was whether their basic needs were being met. And that was it.

Let me tell you: adopting a "screw it" attitude was unbelievably freeing. It absolved me of the responsibility to make sure everything went perfectly with and for my kids, which drastically reduced my anxiety. Not caring about the fact that Sam spent the majority of my nephew's bar mitzvah fiddling with a rusty chain hanging off the boat (with a rotating cast of adult supervisors, of course) meant that I could actually sort of enjoy the event. I've since adopted this attitude many times, for big events as well as holidays and trips.

A "screw it" attitude can also come in handy when you're crashing with relatives during holidays or vacations. As I mentioned above, staying at other people's homes means subjecting yourself to their house rules, which may be very different from your own, particularly if you and the relative in question have very different parenting values. You can certainly choose to expend significant energy trying to, say, get your 4-year-old down to bed at 8:00 P.M. while her cousins are literally banging on drums in their basement. Or you can say "screw it" and resign yourself to the fact that your kid will probably be on her cousins' (ridiculous) sleep schedule while you are staying at their house. Why not let your daughter join her cousins on the drums while you spend some time catching up with the brother you rarely see?

Set the Bar Low

Along with adopting a "screw it" attitude, setting the bar low will ensure that you aren't disappointed by a special occasion, regardless of how it plays out. Patti recognized that she'd set the bar far too high for Isabelle's flower girl performance: she'd envisioned a pristine, beaming Isabelle gracefully throwing flowers as onlookers oohed and aahed. When none of this transpired, she was crushed.

For her nephew's communion, she decided to set the bar far lower. Her one goal was to be physically in the church at the moment her nephew received his first communion. That was it. She and her husband agreed ahead of time that he would be on "Isabelle duty," ensuring that she'd be able to remain in church.

Happily, Patti was able to meet her modest goal. And surprisingly, Isabelle actually made it through the entire service—sure, she was making her Ariel and Belle dolls "dance" in the pews, but she wasn't so disruptive that she needed to be taken out. By setting the bar low, Patti set herself up for success.

Here are some other examples of low-bar goals:

1. Spend 10 minutes on the beach without interruption.
2. Get one good picture at a family wedding.
3. Make Christmas cookies that are edible, if supremely unattractive.
4. Sit for 10 minutes at the Passover seder table.
5. Find one activity on vacation that every family member will enjoy (or at least tolerate with minimal discomfort).

As you can see, all of these bars are relatively easy to clear (and if they seem too ambitious for your family, pick ones you think you can manage). Regardless of how chaotic a given event or holiday or vacation is, if you set these types of goals you'll at least feel like you've had some success. If things end up going better than anticipated, as was the case with Isabelle's behavior in church, you'll consider it a major mom win.

And speaking of mom wins, remember in Chapter 8 when I recommended keeping track of mom wins every day? Keeping track of any and all wins (however small) during vacations, holidays, and special events can be particularly helpful. When you're thinking about your next special occasion, you can revisit your "wins" list from previous occasions. It will remind you that special occasions don't usually turn out to be nearly as catastrophic as you think they will be and that even the worst occasions end up having some redeeming qualities.

What's Really Most Important to You?

Take a minute to revisit the "holidays and special events" and "family vacations" sections of your values worksheet (discussed in Chapter 3). What features of vacations, holidays, and special events are important to you? Do you value being around family? Hosting events yourself? Involving your kids in holiday traditions?

Remembering your values can help you make peace with some of the less than optimal aspects of special occasions with kids. We tend to get so wrapped up in the small details of these things (gift purchasing, getting reservations for the best vacation excursions, picking the most appealing items for the birthday party goodie bag) that we lose sight of the bigger picture. Our values can help remind us of what's truly important to us. I know, I know—I sound like the wide-eyed little girl reminding all of her cynical, materialistic adult relatives to remember the true meaning of Christmas. But truly, thinking about what actually matters to you can help you when you can't stop sweating the small stuff.

Considering my values helped me manage my stress about holiday gifts. In the early years I got really overwhelmed when various relatives asked me for gift lists for my kids. I honestly had to do a lot of research and work really hard at these lists; when my kids were babies they vastly preferred empty shampoo bottles and garbage cans to any actual baby toys. At some point I took a step back and considered my values and what I truly loved about Christmas and Hanukkah with my family—which was *not* ensuring that my sons got tons of super-optimal gifts. So I vowed to spend less time on the gift lists and focus instead on things that mattered to me, like involving my sons in holiday traditions.

In addition to reminding you about what's important to you, your values will help guide you as you're planning ahead for what you might want your special occasions to look like. Below, we'll talk more about planning ahead, as well as other effective behavioral strategies.

Dare to Prepare

There are clearly many things you need to accept when you mix kids and special occasions. As always, however, acceptance needs to be balanced with change. Yes, there's a lot you can't control about occasions with kids, but there are some things you can at least try to control. By implementing behavioral change strategies like advance planning, setting schedules, coping ahead for stressful interactions, and focusing on self-care, you will maximize the chances that your trip or holiday will go well. At the very least, you'll feel better and more empowered if you're actively working toward change.

Make a Game Plan

Throughout the book, we've talked about how moms can manage their feelings of being overwhelmed by planning ahead of time and breaking big tasks into smaller pieces. Advance planning and task management are especially helpful where special occasions are concerned because these events tend to be very labor-intensive for moms. Spreading this labor out over a period of time and approaching special occasions with a "game plan" will significantly reduce the stress you'll experience, both before and during the occasion. It will also hopefully ensure that you're able to honor at least some of your values.

Whether you're planning for a party, holiday, vacation, or school break, the same rules apply. Several weeks ahead, spend some time listing everything you need to get done. Depending on what you're planning for, this might include shopping for supplies or gifts, house cleaning, food preparation, packing for travel, making reservations for meals or excursions, or contacting relevant family members to get a sense of their plans. Next, break this list down into several discrete, manageable steps and assign yourself one or more of these steps each week for the weeks leading up to the occasion.

Caitlyn used a detailed list to help her manage her Christmas hosting duties. Immediately after having her first baby, Caitlyn invited her family and her wife's family to have Christmas dinner at their house. She wanted all of her son's nearest and dearest to be able to celebrate his first Christmas with him at home. But once Thanksgiving rolled around, Caitlyn began to get nervous. She was expecting a crowd of 15—including three small children—at her house, and her parents and in-laws were staying with her. Plus her son was still not sleeping, leaving her with little patience and energy.

To cope with her stress, Caitlyn created a Christmas game plan, featured in the box on the next two pages. As you can see, Caitlyn listed out every possible Christmas-related task and broke each of these tasks down into component parts. She assigned herself certain tasks for each week in the weeks leading up to Christmas. At the start of each week, Caitlyn broke her list down even further, noting which tasks she would complete on which days of that week.

You'll notice that Caitlyn delegated several of these tasks to her wife and asked her guests to bring food. We've talked before about the importance of delegating, and I want to underscore that point again here. I can't tell you how many moms have insisted that their spouses or parents or other family members can't possibly help them prepare for holidays or trips or

Caitlyn's Christmas Game Plan

Week of December 2–8

1. Gifts
   a. Order online for:
      i. Thomas
      ii. Mom and Dad
      iii. Nora's parents (Nora)
      iv. Niece and nephews (Nora)
   b. Send Christmas list for Thomas to parents, in-laws
2. Design and order holiday cards online
3. Buy tree (me and Nora)
4. Decorate house (Nora)

Week of December 9–15

1. Decide on meal plan
   a. Reach out to Brian and ask what his kids like to eat
   b. Draw up grocery list
   c. If planning to purchase anything ready-made, order it
   d. Email guests and let them know what they can bring
2. Go to home goods store to pick out tablecloths, folding table, any serving pieces that we don't already have (Nora)

Week of December 16–22

1. Big clean of house
   a. Move playroom furniture around to accommodate Nora's parents (me and Nora)
   b. Make sure there are enough clean sheets and towels; if not, wash them (me and Nora)
   c. Take out dishes, serving pieces
2. Make Christmas cookies

December 23

1. Go to grocery store in the morning to buy food on list (Nora)
2. Make items that can be done ahead of time
   a. Appetizers
   b. Desserts
3. Set hour-by-hour cooking schedule for 12/25 (what needs to go in the oven when)

December 24

1. Prep and make food
   a. Turkey (defrost, brine)
   b. Salads
   c. Cut vegetables
2. Lay out gifts

December 25

1. 7 A.M. on: Make remaining food during the morning before guests arrive (Nora on kid duty)
2. 11 A.M.: Put out appetizers
3. Put food into oven according to schedule

---

parties. To them I say: Can your family members use the Internet? Can they go to the store? If so, they can absolutely help you. Assign them specific tasks that play to their personal strengths, let them know when these tasks need to be completed, and send them on their way.

Set Your Schedule (Even If You're Not Sure You Can Follow It)

After setting a game plan for the weeks leading up to an occasion, you can create a schedule for you and your kids to follow on the actual day(s) of the occasion. OK, so I know I previously encouraged you to say "screw it" and abandon yourself to the inevitable madness. But I also think it's helpful to try to set a loose schedule and routine for these days, even if you ultimately aren't able to adhere to your schedule at all. As we discussed in Chapter 3, schedules are a big-time anxiety reducer. Schedules provide you with a road map so that you aren't staring down hours upon hours' worth (or in the case of vacations, days upon days' worth) of empty space to fill. Further, setting schedules increases the chances that your values-driven goals will be met.

After Vanessa's disastrous beach vacation, she made a commitment to set a schedule in advance of her next trip. A few weeks before the trip, she did some advance planning to figure out where her family might like to eat and excursions they might enjoy. About a week before the trip, she took a look at the weather forecast and made a rudimentary daily schedule for her family. You can see her schedule in the box on the next page.

As you can see, Vanessa doesn't have things scheduled on an hour-by-hour basis. She planned just enough to give each day a shape. Having learned the hard way that her younger son didn't like to spend a lot of time on the beach, Vanessa planned a variety of activities that would appeal to him and his brother. Vanessa knew that her son would be able to tolerate the beach if their trips to the beach were interspersed with swimming in the pool and other activities.

Every night on vacation, Vanessa shared her schedule for the next day with her kids. I highly recommend doing this. We know that kids benefit from schedules and routines and, like us, can become unmoored when their

---

Vanessa's Vacation Schedule

<u>August 20</u>
1 P.M.: Arrive, unpack
Afternoon: Have lunch by pool, swim in pool
Evening: Dinner at hotel restaurant

<u>August 21</u>
Morning: Breakfast, pool/beach
Afternoon: Lunch by pool, pool/beach
Evening: Dinner at Joe's

<u>August 22</u>
Morning: Pirate cruise
Afternoon: Vanessa takes Brayden into town for lunch/shopping, Paul
    takes Carter to play tennis
Evening: Dinner at Casa Mia

<u>August 23</u>
Splash Park all day, lunch there
Evening: Dinner at hotel

<u>August 24</u>
Morning: Pool/beach
Afternoon: Aquarium, lunch there
Evening: Dinner at Seafarer's

<u>August 25</u>
Morning: Pool/beach
Lunchtime: Eat by pool, pack up things
Afternoon: Drive home

routines are upended. Letting your kids know ahead of time what a special-occasion day or week will look like will help minimize their anxiety and give them a sense of control. You can even involve your kids in planning for the next day or for an upcoming trip or occasion.

Two important notes about scheduling different occasions. First, beware of overscheduling! Yes, holidays and vacations are opportunities to expose our kids to new and exciting things. But too many new and exciting things can lead to overstimulation and set the stage for big-time tantrums. I learned this the hard way before I even became a parent. One summer, I decided to take my then-5-year-old niece into New York City for the day and expose her to the best the city had to offer, which included the American Girl store, M&M store, Toys "R" Us, and a Broadway show. Our journey ended with an epic meltdown, during which Bella screamed for an hour about getting rain in the holes of her Crocs. The day was way too much for her (and, quite frankly, for me). In retrospect, I should have chosen one (or, at most, two) of those activities, instead of all of them.

Second, you need to remember that schedules set for vacations, holidays, and special events are subject to *significant* change (see above re: the impossibility of control during these occasions). You've got to be prepared to abandon your schedules at a moment's notice. It's best to think of special-occasion schedules as loose guides, there to help you minimize your preoccasion anxiety.

If your carefully constructed schedules start blowing up in your face, and you feel overwhelmed and stressed as a result, try taking an adult time-out and engaging in an acceptance-based mindfulness activity. You can modify the "leaves on a stream" exercise for this purpose; imagine that you're writing your best-laid plans on leaves and allowing them to float down the stream, away from you. Just observe your plans drifting away, without pressuring yourself to try to salvage them. Accept that they're gone and move on to thinking about how you (and your kids) can adapt.

I've found that preoccasion scheduling can be particularly helpful during the summertime. See the box on the next page for more on summer scheduling.

Prepare Yourself for Great-Uncle Ron

I don't think you need me to tell you that holidays, special events, and vacations can be breeding grounds for familial and marital conflict. There are a number of reasons for this: we're all stressed during these times and therefore aren't usually our best/most polite/most diplomatic selves; certain family

---

Summertime Scheduling

Summers can be exceedingly stressful for parents because there are typically far fewer structured activities for kids than there are during the school year. This is true not only for school-age kids but also for little ones. Kiddie camp hours tend to be very limited, and many kid classes and activities offered during the school year aren't offered in the summertime.

I am a huge proponent of setting a summer schedule for your family. You don't need to put anything earth-shattering on the schedule; it can just be the things you generally do each day (e.g., trip to the pool, trip to the park, day camp). Further, you don't have to plan way in advance; you can set the schedule for a given day the night before, when you have a good sense of what the weather will be like and what your kids' (and your own) mood will be. As we discussed in Chapter 3, any type of schedule, even one that's filled with somewhat arbitrary tasks, will reduce the anxiety and boredom that comes with an empty, unstructured day with a little one (or little ones). Again, if your kids are old enough, you can tell them the day's schedule ahead of time and even ask for their input.

---

members may differ wildly in their ideas about how holidays or vacations should go; families who are used to interacting as a small unit may suddenly find themselves surrounded by a cast of thousands; and extended family members who haven't lived under the same roof since the early 2000s may be forced to shack up in one small house for several consecutive days.

It's important to cope ahead for potential interpersonal minefields that you're likely to encounter during a holiday or vacation or celebration. While we can't always predict who will go off the rails at any given event, we can think through some stressors we're likely to encounter, based on our previous experiences with the people in question, and plan accordingly.

One example that immediately comes to mind is navigating political discussions during family events. I can't tell you how many mom patients I've seen in recent years who fret in advance of family occasions, worrying that Great-uncle Ron will once again engage in a monologue/rant about everything that's wrong with our country. I've helped lots of moms devise game plans for managing their respective Uncle Rons. Effective strategies have included assigning one family member to distract Ron when he starts off on one of his rants; thinking ahead of time of several nonpolitical topics that will engage Ron; and even, in one case, establishing a signal with other family members (closely related to the Seinfeldian "head tap" that Jerry and Elaine employed when they needed to be rescued from mind-numbing discussions at a party) to indicate when someone needs a break from Ron.

I've also worked with some moms who've chosen to speak with their Uncle Rons ahead of time, gently requesting that they steer clear of political talk. In fact, I find it can be very helpful to set boundaries and clarify expectations in advance of holidays and trips, whether it be about acceptable conversation topics or the amount of gift purchasing that's reasonable or even who's going to pay for what on a large family trip. I'm not going to take you through another DEAR MAN example (at this point, you probably want to have a DEAR MAN discussion with me about how much I'm recommending DEAR MAN). But I do want to remind you to use DEAR MAN, along with the other interpersonal effectiveness skills we discussed in Chapters 9–11, to set effective boundaries.

Nica decided to have a DEAR MAN conversation with her mother about her daughter's first birthday party. Nica's mother started purchasing supplies two months before the party and had very strong opinions about how her only grandchild's first birthday party should unfold (she was particularly adamant about hiring a group of people to dress up as *Sesame Street* characters). Nica's vision for the party differed significantly from her mom's, and she worried that her mother would steamroll all of her plans, as she had many times in the past.

So Nica asked her mother if they could have lunch and talk about the party. Nica framed it as a planning discussion so that her mother would feel involved. She also used "I" statements to assert what *she* wanted, rather than focusing on all of the things that she didn't want (which of course were all of the things her mother wanted). She was willing to compromise with her mother on certain things (e.g., she allowed one life-sized Elmo), and she capitalized on her mother's strengths, assigning tasks to her mother that she knew her mother could perform easily and well.

I'm aware that certain people have very, very strong opinions about holiday traditions and vacations and parties, and I don't believe that a few DEAR MAN conversations will inspire them to completely change their views. However, I do think that such conversations will increase the chances that at least some of your needs will be met and will help you feel more in control of the situation. I also think you'll probably be able to get your family member(s) to budge a little bit, which will feel like a big win.

Take Care of Yourself!

We talked in Chapter 6 about the importance of taking care of yourself and prioritizing your own needs. It can be particularly difficult to focus on self-care during holidays, vacations, and celebrations, when moms often spend their time and energy trying to cater to the needs of everyone else in their family. (This is how moms end up accompanying their kids on perilous water slides and hosting thirty 5-year-olds at trampoline park birthday parties.)

But here's the thing: special occasions take a lot out of you, so you need to be especially vigilant about replenishing yourself during these times. Further, during vacations and holidays you often spend more time with your kids than you do normally. As far as I'm concerned, the more time you spend with your kids, the more critical it is to carve out some time for yourself.

While you're planning out a rudimentary schedule for your celebration day or vacation, make sure to add some self-care to the agenda. As I noted in Chapter 6, your self-care breaks need not be lengthy or complicated. You might decide to go for a walk on the morning of your kid's birthday party or participate in one vacation activity per day that you will genuinely enjoy. All that matters is that you have the opportunity to refresh yourself (in time for the next family-related stressor).

You can also adopt a "lemonade out of lemons" strategy, whereby you do whatever it takes to make stressful occasions as palatable for yourself as possible. The personal example that comes to mind is coping with the summer bathing suit mandate. Before having kids, I didn't realize that once you have small children, you are forced to wear bathing suits all the time—at backyard parties, on the beach, and (most galling of all) at the neighborhood pool, in full view of all your neighbors. I've always been modest and have never felt comfortable wearing a bathing suit in public. But after having Matty, I knew I'd be stuck in a suit in public for years to come. So I did some research and invested in good-quality bathing suits. Now, when I'm forced to be out at the public pool, I know I'll at least feel comfortable in what I'm wearing.

Other potential lemonade-out-of-lemons scenarios include making your own favorite treat to take to a large holiday gathering that you're not looking forward to, signing yourself up for the one adult-only activity at a kid-friendly vacation resort, and using kid birthday parties as an excuse to hang out with friends and family members you haven't seen in a while. No matter how kid focused an occasion is, you can always find small ways to make it bearable.

One more note about self-care and special occasions. It is OK to prioritize your own fun at these things! You can take a break from always catering to your kids and actually cater to yourself for a change. I worked with one mom, Suzanne, who was the matron of honor in her best friend's wedding, which was taking place several states away. Her twin 3-year-olds were in the wedding party, and Suzanne envisioned herself spending the whole occasion chasing them around. She decided that she didn't want to do that—she wanted to enjoy herself without having to worry constantly about her kids. So she asked her best friend to hook her up with a local babysitter who could follow her kids around the wedding and take them back to the hotel whenever they'd clearly had enough. The wedding was a huge success for Suzanne, who reported that she felt "free" for the first time since her twins were born.

While having someone to watch your kids is always helpful, you don't need to hire a babysitter to effectively prioritize your own fun. Sometimes choosing not to care can help you accomplish this. For example, are you a mom who is borderline obsessive about what your kids eat? If you choose not to care about this at, say, Thanksgiving, you can actually enjoy your own food instead of spending the whole dinner force-feeding sweet potatoes to a kid who only has eyes for the pies sitting on the counter. You know that regardless of what they eat, you're going to give the kids dessert anyway (or a sneaky relative will), so why not just focus on your own food for this one meal? Simply deciding to reduce your vigilance around your kids' behaviors (while still acting responsibly, of course) can help you actually sort of enjoy yourself.

For one final time, let me remind you of something I've emphasized often throughout this book: **It is important to consider your own needs.** Try and do what you can to ensure you will enjoy (or at least not loathe) the many special occasions and events you'll experience as a new parent.

APPENDIX

Values Worksheet

Directions

For each valued domain, several sample values are listed, along with several sample values-based statements. First, determine whether you hold any of the values listed, and add any additional values you may hold. Next, review the sample values-based statements, and note which (if any) apply to you. Add any additional statements that reflect the values you previously endorsed.

You can interpret these values in any way that feels meaningful to you. For example, if you're thinking about the value of "supportiveness" in the context of parenting, you can be referring to financial support or emotional support (or both). "Contribution" can refer to contribution of time, attention, or money (or all three).

Also, some of the domains listed may not apply to you (e.g., perhaps you don't really value community engagement or spirituality). Feel free to skip over any domains that aren't important to you.

Finally, if you find that you've circled a large number of sample values within a given domain (e.g., parenting), try to rank-order them and pick the top three or four to use for goal setting.

Parenting

We know that different parents prioritize different things. What kind of parent do you want to be? What do you want your relationship with your kids to be about? What aspects of parenting are important to you?

Sample values: Adventure, Affection, Authenticity, Caring, Connection, Consistency, Contribution, Control, Discipline, Empathy, Encouragement,

Flexibility, Fun, Honesty, Humor, Mindfulness, Nurturing, Open-mindedness, Order, Patience, Reliability, Responsibility, Role modeling, Safety, Spontaneity, Structure, Supportiveness

Can you think of other parenting values that are important to you?

Sample values-based statements

1. I value being physically present for my children.
2. I value being a mindful parent who is tuned in to whatever my kids are doing.
3. I value being on the "front lines" with my children, being the one responsible for taking them to playdates and classes and interacting with nannies/day care.
4. I value being the planner for my kids, managing their schedules, making doctors' appointments, and buying their clothes and gifts.
5. I value being a disciplinarian with my children.
6. I value keeping my kids on a regular routine/schedule.
7. I value being a source of emotional support for my children, who they can turn to in times of need.
8. I value being a source of financial support for my children.
9. I value exposing my children to unique experiences.
10. I value engaging in "fun" activities with my kids.
11. I value imparting my own values to my kids.

Can you think of other statements about what you want your parenting to be like, based on the values you endorsed above?

Work/Career

How large a role do you want your job/career to play in your life? What aspects of work do you wish to prioritize?

Sample values: Accomplishment, Ambition, Balance, Challenge, Community, Contribution, Financial stability, Flexibility, Independence, Initiative, Job security, Learning, Mastery, Recognition, Risk-taking, Service, Teamwork

Can you think of other work values that are important to you?

Sample values-based statements

1. I value having a career that allows me to be available for my children whenever they need me.
2. I value being at home with my children.

3. I value being committed to and engaged with my career.
4. I value having opportunities to get out of the house and interact with other adults.
5. I value being challenged intellectually.
6. I value engaging in creative tasks.
7. I value helping people/making a difference.
8. I value making as much money as possible.
9. I value having a job/career that gives me flexibility.

Can you think of other statements about what you want your work life to be like, based on the values you endorsed above?

Health/Self-Care

What are the types of things you want to be doing to take care of yourself?

Sample values: Accomplishment, Achievement, Assertiveness, Assistance, Beauty, Challenge, Change, Commitment, Confidence, Control, Drive, Fitness, Mental health, Organization, Rituals, Self-definition, Self-discipline, Wholeness

Can you think of other health/self-care values that are important to you?

Sample values-based statements

1. I value devoting significant time and energy to a challenging exercise regimen.
2. I value moving my body in some capacity on a regular basis.
3. I value actively working on my mental health through self-help or therapy.
4. I value regularly practicing mindfulness/yoga.
5. I value looking nice and "put-together."
6. I value healthful eating.
7. I value treating myself to activities that help me look and feel good (e.g., regular hair appointments, manicures, pedicures, massages, facials, body work).
8. I value having a clean, organized home.
9. I value being able to say "no" as a form of self-care.
10. I value having regular help with my children, from a nanny/babysitter or from family.

Can you think of other statements about what you want your self-care regimen to be like, based on the values you endorsed above?

Education/Learning

Some moms are happy to have their school days behind them, whereas others always want to keep learning. What role, if any, do you want education to play in your life?

Sample values: Accomplishment, Challenge, Community, Curiosity, Discovery, Growth, Initiative, Knowledge, Mastery, Open-mindedness, Self-definition, Self-development, Truth, Understanding, Wisdom

Can you think of other education/learning values that are important to you?

Sample values-based statements

1. I value consistently learning new things about parenting and keeping up with the latest parenting blogs/websites.
2. I value consistently learning new things that are not at all related to parenting.
3. I value staying informed about the news/the outside world.
4. I value any opportunity to be educated about things I don't know much about.
5. I value feeling intellectually challenged.
6. I value ongoing learning.
7. I value learning with a community of other adults.

Can you think of other statements about what you want your education/learning experiences to be like, based on the values you endorsed above?

Recreation/Leisure/Passions

What things outside of family and work help define who you are as a person? Note: consider those leisure/recreational activities that you are passionate about and substitute these things in for "my passion" in the following values statements.

Sample values: Accomplishment, Adventure, Challenge, Community, Connection, Control, Creativity, Curiosity, Excitement, Fun, Growth, Initiative, Inspiration, Mastery, Persistence, Ritual, Self-definition, Self-discipline, Self-expression, Skillfulness, Structure

Can you think of other recreation/leisure/passion values that are important to you?

Sample values-based statements

1. I value being able to define myself as someone who pursues my passion.
2. I value being able to engage with my passion on a regular basis.
3. I value continually working to improve at my passion.
4. I value the stress relief/mental break that comes with pursuing my passion.
5. I value pursuing my passion by myself.
6. I value pursuing my passion alongside other people.
7. I value pursuing my passion in a structured, disciplined manner.
8. I value repeatedly setting and reaching goals relating to my passion.

Can you think of other statements about what you want your recreation/leisure time to be like, based on the values you endorsed above?

Spirituality

Do you consider yourself a spiritual person? Do you wish for some spiritual connection in your daily life?

Sample values: Comfort, Community, Connection, Contribution, Enlightenment, Faith, Gratitude, Humility, Kindness, Mindfulness, Reciprocity, Responsibility, Ritual, Self-development, Tradition

Can you think of other spirituality values that are important to you?

Sample values-based statements

1. I value being part of an organized religious community.
2. I value being able to practice my religion on a regular basis.
3. I value cultivating my spirituality—that is, considering not only myself but also my connection with the larger world/universe.
4. I value spending time with people who are also spiritual.
5. I value maintaining religious rituals.

Can you think of other statements about what you want your spiritual life to be like, based on the values you endorsed above?

Community Engagement/Activism

Are you someone who wishes to be involved in your community, either on a local or more national/international scale?

Sample values: Action, Altruism, Caring, Change, Community, Compassion, Connection, Contribution, Cooperation, Courage, Diversity, Equality, Fairness, Freedom, Justice, Persistence, Pride, Respect, Responsibility, Service, Teamwork

Can you think of other community engagement values that are important to you?

Sample values-based statements
1. I value actively working to better my town/community.
2. I value being able to work for political causes that are meaningful to me.
3. I value being able to work for social justice causes that are meaningful to me.
4. I value connecting with others in my community who are also passionate about the causes I care about.

Can you think of other statements about what you want your community engagement to be like, based on the values you endorsed above?

Relationship with Partner

Different moms want different things from their relationships. What do you want your relationship to look like? What kind of partner do you want to be?

Sample values: Collaboration, Communication, Connection, Consistency, Dependability, Encouragement, Equality, Humor, Independence, Intimacy, Open-mindedness, Passion, Reciprocity, Reliability, Respect, Romance, Safety, Security, Spontaneity, Supportiveness, Teamwork, Vulnerability

Can you think of other relationship values that are important to you?

Sample values-based statements
1. I value communicating openly with my partner, sharing my feelings and perspectives and listening to my partner's feelings and perspectives.
2. I value having the time to work on my relationship with my partner.

3. I value having the opportunity to pursue kid-free social and recreational activities with my partner.
4. I value pursuing social and recreational activities separately from my partner.
5. I value co-parenting with my partner, truly making decisions as a team.
6. I value equality in my partnership, such that we make equal contributions to running the household.
7. I value feeling cared for in my relationship.
8. I value having some space from my partner.
9. I value having distinct functions from my partner, where [he or she] is responsible for taking care of certain things, and I'm responsible for taking care of others.
10. I value "running the household," with minimal input from my partner.

Can you think of other statements about what you want your relationship to be like, based on the values you endorsed above?

Extended Family

New parents vary widely in terms of the types of relationships they wish to cultivate with extended family members. What kind of family member do you want to be, and how do you want your own new family to interact with relatives? Note that you might need to complete this section several times, thinking about several different family members.

Sample values: Assertiveness, Authenticity, Caring, Communication, Connection, Dependability, Empathy, Flexibility, Forgiveness, Gratitude, Honesty, Inclusion, Independence, Loyalty, Obligation, Openness, Patience, Reciprocity, Reliability, Respect, Responsibility, Tradition, Trust

Can you think of other extended family relationship values that are important to you?

Sample values-based statements
1. I value being able to communicate with family members on a regular basis.
2. I value getting input and advice about parenting from extended family members.
3. I value cultivating strong relationships between extended family members and my children.
4. I value respecting extended family members' wishes.

5. I value being able to rely on extended family members for help with my children.
6. I value having some/a lot of distance (physical, emotional, or both) from my extended family.
7. I value being able to make decisions independently, without being influenced by extended family members' opinions.
8. I value having a polite and cordial, but not close, relationship with extended family.

Can you think of other statements about what you want your extended family relationships to be like, based on the values you endorsed above?

Friendships

Moms want different things from friendships. Some want to be part of an intimate, *Sex and the City*–type crew. Others feel too overwhelmed to maintain friendships and just want acquaintances with whom they can carpool. What types of friendships do you want to cultivate? What kind of a friend do you want to be?

Sample values: Assertiveness, Authenticity, Caring, Communication, Community, Connection, Dependability, Diversity, Empathy, Encouragement, Equality, Flexibility, Fun, Generosity, Honesty, Humor, Inclusion, Intimacy, Loyalty, Openness, Patience, Reciprocity, Reliability, Respect, Supportiveness, Teamwork, Trust, Understanding, Vulnerability

Can you think of other friendship values that are important to you?

Sample values-based statements
1. I value having deep friendships with people with whom I can share honest, intimate details of my life.
2. I value having a community of "mom friends" with whom I can "vent" and discuss the ups and downs of parenting.
3. I value having a community of friends who will always volunteer their time to help me or my kids.
4. I value having a community of like-minded friends with whom I share opinions on political/social justice issues.
5. I value having regular opportunities to hang out with friends (without kids present).

6. I value having regular opportunities to hang out with friends (with kids present).
7. I value having "fun" friends who help me escape from the day-to-day life of a mom with young kids.
8. I value having a group of casual acquaintances with whom I can make small talk at kid events and who can help me out with kid-related things (e.g., carpooling, playdates).

Can you think of other statements about what you want your friendships to be like, based on the values you endorsed above?

Holidays and Special Events

What aspects of holidays and special occasions are important to you? How do you want your holidays and special occasions to be?

Sample values: Connection, Contribution, Control, Faith, Family, Generosity, Inclusion, Opulence, Order, Respect, Rituals, Routine, Sacredness, Service, Simplicity, Spirituality, Spontaneity, Structure, Thrift, Tradition

Can you think of other holiday/special event values that are important to you?

Sample values-based statements

1. I value being able to host/celebrate holidays and special events in my home.
2. I value hosting/attending celebrations that are elaborate.
3. I value spending holidays/special events with family and friends.
4. I value celebrating holidays/special events more quietly, with just immediate family.
5. I value passing on traditions to my children.
6. I value being able to have some space from extended family during holidays.
7. I value prioritizing religious/faith-based observances.
8. I value commemorating holidays/special events with charitable activities.
9. I value holidays/events that are scheduled and structured.
10. I value celebrating occasions in a "low-key," less structured manner.

Can you think of other statements about what you want your holidays/special events to be like, based on the values you endorsed above?

Family Vacations

What aspects of family vacations are important to you? How do you want your family vacations to be?

Sample values: Activity, Adventure, Connection, Contribution, Control, Diversity, Excitement, Family, Fitness, Independence, Leisure, Nature, Order, Play, Relaxation, Routine, Self-care, Simplicity, Spontaneity, Structure, Thrift, Tradition

Can you think of other family vacation values that are important to you?

Sample values-based statements

1. I value vacations that are highly scheduled and packed with activities.
2. I value vacations that are slower-paced and more leisurely.
3. I value vacations with a mix of relaxation and activity.
4. I value vacations as opportunities to expose my children to adventure/fitness/nature/different cultures (or all of the above).
5. I value vacations as opportunities for family togetherness.
6. I value elaborate, luxurious vacations.
7. I value simple vacations.
8. I value the opportunity for every family member to pursue personal passions/self-care goals while on vacation.

Can you think of other statements about what you want your family vacations to be like, based on the values you endorsed above?

Resources

Organizations That Provide Support, Mental Health Provider Referrals, and Resources

Association for Behavioral and Cognitive Therapies (ABCT)
http://abct.org
• ABCT provides detailed information about psychological disorders and available evidence-based treatments and has a find-a-therapist service.

Association for Contextual Behavioral Science (ACBS)
https://contextualscience.org
• The umbrella organization for all things ACT. The "for the public" section of the website includes descriptions about ACT, information about finding ACT providers, free audio exercises and videos, and ideas for recommended reading.

Anxiety and Depression Association of America (ADAA)
https://adaa.org
• Provides fact sheets about a wide range of anxiety and depression issues and detailed information about treatment and referral options. ADAA also has its own online community support group.

Behavioral Tech
https://behavioraltech.org/resources/resources-for-clients-families
• The umbrella organization for all things DBT. The site features resources for clients and families, including a description of DBT, recommended books and videos, and information about finding a DBT provider.

Postpartum Support International (PSI)
https://postpartum.net
• PSI is a comprehensive resource for postpartum mental health issues. Includes detailed descriptions of these issues, links to support group options, and information about accessing treatment.

The 4th Trimester Project, out of UNC's Jordan Institute for Families
https://newmomhealth.com
• The 4th Trimester Project has an excellent website for moms. Included on the site is a wealth of information and helpful advice about the gamut of issues facing new moms, from maternal physical and emotional needs to baby care to navigating relationships with family and friends post-baby and connecting with other moms.

The Motherhood Experience

There are literally an endless number of blogs, websites, and podcasts about the motherhood experience. I deliberately did not include any blogs or social media feeds on this list, as they change every day (and I've also found that some blogs/feeds that really resonate with some moms don't work for others). So I just included a few websites and podcasts that have resonated both with me and with the mothers I treat.

Websites

Motherly
www.mother.ly
• Motherly calls itself a "lifestyle brand" for moms. Its site features articles, videos, video essays, and a podcast covering an extensive list of topics (the pregnancy and birth experience, beauty, parenting, maternal challenges, social support).

Motherwell magazine
www.motherwellmag.com
• *Motherwell* includes beautifully written essays by moms from all walks of life, covering every aspect of the maternal experience.

New York Times Parenting
https://parenting.nytimes.com
• The *Times* completely revamped its parenting platform, which now includes excellent evidence-based guides to a variety of parenting issues (some of which are cited below) as well as thought-provoking opinion pieces and personal essays. I particularly love this series of articles: Motherhood changes us all, by Jessica Grose (2020, *New York Times*). *www.nytimes.com/2020/05/07/parenting/motherhood-changes-us-all.html*

On Parenting from the *Washington Post*
www.washingtonpost.com/lifestyle/on-parenting
• A collection of excellent essays and opinions on the parenthood experience, as well as opportunities to seek advice from parenting experts.

Scary Mommy
www.scarymommy.com
• Scary Mommy used to be known primarily for its snark, but in recent years it has broadened its focus. The site now features a large number of articles and personal essays about the maternal experience, as well as an anonymous confessional that allows you to divulge all of your warts-and-all motherhood experiences. There are also a number of funny videos and a Scary Mommy podcast.

Podcasts

Motherhood Sessions
*https://gimletmedia.com/shows/
motherhood-sessions*
• In this podcast, reproductive
psychiatrist Dr. Alexandra Sacks has
intimate conversations with mothers
about a variety of maternal issues.

The Longest Shortest Time
https://longestshortesttime.com
• Sadly, this podcast is no longer
producing new episodes, but you should
absolutely check out its back catalog.
For 9 years the podcast covered every
possible aspect of mothering, with a
wide range of guests including experts
and regular parents.

Mom Brain

Here are some interesting articles discussing what might really be happening in our
"mom brains":

Motherhood brings the most dramatic
brain changes of a woman's life. So
why does prenatal care ignore the topic
altogether?, by Chelsea Conaboy (2018,
Boston Globe Magazine).
*www.bostonglobe.com › magazine ›
2018/07/17 › story*

Reframing "mommy brain," by
Alexandra Sacks (2018, *New York
Times*).
*www.nytimes.com/2018/05/11/well/family/
reframing-mommy-brain.html*

This is your brain on motherhood, by
Jenni Gritters (2020, *New York Times*).
*www.nytimes.com/2020/05/05/parenting/
mommy-brain-science.html*

What "mommy brain" really looks like,
by Katie Heaney (2018, *The Cut*).
*www.thecut.com/2018/05/science-of-
brain-after-giving-birth.html*

Working Moms and Child Care

There is a tremendous amount of writing out there about working motherhood.
Here are some highlights.

Books

Brody, L. S. (2017). *The fifth trimester:
The working mom's guide to style, sanity, and success after baby*. New York:
Doubleday.—I also want to shout out
the excellent Resources section on the
website (*www.thefifthtrimester.com*),
which provides detailed information

about accessing child care, career
development, and organizations that
advocate for working moms.
Downey, A. (2016). *Here's the plan: Your
practical, tactical guide to advancing
your career during pregnancy and parenthood*. Berkeley, CA: Seal Press.

Fey, T. (2011). *Bossypants*. New York: Little, Brown.—I just love what Tina Fey has to say about working motherhood (and about every other topic, for that matter). Sadly, I've never had Oprah tell me that I'm spreading myself too thin, but I can absolutely relate to Fey's struggles as an ambitious working mom.

Mihalich-Levin, L. (2017). *Back to work after baby: How to plan and navigate a mindful return from maternity leave.* Mindful Return. Accompanying website: *www.mindfulreturn.com.*

Articles

A mother's clock, by Lydia Kiesling (2019, *New York Times*). *www.nytimes.com/2019/05/11/style/mothers-day-working-moms-parental-leave.html*
• This wonderful piece by writer Lydia Kiesling, accompanied by gorgeous photos of moms of all varieties, speaks to being a mother who wants to work and the attendant guilt that comes with that.

How to be mostly O.K. (and occasionally fantastic) at the whole working mom thing, by Lauren Smith Brody (2019, *New York Times*). *www.nytimes.com/guides/working-womans-handbook/how-to-be-a-working-mom*
• An excellent guide to navigating working motherhood, covering topics such as coping with working mom guilt, avoiding being penalized at work for being a mother, finding balance, and advocating for working moms.

I've picked my job over my kids, by Lara Bazelon (2019, *New York Times*). *www.nytimes.com/2019/06/29/opinion/sunday/ive-picked-my-job-over-my-kids.html*
• An op-ed from a working mom who openly and unapologetically admits to prioritizing her work over her children.

Why American moms are seriously struggling, by Alia E. Dastagir (2019, *USA Today*). *www.usatoday.com/in-depth/news/nation/2019/05/09/working-moms-motherhood-stress-parenting-good-mom-childcare-daycare-costs-maternity-leave-gender-gap/ 3586366002*
• An interesting review of the economic, cultural, and social factors conspiring against working mothers.

America's child care problem is an economic problem, by Anna North (2020, *Vox*). *www.vox.com/2020/7/16/21324192/covid-schools-reopening-daycare-child-care-coronavirus*
At what cost? The brutal math of caring for children in America, by Katie Reilly and Belinda Luscombe (2019, *Time*). *https://time.com/child-care-crisis/*
• Both of these pieces discuss the significant issues with childcare in America.

Perinatal Mood and Anxiety Disorders and Maternal Anxiety

Books

Cowan, K. (2017). *When postpartum packs a punch: Fighting back and finding joy.* Amarillo, TX: Praeclarus Press.

Kleiman, K., & McIntyre, M. (2019). *Good moms have scary thoughts: A healing guide to the secret fears of new mothers.* Sanger, CA: Familius.

Kleiman, K., & Raskin, V. D. (2013). *This isn't what I expected: Overcoming postpartum depression.* Philadelphia: Da Capo Press.

Kleiman, K., & Wenzel, A. (2011). *Dropping the baby and other scary thoughts: Breaking the cycle of unwanted thoughts in motherhood.* New York: Routledge.

Wiegartz, P. S., & Gyoerkoe, K. L. (2009). *The pregnancy and postpartum anxiety workbook: Practical skills to help you overcome anxiety, worry, panic attacks, obsessions, and compulsions.* Oakland, CA: New Harbinger.

Articles

Mom, the designated worrier, by Judith Shulevitz (2015, *The New York Times*). *www.nytimes.com/2015/05/10/opinion/sunday/judith-shulevitz-mom-the-designated-worrier.html*

Websites Offering Support and Referrals for Mothers with PMADs

Postpartum Support International
https://postpartum.net

Postpartum Progress
https://postpartumprogress.com

Seleni Institute
www.seleni.org

General Overviews of CBT, DBT, and ACT

Gillihan, S. J. (2018). *Cognitive behavioral therapy made simple: 10 strategies for managing anxiety, depression, anger, panic, and worry.* Emeryville, CA: Althea Press.

Greenberger, D., & Padesky, C. A. (2015). *Mind over mood: Change how you feel by changing the way you think* (2nd ed.). New York: Guilford Press.

Harris, R. (2019). *ACT made simple: An easy-to-read primer on acceptance and commitment therapy.* Oakland, CA: New Harbinger.

McKay, M., Wood, J. C., & Brantley, J. (2019). *Dialectical behavior therapy skills workbook: Practical DBT exercises for learning mindfulness, interpersonal effectiveness, emotion regulation, and distress tolerance* (2nd ed.). Oakland, CA: New Harbinger.

CBT, DBT, and ACT for Anxiety

Books

Abramowitz, J. S. (2018). *Getting over OCD: A 10-step workbook for taking back your life* (2nd ed.). New York: Guilford Press.

Antony, M. M., & Swinson, R. P. (2009). *When perfect isn't good enough: Strategies for coping with perfectionism.* Oakland, CA: New Harbinger.

Antony, M. M., & Swinson, R. P. (2017). *The shyness and social anxiety workbook: Proven, step-by-step techniques for overcoming your fear* (3rd ed.). Oakland, CA: New Harbinger.

Chapman, A. L., Gratz, K. L., & Tull, M. T. (2011). *The dialectical behavior therapy skills workbook for anxiety: Breaking free from worry, panic, PTSD, and other anxiety symptoms.* Oakland, CA: New Harbinger.

Forsyth, J. P., & Eifert, G. H. (2016). *The mindfulness and acceptance workbook for anxiety: A guide to breaking free from anxiety, phobias, and worry using acceptance and commitment therapy* (2nd ed.). Oakland, CA: New Harbinger.

Minden, J. (2020). *Show your anxiety who's boss: A three-step CBT program to help you reduce anxious thoughts and worry.* Oakland, CA: New Harbinger.

Owens, K., & Antony, M. M. (2011). *Overcoming health anxiety: Letting go of your fear of illness.* Oakland, CA: New Harbinger.

Tirch, D. D. (2012). *The compassionate-mind guide to overcoming anxiety: Using compassion-focused therapy to calm worry, panic, and fear.* Oakland, CA: New Harbinger.

Tull, M. T., Gratz, K. L., & Chapman, A. L. (2017). *The cognitive behavioral coping skills workbook for PTSD: Overcome fear and anxiety and reclaim your life.* Oakland, CA: New Harbinger.

Apps for Monitoring Anxiety (and All Other Moods as Well)

Apps featuring CBT, DBT, and ACT seem to proliferate on a daily basis. Many of them will be gone by the time this book goes to press. I'm listing a few mood-tracking apps that I routinely recommend, because they're easy to use and were developed by reputable sources. I also recommend checking out *https://psyberguide. org/apps* if you are interested in up-to-date, helpful reviews of mental health apps.

MoodKit and MoodNotes
https://moodnotes.thriveport.com
www.thriveport.com/products/moodkit
• Both of these apps allow you to track mood as well as categorize distorted thoughts and challenge them. MoodKit also includes several modules aimed at helping you pursue goal-directed (and mood-enhancing) activities.

T2 Mood Tracker
https://apps.apple.com/us/app/t2-mood-tracker/id428373825
• This is a basic mood tracker app, with opportunities for you to record your mood and make related notes.

CBT, DBT, and ACT for Depression

Marra, T. (2004). *Depressed and anxious: The dialectical behavior therapy workbook for overcoming depression and anxiety.* Oakland, CA: New Harbinger.

Rego, S., & Fader, S. (2018). *The 10-step depression relief workbook: A cognitive behavioral therapy approach.* Emeryville, CA: Althea Press.

Strosahl, K. D., & Robinson, P. J. (2017). *The mindfulness and acceptance workbook for depression: Using acceptance and commitment therapy to move through depression and create a life worth living* (2nd ed.). Oakland, CA: New Harbinger.

Teasdale, J., Williams, M., & Segal, Z. V. (2014). *The mindful way workbook: An 8-week program to free yourself from depression and emotional distress.* New York: Guilford Press.

Mindfulness and Self-Compassion

Books

Kabat-Zinn, J. (2013). *Full catastrophe living: Using the wisdom of your body and mind to face stress, pain, and illness* (rev. ed.). New York: Bantam Books.

Katz, A. (2018). *One minute to zen: Go from hot mess to mindful mom in one minute or less.* New York: Skyhorse.

Moralis, S. (2017). *Breathe, mama, breathe: 5-minute mindfulness for busy moms.* New York: The Experiment.

Neff, K., & Germer, C. (2018). *The mindful self-compassion workbook: A proven way to accept yourself, build inner strength, and thrive.* New York: Guilford Press.

Pollak, S. M. (2019). *Self-compassion for parents: Nurture your child by caring for yourself.* New York: Guilford Press.

Vieten, C. (2009). *Mindful motherhood: Practical tools for staying sane during pregnancy and your child's first year.* Oakland, CA: New Harbinger.

Apps

There are a huge number of mindfulness apps available. Here are two that have endured (and that the majority of my patients use):

Calm
www.calm.com

Headspace
www.headspace.com/headspace-meditation-app

Sleep

Books

Carney, C. E., & Manber, R. (2013). *Goodnight mind: Turn off your noisy thoughts and get a good night's sleep.* Oakland, CA: New Harbinger.

Harris, S. (2019). *The women's guide to overcoming insomnia: Get a good night's sleep without relying on medication.* New York: Norton.

Mindell, J. A. (2005). *Sleeping through the night: How infants, toddlers, and their parents can get a good night's sleep* (rev. ed.). New York: HarperCollins.

—This is my personal favorite of all of the baby sleep books. Has great advice for parents as well as for babies!

App

CBT-i Coach
https://mobile.va.gov/app/cbt-i-coach
• This is a great app from the VA that takes you through the steps of CBT for Insomnia (CBT-i).

Eating and Body Image

Books Focused on Healthful Eating (Not Dieting)

Bays, J. C. (2017). *Mindful eating: A guide to rediscovering a healthy and joyful relationship with food* (rev. ed.). Boulder, CO: Shambhala.

Willett, W. C., & Skerrett, P. J. (2017). *Eat, drink, and be healthy: The Harvard Medical School guide to healthy eating.* New York: Free Press.

Books Focused on Body Image

McCabe, L. S. (2019). *The recovery mama guide to your eating disorder recovery in pregnancy and postpartum.* Philadelphia: Jessica Kingsley.

Mysko, C., & Amadeï, M. (2009).

Does this pregnancy make me look fat?: The essential guide to loving your body before and after baby. Deerfield Beach, FL: Health Communications.

Books Focused on Eating Disorders

Fairburn, C. G. (2013). *Overcoming binge eating: The proven program to learn why you binge and how you can stop* (2nd ed.). New York: Guilford Press.

Safer, D. L., Adler, S., & Masson, P. C. (2018). *The DBT solution for emotional*

eating: A proven program to break the cycle of bingeing and out-of-control eating. New York: Guilford Press.

Thomas, J. J., & Schaefer, J. (2013). *Almost anorexic: Is my (or my loved one's) relationship with food a problem?* Center City, MN: Hazelden.

Websites

Academy of Nutrition and Dietetics
www.eatright.org
• This site features a wide variety of information about nutrition and health, plus a link to find RDNs (Registered Dietician Nutritionists).

EDReferral
www.edreferral.com
• This site's main purpose is to connect people with eating disorder treatment providers, although it also includes a number of articles about eating disorders and related issues.

National Eating Disorders Association (NEDA)
www.nationaleatingdisorders.org
• This site contains a wealth of information about eating disorders and body image issues and available treatment options. It also hosts a variety of forums where interested readers can post and comment.

Exercise

I'm not a fitness expert by any means, but here are a few brief, stay-at-home workout options that my patients have had success with:

https://7minuteworkout.jnj.com
https://seven.app

www.blogilates.com
https://walkathome.com

Moms in a Judgmental, Pressure-Filled Culture

There's been a ton of writing on American motherhood—how our culture takes an excessively judgmental stance toward moms and places us under inordinate amounts of pressure. Here are three of my favorite pieces of writing on the topic, which I consistently recommend to other moms:

Books

Senior, J. (2014). *All joy and no fun: The paradox of modern parenthood.* New York: HarperCollins.—An extremely validating look at the difficulties of modern parenting—including how unrealistic expectations and competing demands can make parenthood so incredibly difficult to navigate.

Warner, J. (2005). *Perfect madness: Motherhood in the age of anxiety.* New York: Riverhead Books.—An absolute classic about the insane pressure placed on American moms. Includes discussions of "sacrificial" motherhood, maternal anxiety, maternal perfectionism and need for control, and inequitable parenting.

Article

The goddess myth: How a vision of perfect motherhood hurts moms, by Claire Howorth (2017, *Time*).
https://time.com/4989068/motherhood-is-hard-to-get-wrong
• The title of this *Time* piece says it all. The article explores the insanely unrealistic expectations placed on American moms and delves into where these expectations come from.

Couples

Books

Dunn, J. (2017). *How not to hate your husband after kids.* New York: Little, Brown.

Fruzzetti, A. E. (2006). *The high-conflict couple: A dialectical behavior therapy guide to finding peace, intimacy, and validation.* Oakland, CA: New Harbinger.

Gottman, J., & Silver, N. (2015). *The seven principles for making marriage work: A practical guide from the country's foremost relationship expert.* New York: Harmony Books.—John Gottman is famous for his pioneering work in his "love lab," where he's studied couples to ascertain what makes relationships work (and what sinks them). Gottman's website (*www.gottman.com*) contains links to his books, a description of his approach, ideas for quick interventions, and information about how to find therapists who practice his approach.

Johnson, S. (2008). *Hold me tight: Seven conversations for a lifetime of love.* New York: Little, Brown.—Johnson developed emotionally focused couples therapy, which is based on attachment theory. The EFT website (*https://iceeft.com*) includes a description of the EFT approach and a find-a-therapist link.

Lockman, D. (2019). *All the rage: Mothers, fathers, and the myth of equal partnership.* New York: HarperCollins.

Rodsky, E. (2019). *Fair play: A game-changing solution for when you have too much to do (and more life to live).* New York: G. P. Putnam's Sons.

Article

How to make your marriage gayer, by Stephanie Coontz (2020, *New York Times*). *www.nytimes.com/2020/02/13/opinion/sunday/marriage-housework-gender-happiness. html*

Sex

Books

Gottman, J., & Gottman, J. S. (2007). *And baby makes three: The six-step plan for preserving marital intimacy and rekindling romance after baby arrives.* New York: Three Rivers Press.

McCarthy, B., & McCarthy, E. (2020). *Rekindling desire* (3rd ed.). New York: Routledge.

Nagoski, E. (2015). *Come as you are: The surprising new science that will transform your sex life.* New York: Simon & Schuster.

Films

Post-Baby Hanky Panky
http://postbabyhankypanky.com
• This is a great series of short films, made by the Couples and Sexual Health Research Laboratory at Dalhousie University, normalizing the challenges of post-baby sex and offering tips for communicating effectively with your partner.

Referrals for Sex Therapists

**Society for Sex Therapy
and Research**
https://sstarnet.org/find-a-therapist

**American Association of Sexuality
Educators, Counselors, and
Therapists**
www.aasect.org/referral-directory

Family

4th Trimester Project
https://newmomhealth.com/familyfriends
• The 4th Trimester Project provides
an excellent guide to navigating family
and friend relationships.

**American Association for Marriage
and Family Therapy**
*www.aamft.org/Directories/Find_a_
Therapist.aspx*
• This is a link to AAMFT's find-a-
therapist service to help you find a
local family therapist.

Grief

Cacciatore, J. (2017). *Bearing the unbear-
able: Love, loss, and the heartbreaking
path of grief.* Somerville, MA: Wisdom.
Devine, M. (2017). *It's OK that you're not
OK: Meeting grief and loss in a culture
that doesn't understand.* Boulder, CO:
Sounds True.

Soffer, R., & Birkner, G. (2018). *Modern loss: Candid conversation about
grief. Beginners welcome.* New York:
HarperCollins.—I recommend this
book and especially recommend the
Modern Loss website (*https://mod-
ernloss.com*), an extremely valuable
resource for anyone experiencing
grief. It provides detailed information about all kinds of loss, moving
personal essays, practical information about things like dealing with a
loved one's estate, and links to support groups and services.

Parenting

"Expert" parenting sites and books abound. The books and sites I recommend here
utilize evidence-based principles, are user friendly, and take a realistic/nonalarmist
approach to guiding parents through parenting challenges and teaching parents
how to understand the minds of young children. These books and sites help reduce
maternal stress (as opposed to some other "expert" parenting writing, which I find
increases it!).

Books

Hershberg, R. S. (2018). *The tantrum survival guide: Tune in to your toddler's mind (and your own) to calm the craziness and make family fun again.* New York: Guilford Press.

Leahy, M. (2020). *Parenting outside the lines: Forget the rules, tap into your wisdom, and connect with your child.* New York: TarcherPerigee.

Naumberg, C. (2019). *How to stop losing your sh*t with your kids: A practical guide to becoming a calmer, happier parent.* New York: Workman.

Oster, E. (2019). *Cribsheet: A data-driven guide to better, more relaxed parenting, from birth to preschool.* New York: Penguin Press.—Also check out Oster's excellent newsletter, filled with data-driven parenting advice: *https://emilyoster.substack.com*

Siegel, D. J., & Hartzell, M. (2013). *Parenting from the inside out: How a deeper self-understanding can help you raise children who thrive* (10th anniversary ed.). New York: Tarcher/Penguin.—In addition to this book, Dr. Siegel has several other excellent parenting books that are very much worth checking out.

Podcasts

Mom and Dad are Fighting
https://slate.com/podcasts/mom-and-dad-are-fighting
• *Slate* magazine's parenting podcast, hosted by three candid parents, offers humorous takes on common parental trials.

Ask Dr. Lisa
https://podcasts.apple.com/us/podcast/ask-lisa-the-psychology-of-parenting/id1525689066
• Psychologist Dr. Lisa Damour has written two excellent books about raising adolescent girls. In her podcast, she provides evidence-based answers to questions from parents of kids of all ages.

Websites

Aha! Parenting (Dr. Laura Markham)
www.ahaparenting.com

Hand in Hand Parenting
www.handinhandparenting.org

Megan Leahy, Parent Coach
www.mlparentcoach.com

Positive Parenting Solutions (Amy McCready, parenting coach)
www.positiveparentingsolutions.com

Friendships

Website

4th Trimester Project
https://newmomhealth.com/meetmamas
• Excellent advice for connecting with other mothers on social media and IRL, including things to watch out for.

Articles

The cheeky "wine mom" trope isn't just dumb. It's dangerous, by Ashley
  Abramson (2018, *Washington Post*).
*www.washingtonpost.com/news/parenting/wp/2018/09/21/the-cheeky-wine-mom-trope-
isnt-just-dumb-its-dangerous*
• A terrific piece from the *Washington Post* about the dangers of the "wine mom
trope."

The *New York Times* parenting section has published several excellent articles on
mom friendships:

Make your own moms group, by Claire
Zulkey (2019, *New York Times*).
*https://parenting.nytimes.com/
relationships/mom-groups-online*

Making friends with other parents is
like dating, by Lyz Lenz (2019, *New
York Times*).
*https://parenting.nytimes.com/
relationships/new-mom-friends*

The absolute necessity of the new mom
friend, by J. Courtney Sullivan (2018,
New York Times).
*www.nytimes.com/2018/08/18/opinion/
sunday/new-mom-friends-motherhood.
html*

How to handle a mom-friend breakup,
by Pooja Makhijani (2020, *New York
Times*).
*www.nytimes.com/2020/06/25/parenting/
moms-friends-fight.html*

Online Spots to Connect with Other Moms

Meetup
www.meetup.com
• Meetup has information about a wide
variety of groups meeting in your area.
Lots of local moms' groups post their
events on Meetup (or you can post your
own mom event there!).

La Leche League Breastfeeding
Support
www.llli.org/get-help
*www.llli.org/get-help/breastfeeding-
support-facebook-group*
• Don't let my nipple biting experience
dissuade you—nursing support groups
can be a great source of advice and
new friendships. The La Leche League
sponsors a number of support groups
around the country and also has a
virtual support group on Facebook.

Apps

Peanut
www.peanut-app.io

Index

Vacations. *See* Special activities and events
Validation. *See also* Communication
  co-parenting relationship and, 168–170, 171
  extended family relationships and, 186–187,
    195, 197
  identity and, 47
  sharing the household load and, 181
  venting and, 165–166
  worrying about harming your child and,
    103–104
Values Worksheet. *See also* Values-based goals
  big-stuff worrying and, 81
  complete, 243–252
  coping with judging from others and, 139
  exposure techniques and, 94
  extended family relationships and, 185, 188
  friendships and, 205
  passion pursuit and, 120
  returning to work and, 57–59, 244–245
  sharing the household load and, 178
  special events and activities and, 231–232
  values-based goals and, 48–53, 55, 57–58
Values-based goals. *See also* Goals; Values
    Worksheet
  big-stuff worrying and, 80, 81–84
  comparison making and, 135
  co-parenting relationship and, 164
  coping with judging from others and, 139
  exercise and, 113
  exposure techniques and, 94
  extended family relationships and, 185, 188
  identity and, 48–55
  overview, 46
  passion pursuit and, 119–120
  perfectionism and, 146
  self-care and, 109

special events and activities and, 231–232
taking action with what you can control
    and accepting what you can't control,
    81–84
work–life balance and, 57–60
Venting, 165–166, 206
Visualization exercises. *See* Imagery
Volunteering, 122–125

Weight loss, 112, 115
Work–life balance. *See also* Returning to work
  child care decisions and, 61–63
  comparison making and, 128
  identity and, 55–63
  sharing the household load and, 177–183
  Values Worksheet and, 57–59, 244–245
Worksheet, values. *See* Values Worksheet
Worry. *See also* Anxiety; Fears
  big-stuff worrying, 76, 78–84
  COVID-19 and, 105–106
  expectations regarding special events and
    activities, 228–229
  exposure techniques and, 89–96
  nighttime worrying, 75, 77
  overview, 64–68, 85–87
  reassurance seeking and, 100–103
  recognizing thinking traps, 68–69
  sharing the household load and, 178–180
  small-stuff worrying, 69–76
  worrying about harming your child and,
    103–105
Worry time, scheduling, 75–76, 77
Worst-case scenario consideration, 71–72,
    80–81, 227–229
Worthless feelings, 18

About the Author

Ilyse Dobrow DiMarco, PhD, is a clinical psychologist in private practice in Summit, New Jersey. She specializes in helping women use cognitive-behavioral therapy and related evidence-based strategies to navigate the myriad challenges of motherhood. Her writing has been featured in *Motherly, Motherwell, Pop Sugar Moms, Psychology Today, Scary Mommy, The Week,* and *Today Parenting,* as well as on her own blog, *www.drcbtmom.com.* She lives in New Jersey with her husband and two sons.